YOUNG CHILDREN
AND MICROCOMPUTERS

YOUNG CHILDREN AND MICROCOMPUTERS

Patricia F. Campbell
Greta G. Fein

A Reston Book

Prentice-Hall, Inc.
Englewood Cliffs, New Jersey 07632

Library of Congress Cataloging in Publication Data
Main entry under title:

Young children and microcomputers.

   Bibliography: p.
   1. Computers and children. 2. Computer-assisted
instruction. I. Campbell, Patricia F. II. Fein, Greta G.,
QA76.9.C659Y68 1986 001.64'088054 85–8321
ISBN 0–8359–9482–1

A Reston Book
Published by Prentice-Hall, Inc.
A Division of Simon & Schuster, Inc.
Englewood Cliffs, NJ 07632

© 1986 by Prentice-Hall, Inc.
Englewood Cliffs, NJ 07632

10 9 8 7 6 5 4 3 2 1

Printed in the United States of America

CONTENTS

PREFACE

The future of microcomputers in educational settings is uncertain. Their immense potential was imaginable long before it was realizable. The slow and laborious process of research, development, and teacher preparation was short-circuited by a wave of enthusiasm that, within a brief 5-year period, brought microcomputers of some type to almost every school in the nation. Beginning in the secondary schools, microcomputers soon reached the upper elementary grades, then the primary grades, and finally the preschool. By all appearances, the movement is slowing down, if not stalling entirely. This welcomed pause, which may only be temporary, offers an opportunity to ponder basic issues in educational research and practice obscured by the initial enthusiasm.

One purpose of this volume is to delineate the problems and the possibilities of this new technology. Most of the contributors are engaged in microcomputer research and development activities. Even so, they bring to this effort different perceptions of the problems and different conceptual frameworks for addressing them. In a sense, the microcomputer has opened the door to many important ideas about children's education and development. In designing this volume, we tried to present a sampling of these ideas.

The second purpose is to indicate the scope of the research and development work currently in progress. Research findings are becoming available faster than they can be published in professional journals. When published, articles appear in such a great variety of journals and books that it is becoming inordinately difficult to grasp the array of issues that are being addressed. Because contributors to this volume represent diverse research approaches, the volume provides a handy overview of current research issues in the field.

Finally, our aim is to make information about these perspectives available to educators and researchers who are not themselves currently involved in this area. For this reason, contributors to this volume were urged to present their ideas in nontechnical language, whenever possible using anecdotal data to illustrate important theoretical or empirical issues.

Mark Lepper and James Milojkovic (Chapter 2) examine the implications of theories of information processing and motivation for research aimed at the improvement of instructional computer programs. The microcomputer seems to offer unique instructional advantages. How can these advantages be better understood as they are deliberately exploited for instructional purposes?

Karen Sheingold (Chapter 3) acknowledges the concerns of early childhood educators that young children will be forced prematurely into a mechanized, two-dimensional symbolic world. Nevertheless, with its dynamic and programmable properties, the microcomputer might provide children experiences that would not be possible with other, more conventional symbolic media. Perhaps, Sheingold suggests, educational goals need to be reconsidered in light of what children can do with this unique symbolic machine. As Lepper and Milojkovic examine the implications of modifiable program features for enhancing children's intrinsic motivation, Sheingold asks about the educational value of the activities these motivated children will pursue.

I. OVERVIEW: ISSUES IN RESEARCH AND APPLICATION

Part I presents an overview of issues in research and application. Taken together, these chapters stake out the challenge for the future. In Chapter 1, Greta Fein identifies some of the themes that reappear in different parts of the volume. Among these themes, some deal with control; others with individual differences; and still others with classroom organization, the role of the teacher, evaluation, and educational reform.

II. CONCERNS

Because microcomputers in the lives of young children might have negative effects, Part II brings together recent research in this area. Karin Borgh and W. Patrick Dickson (Chapter 4) pose practical questions about whether preschoolers can manipulate a microcomputer keyboard, run programs with little adult assistance, share a computer, and help one another solve program problems. Their observations indicate that a conventional keyboard is not a source of frustration, and that with some initial supervision, children can operate simple programs with little adult help. Moreover, children can share a single unit and cooperate in its use.

Patricia Campbell and Shirley Schwartz (Chapter 5) describe studies of the impact of microcomputers on the play and social behavior of preschool boys and girls. According to these researchers, computers need not encourage solitary activity, and, when programs appeal to the interests of both sexes, boys do not spend more time at the computer than do girls. These investigators note that the response of teachers to the computer may be as important as the software in determining the effects on children. While parents interviewed by these researchers supported the use of computers in the classroom, they were concerned about the violence in some computer games. Steven Silvern (Chapter 6) addresses concerns about the impact of software on children's arousal and aggression. His results support an approach that takes into account the content of the software and the social context of the activity.

These studies are valuable as much for the questions they consider as for the tentative answers they provide. Clearly, young children can manipulate a keyboard, work cooperatively, and continue to pursue traditional classroom activities when the computer is present. Whether the introduction of young children to computer activities encourages solitary pursuits, disrupts the classroom, segregates boys and girls, or precipitates unacceptable behavior depends on the environment in which innovation occurs. This first generation of classroom-computer research suggests that the impact of microcomputers on classroom life will depend on the quality of the software, the attitude of the teachers, the physical and social arrangement, the accessibility of the machine, and probably on other things happening in the classroom. These studies remind us that innovations are never single, isolated events, that classrooms are complex systems, and that educators are ultimately responsible for balancing the parts that make up the whole.

III. VISIONS

Part III deals with visions of the future. A careful, in-depth look at how young children interact with different software offers clues about the kinds of learning that might be occurring. June Wright and Anastasia Samaras (Chapter 7) use a model derived from studies of play to examine how preschool children use open-ended graphics programs. These children were encouraged to explore the medium, to discover its rules, and to make of it what they wished. They did so with zest, imagination, and humor.

Rich Hofmann (Chapter 8) offers a vision of learning and productive thinking in the early primary years. Some of Hofmann's report is eerily reminiscent of O. K. Moore's talking typewriter. The opportunity for a group of second graders to play with a talking touch pad led to the fortuitous discovery of orthographic and phonetic principles. From a simple game stressing one-to-one correspondence, the children discovered the principle of subtraction. Hofmann suggests that some software has an unusually high potential for the discovery of productive principles. Does other software require more guidance from the teacher? How deep is the children's understanding and how widely will it apply?

Judy Kull (Chapter 9) gives us an intimate portrait of young children learning Logo. Here, too, we find children mastering a complex micro-environment, solving tricky problems, helping one another, and thinking about their own thinking. Kull finds evidence of different learning styles and of children who design different problems for themselves. Conceivably, intrinsic motivation will be keener when children set their own problems than when they work with problems set by an adult. Kull also identifies some of the mathematical discoveries first-grade children make when using Logo.

Each of these investigators records behavior in keeping with the principles of clarifying educational environments (Moore & Anderson, 1969). The children express a sense of agency and patienthood, they experience reciprocity and find opportunities to make normative judgments. Their interest is maintained by the intrinsic satisfaction of the activity. Their learning is productive, whether it involves commands for a graphics program, Logo, or English orthography. And finally, the environments described by these investigators are responsive. Both software and teachers respond to the children's initiatives, while the children are encouraged to be reflectively responsive to their own behavior. Yes, teachers are very much a part of these microcomputer settings; but the teaching is of a special type worthy of further analysis.

These authors also offer insights about how children experience the microcomputer. One recurring theme is that the children feel they are in control. Another is the children's discovery that an exacting system permits an enormous variety of outcomes. Still another theme is that children approach the task in different ways and probably take from it different things. When children are in charge of their own learning, they may learn things that adults would never think to teach. Because studies of children interacting with microcomputers may provide a new understanding of how young children think and learn, these studies may provoke new models of how children might be taught.

IV. CURRICULUM APPLICATIONS

Part IV presents different approaches to developing curricula and devices for young or handicapped children. Marilyn Church and June Wright (Chapter 10) describe a comprehensive microcomputer curriculum for normal preschool children. These educators share the numerous considerations that en-

tered into seemingly mundane decisions about software, sequencing, timing, and setting. But each decision constituted these educator's best guesses about microcomputer activities and arrangements likely to contribute to the broader educational and social goals of a particular preschool program.

McConville, McGregor, Panyan, and Tobin (Chapter 11), illustrating a different approach, begin with the problems of children with different handicapping conditions. The advantages of microcomputer assisted instruction, discussed by Lepper and Milojkovic in Chapter 2, have special relevance for children with attentional, memory, and other deficits. From the perspective of special education, the advantage of microcomputers is that they are nonjudgmental, predictable, and patient. Perhaps the most dramatic microcomputer applications will be in the education of multiply handicapped children, especially those whose handicaps would ordinarily mean a lifetime of passive dependency.

Investigators in this section remind us that microcomputers will be most profitable when they are integrated into the broader goals of an early childhood program, and when applications take into account the special characteristics of the children involved. A microcomputer curriculum is more than one software package or peripheral device. A curriculum must be planned, coordinated with children's other life experiences, and implemented in a way that supports other aspects of the educational program. The microcomputer is not an educational panacea or a substitute for intelligent and sensitive adults.

V. SOCIAL REALITIES

The first four sections of this volume explore different aspects of microcomputers in early childhood settings. These sections touch issues concerning motivation; educational aspirations; negative effects; and aspects of cognitive, social, and personal development that might be affected by children's computer activities.

Part V deals with educational and social realities. What is known about the benefits of computer assisted instruction (CAI)? James Kulik (Chapter 12) offers an historical perspective, describing improvements in the effectiveness of programmed instruction that followed improvements in the technology. In spite of early disappointments, a long view spanning almost two decades of evaluation reveals gradual improvement in the effectiveness of computer assisted instruction in traditional academic areas. Interestingly, the data suggest that younger children may benefit more than older children, a finding worth investigating further.

In some respects, evaluations of deeper educational aims today resemble the early evaluations of CAI. Even though the use of CAI in the learning of mathematics, reading, and spelling seems to be straightforward, it required much sophisticated development to yield the learning outcomes reported by Kulik. Another decade or two might be needed to achieve and assess the deeper social, cognitive, and personal outcomes of newer approaches.

Logo offers an informative example of these problems. Systematic studies of Logo are few, and often ambiguous in design, limited to select groups of children, and hazy about the learning opportunities provided. A rather major problem concerns the reliability or validity of instruments used to assess student outcomes, especially when investigators fail to find significant effects. One of the most prominent of these studies was reported by Bank Street researchers in a series of technical reports (Pea, 1983; Pea & Kurland, 1984a, 1984b). In Chapter 13, Seymour Papert discusses this research, addressing specifically the classroom conditions needed to support Logo learning and the instruments needed to assess the learning that has occurred. Logo can be "known" at different levels, and it seems too early in the research effort to expect 20, 30, or even 60 hours of Logo experience to match one or another particular level of knowing. Papert's position touches a central issue in the evaluation of Logo and of other sophisticated, openminded computer activities. The difficult challenge is to identify the cognitive processes used to define and solve Logo problems (see Kull, this volume).

Unfortunately, many of the battles about the value or futility of microcomputers in education are being fought in the popular media rather than in scientific journals. More so than with any other educational issue, the role of microcomputers in education has become a public matter. Lois-ellin Datta (Chapter 14) examines public and private policies that currently determine in part whether microcomputers will be available to all or only to some children. This meticulous analysis presents the small and barely noticeable practices that bias the educational use of microcomputers toward older, more affluent children. An important implication of this chapter is that educational inequity occurs in small, inconspicuous, but cumulative steps. In effect, while the debate about the efficacy of computer experiences continues, some children will have opportunities denied to others if affluent parents are willing to bet on positive outcomes.

The future of microcomputers in educational settings will most likely depend on the imaginativeness, flexibility, and depth of the software; on the enthusiasm of students; on the skills and openness of teachers; on the willingness of school administrators and parents to tolerate fundamental changes in the way children are educated; and on public policies that support access and quality for all children. These components of the larger educational enterprise present different problems, each in need of careful analysis.

Several individuals contributed in special ways to this volume. Carol King, as a Reston Editor, provided initial support for this project. Ann Mohan was a superb copy editor, adding a professional touch to the final product. We also want to thank Shirley Schwartz, who was always available when needed. Finally, we are indebted to those who contributed their insights and viewpoints to the chapters that make up this book.

REFERENCES

Moore, O. K., & Anderson, A. R. (1969). Some principles for the design of clarifying educational environments. In D. Goslin (Ed.), *Handbook of socialization theory and research* (pp. 571–613). Chicago: Rand McNally.

Pea, R. D. (1983). *Logo programming and problem solving* (Technical Report No. 12). New York: Bank Street College of Education, Center for Children and Technology.

Pea, R. D., & Kurland, D. M. (1984a). *Logo programming and the development of planning skills* (Technical Report No. 16). New York: Bank Street College of Education, Center for Children and Technology.

Pea, R. D., & Kurland, D. M. (1984b). *On the cognitive effects of learning computer programming: A critical look* (Technical Report No. 9). New York: Bank Street College of Education, Center for Children and Technology.

TRADEMARKS

YOUNG CHILDREN
AND MICROCOMPUTERS

PART I

OVERVIEW:
ISSUES
IN RESEARCH
AND APPLICATION

CHAPTER 1

MICROCOMPUTERS AND YOUNG CHILDREN: AN INTERACTIVE VIEW

Greta G. Fein
College of Education
University of Maryland
College Park, Maryland 20742

We who live in advanced industrial nations may well be in the eye of a transformation whose momentum is quickening and whose scope is widening, a transformation likely to etch enduring changes on the contours of human civilization.

Over the past 100 years, we have seen the second great transformation of the physical scenery; as farmland once replaced verdant forests, so now highways and suburban housing are replacing farms, swamps, and marshes. The social scenery is changing as well. A declining birth rate means smaller families with a higher ratio of wage earners; each child born will cost more to rear, but in exchange will produce more goods and services over a longer life span. These children will live increasingly secluded and private lives, in dwellings that occupy a larger percentage of the nation's physical space, equipped with devices providing household services, information, and entertainment at the press of a switch.

Consider changes in the nature of work. No longer the leading world producer of steel, automobiles, or countless other goods, our nation has become a producer of services, ideas, and new technologies likely to alter the relationship of human beings to the environment, to industry, and to one another. Work has become less a matter of physical strength and more a matter of technical sophistication. Less physical labor is required to grow a field of potatoes, and fewer fields to feed the nation. Less social skill is required to manage a large corporation, and less mental effort to balance a check book. Problems in farming, management, and the conduct of personal matters can now be solved by sophisticated techniques far removed from immediate encounters with soil, paper, or people. At one time, industry required a disciplined and compliant work force; now it requires devices that may soon enhance even the limited communication capacities of severely handicapped individuals (McConville, McGregor, Panyan, & Tobin, this volume).

One sign of this transformation is the microcomputer, a remarkable machine cheap enough and simple enough to be used by young and old for a variety of purposes. In a strange, unprecedented way, the microcomputer is a machine that permits symbols to be manipulated to yield objects serving as books, bulletin boards, calculators, pencils, musical instruments, easels, and even simulations of the makers of such things (Sheingold, this volume). These mental objects, in which form is severed from function, are known by their schematic blueprint to a producer, by their practical outcomes to a user, and by appearance of assorted peripherals to an observer. Edward Sapir (1921), the noted linguist, once commented that human language was like a dynamo hooked up to a doorbell. We now know that the dynamo is the human capacity for symbolization and that this dynamo, when hooked into systems such as the computer, is far more powerful than human language, but, as yet, less powerful than the human mind. Although Plato would have shuddered at the thought, we may someday exchange ideas with an electronic Socrates.

As parents, teachers, and researchers we sense these larger issues, but because we are in the eye of the storm we cannot easily assess its momentum, discern its scope, or guess its path. We suspect that the presence of microcomputers in the lives of young children is an important issue because of its relationship to these larger changes. In trying to understand and direct this one small sign of change, we may illuminate the others. Perhaps if we can grasp the powerful ideas embedded in this device as it is used by young children, we may come a little closer to grasping the impact of technology on the world we live in.

The purpose of this chapter is to summarize some of the issues facing those engaged in understanding the proper role of microcomputer technology in the education of young children. Interactive issues are stressed, such as the child's perceptions of control over the machine, individual differences in children's styles of interacting with the environment, collaboration among peers, the teacher's role in designing an intellectually appropriate and stimulating microcomputer experience, the contribution of research, and the impact of the broader culture on educational decisions.

PERCEIVED CONTROL

"Hey, look what I did!" says a 4-year-old using a graphics program (Wright & Samaras, this volume). "I knew it! I just knew he would go 22!" says a 6-year-old learning Logo (Kull, this volume). In a simple graphics program, children quickly recognize the relationship between their actions on a joystick, knob, or button pad and events on the monitor (Wright & Samaras, this volume). In Logo, the relationship between action and outcome is even more precise (Kull, this volume). When control is lacking, cooperative efforts soon become a source of frustration and conflict (Silvern, this volume). Some software seems to promote children's sense of being in control of the computer, rather than being controlled by it.

As Hofmann (this volume) notes, children's perceptions of control are related to the type of control exercised by the software. In subtle-control software, children have considerable choice in their interactions with the software and they have an opportunity to discover new interactive possibilities as they use it.

What aspects of the software encourage children to attribute outcomes to their own actions? The opportunity to choose outcomes might be one such feature. Some software is productive because its commands and rules permit different ways of generating immensely divergent effects. Graphics programs, Logo, and word processing programs are examples of software with this

characteristic. In the talking touch pad described by Hofmann (this volume), children choose the combination of letters to be spoken by the device, and in the language arts program described by Church and Wright (this volume), children develop their own stories and illustrative pictures. One aspect of control may have to do with the diversity of outcome possibilities and the scope of choices available to the child.

A choice between different means may also enhance feelings of control. Some programs offer different ways of obtaining the same result. In a simple graphics program, there may be more than one way of erasing or filling a form with color; in Logo, there are increasingly elegant ways of constructing procedures yielding the same configuration. Perceptions of control may increase when children discover that they may choose different ends or different means to achieve the same end.

Predictability (McConville et al., this volume) may be as basic as diversity of outcomes and diversity of means. Choice gains teeth when there is a dependable relationship between action and outcome. According to several authors in this volume, children quickly appreciate the preciseness of a program's command structure and quickly learn the causal connections embedded in this structure. The immediacy of the microcomputer's response to the child's actions (Lepper & Milojkovic, this volume) may also enhance the child's perception of controlling an event, as it facilitates the learning of specific content in reading, mathematics, or whatever else the software would teach.

LEARNING STYLES

When faced with a new and intricate object, children will explore its salient features. Some children explore exhaustively, moving methodically from one feature to the next, while others get hooked on one or two features, exploring those in depth before moving on to the next (Hutt, 1979; Vandenberg, 1984). Although children's exploratory behavior with sophisticated software has not been systematically studied, several chapters in this volume (Kull; Hofmann; Wright & Samaras) indicate that studies of this type might be fruitful.

For example, Wright and Samaras describe a process of discovery that begins with an arrangement that controls the lines and colors appearing on a monitor. Similarly, Hofmann begins with a keyboard that prints letters and a touch pad that translates these letters into sounds. The teacher draws children's attention to these physical entities and what they can do. Church and Wright, Borgh and Dickson, Hofmann, and Kull explain how children are introduced to the basic capabilities of the equipment and the software. Once introduced, the children are encouraged to explore on their own.

As might be expected from previous research, some children quickly discover new capabilities (e.g., the button pad or the space bar), new combinations of old commands, or even a more differentiated discrimination within the old (upper and lower case letters, different ways of erasing). These children survey the larger domain before deciding what to do, and they are ever alert to new possibilities. Other children prefer to stay with a few familiar commands, using what they already know to create effects that have symbolic meaning (writing the letters of one's name in Logo or drawing a car driving down a road in Scribbling®). These children seek new information only when it helps them do what they have already set out to do.

Missing in our theories of learning is a theory of "discoverable information." If the children observed by Wright and Samaras had not been free to explore the button pad, the divergent explorers could not have discovered how to animate their graphics; if the children described by Papert (this volume) had not been free to observe the work of

older children, they would not have had an opportunity to discover the dynamic turtle. In each case, the teachers had no reason to believe that the children could understand and use this information. In each case, the information was there and a few children reached out for it. And, in each case, the information was eventually assimilated by others in the group.

These observations have important implications for the organization of the classroom, the design of curricula in areas other than computers, and the study of children's learning. What conditions of discovery yield this kind of field learning? What kind of information is discoverable in this manner? Answers to the second question might contain notions of relevance (i.e., the new information must be relevant to the old) or productivity (i.e., the new information must increase the productivity of the old). Answers to the first question might contain notions about the presence of explorer children in the classroom, a classroom that encourages divergent exploration, and, of course, one that contains discoverable information.

SOCIAL ORGANIZATION OF THE CLASSROOM

The notion that children bring different learning styles to microcomputer activities has important implications for the design of classroom environments. One possibility, suggested by several authors in this volume (Borgh & Dickson; Campbell & Schwartz; Wright & Samaras), is to present the microcomputer as a regular classroom activity that children may engage in as they engage in blocks, dramatic play, or art. The microcomputer would be a normal part of the preschool or primary classroom life.

These studies also suggest that the social organization of the classroom will determine whether or not the fruits of different learning styles will be shared by the children

(Borgh & Dickson; Kull; Sheingold; Wright & Samaras). If children are encouraged to express preferred styles of learning, and to share their discoveries, new ideas and insights may quickly become the property of the entire group. The children described by Hofmann might not have made their orthographic discoveries had they not been allowed to use toilet graffiti as a source of text and had the classroom setting not encouraged the children to share ideas with one another. Complex microcomputer environments and expansive classroom settings may optimize the transmission of skills and understanding within the peer group. Translated into a research question, we might ask whether some children are natural detectors of useful information and whether these children use special communicative devices to disseminate this information to others.

As Papert (this volume) notes, what children learn from the microcomputer depends on the culture of the classroom and the school. How computer activities are presented may be as important as the software. In a classroom sensitive to the social organization of work, the microcomputer can provide an opportunity for children to work cooperatively in small semiautonomous teams (Borgh & Dickson; Kull; Wright & Samaras, this volume). In a classroom sensitive to children's strivings for autonomy and success, teachers will guide without precluding discovery and encourage discovery without permitting children to flounder. One consensus of those contributing to this volume is that the classroom context will influence what children learn from or about the software just as it influences what children learn from other educational devices.

TEACHERS

Teachers ordinarily do not determine whether microcomputers will be provided in their classrooms. However, once these machines are available, teachers determine when and how they will be used. More important, they determine their own role in guiding children's interactions with the computer and with one another (Campbell & Schwartz, this volume).

How teachers perceive this role depends upon their vision of what computers can and ought to do. One vision might stress independent student learning of basic academic skills. The data discussed by Kulik (this volume) and the research program described by Lepper and Milojkovic (this volume), indicate that software that enhances intrinsic motivation while providing opportunities for learning or practice may serve this purpose. Cast in this role, the teacher must be a software connoisseur, wisely choosing programs that are intellectually sound and appropriately motivating (Silvern, this volume).

However, individualized instruction and independent study may not provide the ideal setting for all kinds of learning. Because in some areas students working together learn better than students working alone, the teacher might need to provide opportunities for children to work in groups (Borgh & Dickson; Campbell & Schwartz, this volume). One aspect of the teacher's role is to manage the social framework in which learning occurs.

As programs become more open-ended, the teacher's role becomes more delicate. In the vignettes discussed by Wright and Samaras (this volume), we see an off-stage teacher asking thought-provoking questions: Does it make a difference if you turn it fast or slow? Does pushing the button make it change? These questions draw children's attention to important features of the microworld, especially the relationship between actions on the controls and events on the monitor. Interestingly, these teacher behaviors resemble those of mothers who are especially adept in teaching their children content-specific material (Price, 1984).

The off-stage teacher is also a presence in the protocols used by Kull (this volume). In this program, pre-Logo exercises were used to introduce the children to basic Logo concepts. The teachers prepared charts to introduce new Logo commands. But beyond these structured teaching activities, the protocols document the ongoing interaction between teachers and students as the Logo experience developed. "What would happen if you used CS?" asks the teacher. "Is that what you want to do?" "Do you know how to erase a line?" Note the teacher's use of metacognitive terms such as *want* and *know*. These terms reflect the basic intention of the questions: They urge the children to reflect on "if-then" contingencies and to take responsibility for making choices, and they offer technical information when it is likely to be most meaningful to the child. In the third example, the child had previously erased a line by retracing with the background color and the teacher was trying to determine whether or not he remembered this strategy.

These observations pose questions of considerable practical and theoretical importance. Suppose that some computer-based learning is not independent of the quality and sensitivity of teaching? Suppose, further, that software program and style of teaching interact to enhance specific learning or broader cognitive outcomes? One example is the debate about Logo provoked by the Bank Street studies (Papert, this volume). It may well be that children in an unstructured classroom, presumably designed in accordance with a discovery model of learning, will not achieve the kind of learning needed to understand Logo. It may even be that peers as teachers will not yield this learning because the children, themselves, have only a dim appreciation of what they know.

One answer is formal instruction in which the children systematically move through an organized Logo curriculum, completing teacher-assigned tasks, with little left to chance or the children's imagination. Another is illustrated in the teacher-child interactions just described—an interactive, intellectually stimulating program. In sub-

scribing to this option, however, we return the teacher to the teaching process, and learning is no longer completely independent of an interactive adult. Not all educational software may require an off-stage teacher; drill and practice programs are likely to work on their own, while other types may require minimal teacher intervention. Conceivably, the depth of learning attainable in a microcomputer activity will be related to the kind of teacher involvement needed to produce the best outcomes.

EVALUATION

Several generations of technological innovation were needed before the programmed instruction envisioned by Skinner became possible (Kulik, this volume). Unique properties of the microcomputer—its interactiveness, its potential for individualizing instruction, and its quick response in multiple modes (Lepper & Milojkovic, this volume)—contribute to its usefulness as a teaching device. However, the Skinnerian model of learning applies only to the learning of material in which some responses are clearly right and others clearly wrong. What needs to be learned is established beforehand, and opportunities for serendipitous discovery are either limited or entirely absent. Can we aspire to more?

Most of the contributors to this volume say "yes." Hofmann stresses the notion of productive thinking. Kull describes children who devise ingenious solutions to problems they have defined for themselves, and Wright and Samaras describe even younger children who discover novel combinations as they explore the machine's capabilities. Papert notes the concrete and formal operational schemas built into Logo mastery. Beyond these cognitive outcomes, we have the possibility of improved attitudes toward learning, enhanced self-confidence, and the cultivation of other personal characteristics associated with effective functioning in the world outside of school. If it took several decades for technology to contribute to academic learning, it may take several more for this contribution to be extended to these broader and less easily measured aspects of educational outcomes.

PASSING FANCY OR EDUCATIONAL TRANSFORMATION?

Will the microcomputer reform the way children are taught in today's schools? Some observers predict a sweeping educational transformation (Kulik, this volume), or at least the possibility of one (Papert, this volume). Others are more skeptical, noting that other technological inventions (the motion picture, television) were absorbed by the society at large without achieving a visible presence in the schools (Datta; Lepper & Milojkovic, this volume). Unfortunately, we do not know why these technologies failed to influence school instruction, and we lack a useful theory of technological impact to guide our present efforts.

In thinking about the impact of microcomputers on schooling, a third possibility merits attention. Suppose we are in the midst of a transformation of education comparable to the inventions of schooling, writing, and the printing press (Kulik, this volume). Suppose this transformation is embedded in a far broader cultural and economic transformation as consequential as those that gave us tools and towns, transportation and commerce, machines and mass production. When scholars a millenium from now look at the 20th century, they may see a radical technological transformation quickly absorbed into traditional educational practices. As today we are barely conscious of pencils and mimeographed worksheets, so tomorrow we might be barely conscious of the microcom-

puters on our children's desks. Just as pencil and paper may be used for writing stories or drawing pictures, they may also be used to complete, senseless exercises on cheaply reproduced drill-and-practice worksheets. As we once joined pencil and paper to dull children's minds, we many now join mouse and monitor to the same end.

Unlike earlier transformations, however, we are debating, studying, and experimenting with the educational potential of the microcomputer. If children already show a 5-month gain in basic skills as a result of computer-assisted instruction (CAI) (Kulik, this volume), improved CAI programs might do better as they add features that enhance children's interest in learning (Lepper & Milojkovic, this volume). More children may master the basic skills of arithmetic, reading, and writing sooner and with less pain. However, when the microcomputer is used only to achieve these ends, it is essentially serving an old, though commendable goal, the extension of functional literacy in arithmetic and reading to the entire population. The transformation begun by the printing press may be completed by the computer.

If microcomputers yield only more efficient traditional learning, an educational transformation has not taken place. At the very least, we need to be concerned about the transition from basic skills to expressive literacy, the use of words to convey intricate ideas, and the edifice of aesthetic sensitivity that might be erected on these foundation skills (Sheingold, this volume). At the most, we would be concerned about the potential for the microcomputer to enhance children's capacity for divergent and productive thinking (Hofmann; Kull; Sheingold; Wright & Samaras, this volume); their mastery of powerful mathematical ideas (Kull; Papert, this volume); and, more broadly, their acquisition of the capacity as adults to understand national debates about the federal budget, arms control, environmental policy, and other matters of vital interest to the citizenry of a democratic society.

REFERENCES

Borgh, K., & Dickson, W. P. (1986). Two preschoolers sharing one microcomputer: Creating prosocial behavior with hardware and software. In P. F. Campbell & G. G. Fein (Eds.), *Young children and microcomputers* (pp. 37–44). A Reston Book. Englewood Cliffs, NJ: Prentice-Hall, Inc.

Campbell, P. F., & Schwartz, S. S. (1986). Microcomputers in the preschool: Children, parents, and teachers. In P. F. Campbell & G. G. Fein (Eds.), *Young children and microcomputers* (pp. 45–59). A Reston Book. Englewood Cliffs, NJ: Prentice-Hall, Inc.

Church, M. J., & Wright, J. L. (1986). Creative thinking with the microcomputer. In P. F. Campbell & G. G. Fein (Eds.), *Young children and microcomputers* (pp. 131–143). A Reston Book. Englewood Cliffs, NJ: Prentice-Hall, Inc.

Datta, L. (1986). Microcomputers and young children: A public or private affair? In P. F. Campbell & G. G. Fein (Eds.), *Young children and microcomputers* (pp. 181–197). A Reston Book. Englewood Cliffs, NJ: Prentice-Hall, Inc.

Hofmann, R. (1986). Microcomputers, productive thinking, and children. In P. F. Campbell & G. G. Fein (Eds.), *Young children and microcomputers* (pp. 87–101). A Reston Book. Englewood Cliffs, NJ: Prentice-Hall, Inc.

Hutt, C. (1979). Exploration and play. In B. Sutton-Smith (Ed.), *Play and learning* (pp. 175–194). New York: Gardner Press.

Kulik, J. A. (1986). Evaluating the effects of teaching with computers. In P. F. Campbell & G. G. Fein (Eds.), *Young children and microcomputers* (pp. 159–169). A Reston Book. Englewood Cliffs, NJ: Prentice-Hall, Inc.

Kull, J. A. (1986). Learning and Logo. In P. F. Campbell & G. G. Fein (Eds.), *Young children and microcomputers* (pp. 103–128). A Reston

Book. Englewood Cliffs, NJ: Prentice-Hall, Inc.

Lepper, M. R., & Milojkovic, J. D. (1986). The "computer revolution" in education: A research perspective. In P. F. Campbell & G. G. Fein (Eds.), *Young children and microcomputers* (pp. 11–23). A Reston Book. Englewood Cliffs, NJ: Prentice-Hall, Inc.

McConville, L., McGregor, G., Panyan, M., & Tobin, D. (1986). Educational matching: Microcomputer applications in the education of handicapped children. In P. F. Campbell & G. G. Fein (Eds.), *Young children and microcomputers* (pp. 145–156). A Reston Book. Englewood Cliffs, NJ: Prentice-Hall, Inc.

Papert, S. (1986). Are computers bad for children? In P. F. Campbell & G. G. Fein (Eds.), *Young children and microcomputers* (pp. 171–180). A Reston Book. Englewood Cliffs, NJ: Prentice-Hall, Inc.

Price, G. (1984). Mnemonic support and curriculum selection in teaching by mothers: A conjoint effect. *Child Development, 55,* 659–668.

Sapir, E. (1921). *Language: An introduction to the study of speech.* New York: Harcourt, Brace & World.

Sheingold, K. (1986). The microcomputer as a symbolic medium. In P. F. Campbell & G. G. Fein (Eds.), *Young children and microcomputers* (pp. 25–34). A Reston Book. Englewood Cliffs, NJ: Prentice-Hall, Inc.

Silvern, S. B. (1986). Video games: Affect, arousal, and aggression. In P. F. Campbell & G. G. Fein (Eds.), *Young children and microcomputers* (pp. 61–70). A Reston Book. Englewood Cliffs, NJ: Prentice-Hall, Inc.

Vandenberg, B. (1984). Developmental aspects of exploration. *Developmental Psychology, 20,* 3–8.

Wright, J. L., & Samaras, A. S. (1986). Play worlds and microworlds. In P. F. Campbell & G. G. Fein (Eds.), *Young children and microcomputers* (pp. 73–86). A Reston Book. Englewood Cliffs, NJ: Prentice-Hall, Inc.

CHAPTER 2

THE "COMPUTER REVOLUTION" IN EDUCATION: A RESEARCH PERSPECTIVE

Mark R. Lepper
James D. Milojkovic
Department of Psychology
Stanford University
Stanford, California 94305

Revolutionary advances in microelectronics have led to the arrival of the powerful, yet inexpensive personal computer—a technology that has begun to transform our society. Since its commercial introduction only 10 years ago, the personal computer has become familiar, indeed commonplace, in the workplace, at home, and in our schools. By the time today's preschoolers have finished their schooling, they will have had more direct experience with computers than 95% of today's adults.

With this influx of computer technology into our society comes a plethora of research questions and opportunities for students of psychology, education, sociology, and communications (e.g., Condry & Keith, 1983; Lepper, in press; Papert, 1980; Taylor, 1980; Walker, 1983). Grand claims concerning both the potential benefits and the potential costs of widespread acceptance of microcomputers have proliferated. To many proponents, the significance of the computer revolution seems likely to compare favorably to that engendered by Gutenberg's invention of movable type and the printed page. To opponents, discussions of *1984* and *Brave New World* seem more in order. Even among advocates of the technology, competing—and often mutually exclusive—recommendations are being offered concerning the ways in which computers ought to be used to accomplish particular educational, industrial, or societal goals.

It is particularly important for us to realize that some of the questions posed by this new technology and some of the social debates it has generated need to be addressed in the near future. Soon the "research window" will close. Once the computer has become truly ubiquitous, it will become func-

tionally impossible to study issues of its general impact on children's intellectual or social development. As the history of research on the social and cognitive effects of television so vividly illustrates, research options become increasingly limited as a new medium becomes universally available (Hornik, 1981; Lepper, in press). Similarly, the current stage of experimentation and flexibility—during which research can have its most significant impact on policy—will soon be ended. In the next few years we are likely to see the entrenchment of particular models of computer usage with children, the development of a body of conventional "wisdom" about computers and children, and the establishment of emotionally and intellectually vested interest groups.

In this chapter, we shall sketch out a few of the research areas that should be of particular interest to educators, parents, and psychologists and examine some of the competing hypotheses that are being offered about the consequences of the increasingly widespread influence of computer technology in our lives. In particular, we will focus on a set of issues concerning the potential effects of frequent exposure to the computer as a medium of learning and instruction.

INSTRUCTIONAL ISSUES

Consider, first, the educational possibilities offered by the microcomputer—its potential as a device for the delivery of interactive and individualized instruction, a technology for motivating and interesting students in learning, and a medium for the creation of environments that encourage indirect, inductive, or experiential learning. To many, these possibilities seem limitless. Alfred Bork (1980), from the University of California at Irvine, has made the following prediction about the use of computers in the schools of the future:

Preparation of this paper was facilitated by support from research grants HD–MH–09814 and HD–17371 from the National Institute of Child Health and Human Development and from the Stanford Center for the Study of Youth Development.

We are at the outset of a major revolution in education, a revolution unparalleled since the invention of the printing press. The computer will be the instrument of this revolution. . . . By the year 2000, the major way of learning at all levels, and in almost all subject areas, will be through the interactive use of computers. (p. 53)

Patrick Suppes (1966), at Stanford, has made an even more impressive claim concerning the opportunities this medium affords:

One can predict that in a few more years millions of school children will have access to what Philip of Macedon's son Alexander enjoyed as a royal prerogative: the personal services of a tutor as well-informed and responsive as Aristotle. (p. 207)

What are the characteristics of computers that lead to such optimistic assessments? Certainly, the history of technological innovations in education is not one that we should find encouraging. Time and again, new technologies have been introduced with fanfare and enthusiasm, but years later have left little of a lasting impression on the face of education in America. Instructional television, filmstrips, programmed learning, language laboratories, and teaching machines have all met a similar sad fate. Why should computers be an exception to this rule?

The justification for enthusiasm, we believe, lies in the interaction of three characteristics of this medium—its interactivity, its intelligence, and its multifunctionality. These features offer the promise of enhancing student learning in a variety of domains and through a variety of methods. The computer can be used as a machine for facilitating rote learning through guided drill and practice or more complex forms of learning through intelligent computer-assisted instruction (CAI) tutorials and computer coaching. It can also be used to present educational materials in the form of games designed to enhance motivation or simulations designed to promote active and inductive learning. It produces as well—for word processing, data analysis, visual representation—tools that may facilitate learning in many areas. And, when connected to appropriate telecommunications systems, it affords students access to new worlds of information.

What sorts of research issues are raised for the educator and the psychologist by this new learning medium?

Instructional Advantages

Let us examine, first, the potential instructional advantages of the computer, as viewed from a cognitive or information processing perspective. Across many possible educational programs, there are at least five common characteristics of learning via this medium that might be expected to facilitate instruction.

Interactivity of Learning. The most obvious distinguishing characteristic of the computer as an instructional device is its interactivity. Unlike other inanimate instructional media, the computer is able to receive, seek, and interpret information from the learner and is capable of differential responding contingent upon information obtained from the learner. Like a human tutor, in principle, it can query the learner, provide hints, offer help, or intervene when the student seems to need additional help. Unlike many human tutors, in practice, it can also be almost continuously responsive, attentive, and available to the learner. In sophisticated systems, moreover, the learner may actively question the computer, ask for a fuller explanation, or request more information when he or she is having difficulties (Sleeman & Brown, 1982).

The fact that the medium encourages, or may even require, active response and participation on the part of the learner may itself produce instructional benefits. Thus, active processing has been hypothesized to produce a greater investment of mental effort, an increased likelihood of mental elaboration, or a more complete integration of new information with past knowledge (e.g., Condry & Chambers, 1978; Moore & Anderson, 1969; Salomon, 1983). At the same time, however, the interactivity of the computer also provides the basis for several other possible advantages of this medium for learning.

Individualization of Learning. The most significant further consequence of the interactive character of computer-based learning lies in the opportunities it provides for the individualization of instruction. Educational decisions concerning the amount of direct instruction to be provided, the sequencing of problems to be presented, and the feedback to be given can all be made contingent upon a model or analysis of the learner's strengths and weaknesses in the domain being taught. Individual students, differing in their styles of learning or their rates of progress, can be presented with different materials tailored to their personal skills and proclivities. Extra assistance can be provided, for example, on those particular problems or concepts with which an individual student is having the greatest difficulties.

Indeed, since the earliest days of computer-assisted instruction, programs employing the computer as a device for teaching have routinely made use of this potential (e.g., Atkinson, 1972; Suppes, 1966). As the technology has become more sophisticated, even more powerful techniques for individualizing instruction are becoming available. The push toward "intelligent" computer-assisted instruction or intelligent tutoring systems, for example, involves the attempt to use tech-

niques taken from the field of artificial intelligence to create more detailed and informative models of the learner's current state of understanding, the gaps in that understanding, and his or her misconceptions in order to more closely match the instruction offered to the learner's needs and capabilities (Sleeman & Brown, 1982). Eventually, such systems, with their vast memories, may be better able to chart and monitor student progress than most human teachers.

Immediacy of Response. A second characteristic of the interactive potential of the computer is its ability to respond to input from the learner almost instantaneously. Again, the immediacy of response feedback, based on prior research, may have general beneficial effects on learning—even if that feedback involves no more than an indication of the correctness of one's responses (Moore & Anderson, 1969). Yet the computer also offers additional opportunities. It makes it possible to receive immediate feedback across a variety of dimensions on which feedback often is not systematically provided, such as speed of response or the quality of one's performance on individual lessons compared to social norms or one's own past performance.

Multiple Response Modes. In a similar vein, the computer also makes available a variety of modes of communication with and response to the learner through which instruction might be carried out, for example, text, graphics, animation, voice synthesis, music, and the like. As a result, it is possible to present information to students in many forms, either simultaneously or in sequence.

At the simplest level, this facility seems likely to enhance learning by providing the learner with multiple possible channels for encoding and retrieving information or by improving the potential "match" between instructional techniques and students' preferred modes of learning. For instance, the computer can present an animated visual display with accompanying written text that is simultaneously being read aloud to the student, enhancing the probability that the student will absorb the information through at least one of these channels.

At a somewhat higher level of analysis, the computer also provides a chance for the use of highly sophisticated devices for the presentation of information that may encourage new forms of learning. For example, many simulations allow the learner to take the role of a participant in some social system, thereby seeing that system through different eyes. Others allow the learner to experiment with counterfactual thinking—to see what would happen to the solar system, for example, if the laws of gravity operated differently. The computer can place complex animations or devices for the representation of data under the student's personal control. It could be used to teach concepts and distinctions via programs that successively "fade out" hints and clues that are no longer needed by the learner. Such possibilities are manifold.

Independence of Learning. Finally, because the computer is an interactive learning medium that can be controlled by the student, it offers rich possibilities for independent learning. With the computer, the student can proceed at his or her own pace, receiving informative feedback that provides a continuous test of the student's understanding of the material. Learning of this sort may take place in many circumstances—alone at home, with a friend after school, or with a class in summer camp. Because the computer is also a particularly effective device for maintaining student motivation, as we shall indicate later, students may persist in working on their own with activities that will have educational benefits.

Research Opportunities. There are several respects in which the computer provides an especially useful tool for the study of how

children learn. First, the computer makes it possible to examine directly the role that variables such as active participation or immediate response feedback might play in the learning process. For example, computer-based lessons of different sorts could be compared with noncomputerized treatments of the same material to discover whether there are ways in which this medium offers truly unique opportunities for instruction (Salomon, 1979). The interaction of learner aptitudes and instructional treatments (e.g., Cronbach & Snow, 1977) could be studied with much greater precision, making use of the capacity of the computer to track student progress continuously and to tailor instruction to past performance. The computer could have *indirect* beneficial effects on educational research as well. Because the design of any educational program for the computer requires a detailed and concrete analysis of instructional goals and techniques, it is likely to force us to think more clearly about the pedagogical choices and decisions we make and their potential consequences for students.

Motivational Advantages

In addition to potential information processing advantages, the computer also offers a number of possible motivational advantages as a medium for instruction and learning (Malone, 1981a, 1981b; Malone & Lepper, in press). Its technical capabilities provide opportunites for enhancing four primary determinants of intrinsic motivation: challenge, curiosity, control, and fantasy.

Challenge. Those theorists who have discussed intrinsic motivation primarily in terms of concepts such as challenge, mastery, or effectance motivation, for example, suggest that we find activities intrinsically interesting to the extent that they present us with meaningful challenges of intermediate difficulty. In this view, we prefer tasks that are neither impossibly difficult nor trivially easy—tasks in which goal accomplishment is uncertain (e.g., Csikszentmihalyi, 1975; Deci, 1975; Harter, 1978; White, 1959).

The most obvious opportunity offered by the computer in this area is one of continuous adjustment of the level of challenge provided by an activity through the use of variable levels of difficulty. As students engage in successful educational activities, their skills and knowledge increase. What was once difficult or challenging can quickly become simple and boring. A good instructional program, however, will be able to track the learner's accomplishments and vary the problems presented accordingly.

The technical capabilities of the computer also make it an excellent tool for producing activities involving uncertain goals through the use of other techniques. For instance, the computer is clearly well-suited to the use of random elements, hidden information, or hierarchical goal structures.

Curiosity. Other theorists have thought about intrinsic motivation primarily in terms of ideas such as curiosity, discrepancy, or incongruity (e.g., Berlyne, 1960, 1966; Hunt, 1965; Piaget, 1952). From this perspective, the central issue is the extent to which activities provide an optimal, intermediate level of discrepancy or incongruity between the learner's current knowledge or expectations and the information to be learned. Variability, novelty, and complexity are cited here as determinants of the intrinsic motivational appeal of an activity.

Again, the computer may provide a particularly effective tool for the creation of learning materials that heighten children's curiosity. On the one hand, the inherent interactivity of the medium and its ability to produce a wide variety of audio and visual effects provides an opportunity for heightening sensory curiosity. On the other hand, a more intelligent computer-based system may also be able to enhance cognitive curiosity by highlighting areas of inconsistency,

incompleteness, or unnecessary complexity in a student's understanding of some body of material.

Control. Yet a third set of traditional theories about intrinsic motivation has focused on issues of perceptions of personal control and self-determination. Intrinsic motivation, in this view, arises from activities that provide us with a sense of personal control over meaningful outcomes (e.g., Condry, 1977; deCharms, 1968; Deci, 1975, 1981).

Once more, the computer seems an especially useful medium for increasing students' feelings of control and self-determination. Interactive computer-based learning environments are inherently responsive to the students' responses. It is also easy to create programs in which it is possible for the learner to produce spectacular effects. Similarly, with the computer it is easy to produce learning activities that incorporate high levels of choice and learner control over the format and pacing of learning.

Fantasy. Not only does the computer provide opportunities for exploiting the motivational principles embodied in our traditional theoretical models, it also suggests further perspectives on the determinants of intrinsic motivation. Most prominently, observations of children's interactions with computer-based activities point immediately to the obvious motivational effects of promoting an involvement in a world of fantasy or an identification with fictional characters (cf. Singer, 1973). The technical capabilities of the computer that permit the production of interactive story plots, animated action sequences, effective sound effects, and the like, make this a medium that lends itself to the creation of games and activities likely to produce high levels of intrinsic motivation (Lepper, in press; Malone, 1981a, 1981b).

Research Opportunities. The computer raises two sorts of research possibilities in the domain of motivation. On the one hand, it provides a highly felicitous laboratory for investigating the determinants of intrinsic motivation (Lepper & Greene, 1978; Malone, 1981a, 1981b; Malone & Lepper, in press)—for asking the question: How can we make learning fun? The effects of features hypothesized as critical by different theoretical models can be studied both systematically and simultaneously. On the other hand, the computer also offers the opportunity for contrasting the effects of educational programs that employ such features with comparable programs that do not make use of these technical capabilities to enhance motivational appeal.

Motivational Appeal and Instructional Value

Once the opportunities for enhancing motivation that the computer affords are understood, a third set of fundamental research questions becomes apparent. If manipulations can be devised that have a significant impact on the motivational appeal of an educational activity but are simultaneously independent of the actual instructional content of the activity (e.g., the information presented, the sequencing of problems and activities, the feedback provided), then the general question of how intrinsic motivation affects learning can be asked (Lepper, in press; Lepper & Malone, in press).

Such a question has two forms. One involves contexts in which intrinsic motivation serves as a precondition for engagement in the activity itself—free-choice settings in which children will not approach or persist at an activity unless it is intrinsically motivating. In such situations, learning from a particular program will obviously be heavily, or completely, dependent on the motivational appeal of that program. One cannot learn from an activity, no matter how educational, if one chooses not to engage in it. Such considerations should be crucial, for example, in the case of computer-based

learning in the home or in voluntary clubs or classes.

The second form of this question, however, involves contexts in which engagement in the activity is constrained or required. Here learning might occur whether or not the activity proves intrinsically motivating to students, and it is here that the question of the relationship between motivational appeal and instructional value becomes most pointed and most theoretically significant. Does it make a difference—do we learn better, or worse, or perhaps just differently—if we find the activity from which we are learning interesting and exciting rather than dull and boring?

Instructional Games. A first context in which questions about the instructional consequences of increases in intrinsic motivation may be asked involves the study of instructional games. Consider two parallel educational programs, each presenting the same instruction, problems, and feedback, but varying in their motivational features. In the first such case, material about the addition of fractions might be presented in the form of a standard drill-and-practice program. In the second, the same material might be presented in the form of an entertaining game—one in which the student is confronted with problems involving the addition of fractions whose solution permits the learner to navigate a spaceship through the galaxy, serve hungry customers as the manager of a pizza parlor, or win a race against an animated robot.

What consequences might the use of such motivational enhancements have? Current social debates concerning the educational utility of instructional games present two antithetical views of the effects of the addition of such motivational embellishments to standard instructional programs (Lepper, in press; Lepper & Malone, in press).

On the one hand, how might the addition of these sorts of motivational devices influence learning from the program? Will the addition of motivational elements heighten attention and involvement, producing enhanced learning? Or will their addition prove distracting and likely to impair learning?

On the other hand, how might such devices affect student motivation? Even if it can be shown that students do find the presentation of material in the form of a game to be more entertaining and intrinsically motivating, there is a second, and perhaps more significant, motivational question to be asked. Do such games increase students' intrinsic motivation *outside* of the computer context as well as within it? Or do students learn to find the material itself to be dull and boring when presented outside of the computer domain?

Discovery Learning. A second context in which loosely related research issues arise involves the design and evaluation of computer-based discovery learning environments. Once again, the particular technical capabilities of the computer seem to be especially well-suited to the creation of intellectually complex, interactive learning environments in which exploratory, self-paced, and self-directed learning might flourish. Indeed, it might well be argued that the computer offers the opportunity for the creation of learning activities that more effectively capture the conditions under which discovery learning *ought* to occur than any of those examined in past research in this area (Brown, 1983; Lawler, 1982; Lepper & Malone, in press).

Classic controversies about the relative merits of discovery-based versus more direct and didactic teaching methods (Bruner, 1966; Shulman & Keislar, 1966) are being revived by the advent of powerful personal computers. Do children learn material more deeply or effectively when they are permitted to discover or induce ideas than when they are taught those same ideas directly? Or is such a self-directed approach useful only for a select sample of already motivated stu-

dents or an inefficient waste of instructional resources for all concerned?

Research Opportunities. In both these areas, the contrasting theoretical positions embodied in different approaches to the design of educational software pose obvious research challenges. In a sense, the computer provides a medium, a laboratory, for comparing and evaluating conflicting philosophies of instruction (Lepper & Malone, in press). Under what conditions will one approach prove superior to another? Are some forms of instructional games or discovery learning environments superior to others? Are there certain children for whom such motivational embellishments are likely to prove particularly powerful, or functionally irrelevant? The ease with which such learning environments can be produced and explored using the computer makes it an ideal device for the study of these classic educational controversies.

SOCIAL ISSUES

A consideration of the individual instructional issues outlined here tells only part of the story. It speaks to the *potential* of this medium under ideal, or at least supportive, conditions. It tells us little, however, about the ways in which such developments are likely to be influenced by, and in turn influence, social and societal pressures. In this second section, we briefly examine three sets of social impact or social policy issues that arise from a consideration of the educational potential of microcomputers.

Educational Equity

One significant controversy concerning the potential social consequences of increased educational uses of microcomputers involves fundamental issues of social equality (Lepper, in press). To some, computer technology seems most likely to multiply the advantages of the already privileged segments of our society, further enhancing existing inequalities in the opportunities available to the rich and to the poor. To others, the personal computer is perceived as a tool for achieving social equality, making available to all children the sorts of opportunities now available to only a few.

The frequent vision of the computer as a technology likely to promote further educational inequality is based primarily on economic and related demographic considerations. If only some families or some schools are able to afford state-of-the-art hardware or effective educational software, then the gap between rich and poor is likely to be increased by this new learning medium. Likewise, if only in middle class homes or schools are there adult models to guide and support educational uses of the computer, the relative advantage already enjoyed by these homes and schools seems likely to increase. Or if, as seems to be the case at the moment, computers are used in different ways with different groups of children in schools—for drill and practice with lower class children, but for teaching computer programming with middle class children—such differential treatment may exacerbate the differences it initially reflected.

By contrast, the argument for the computer as an essentially egalitarian technology usually begins with the premise that computers will become sufficiently inexpensive and attractive so that, as in the case of television, economic constraints will not play a significant role. Then, once such factors have been minimized, the egalitarian potential of the medium can be realized. In this second view, the computer is seen as a particularly effective instructional tool for students who would not normally fare well in our educational system. From this perspective, the computer is seen as affording a me-dium for providing the patient, nonevaluative, and individualized attention that less able students require. Through the use of instructional games and simulations, it may also provide a means of enhancing academic motivation among those students who do not ordinarily find schoolwork interesting or relevant. As a result, at least some common forms of computer-based instruction may prove especially effective with children who come from currently disadvantaged segments of society.

Educational Goals

A second class of larger social issues raised by this new technology involves the ways in which the future widespread availability of the microcomputer might alter the educational goals we choose to set for our children. There are two sides to this coin—the computer may supplement or supplant existing curriculum goals and priorities.

On the first side of the coin, the computer may suggest an expansion of traditional curriculum offerings in some areas. Some such additions may involve skills necessary for using computers themselves—the principal assumption underlying current discussion of concepts such as computer literacy. To some advocates, these added skills involve simply the learning of computer programming; to others, the relevant skills comprising computer literacy involve the ability to employ applications programs that permit the computer to be used as a tool to accomplish other ends (e.g., word processing, data analysis, or interactive simulations).

Other additions to the curriculum may be occasioned by the capabilities the computer affords for teaching in new domains or with new methods. For example, the availability of simple and inexpensive word processing programs for children may permit instruction in techniques of writing and editing or aspects of rhetoric that could not have been easily incorporated into the previous curriculum, in which a continued, laborious reworking of essays by hand was required. Or, the availability of a programming language such as Logo may offer a tool that will facilitate the incorporation of general planning and problem-solving abilities as a specific segment in the school curriculum.

On the flip side of the coin, a universal availability of computer technology to children may raise questions about topics that are already central to the present curriculum. One classic example is mental arithmetic. How critical will it be for children of the future to be able to do simple arithmetic operations quickly in their heads, when they might instead have learned to do such problems more easily and effectively using a simple calculator? Similarly, how important will spelling skills or penmanship be in the future, if all significant writing is to be done using word processors with built-in printers and automatic spelling checkers? Obviously we do not want to leave children entirely dependent upon the technology and unable to solve a simple problem or spell a word themselves. The critical, and quite difficult, question for the future is one of priorities and the relative investment of time in learning, practicing, and polishing skills that may retain less functionality as computers become more widespread.

Educational Institutions

Finally, there are a variety of issues that arise concerning the potential social impact of an increasing reliance on microcomputers in our educational institutions. Again, there are several different positions common in current debates.

At one extreme, there is a "minimalist" position, in which computers are seen as likely to have little impact on the process of formal education—once all the initial hoopla and misguided hyperbole is over. To advocates of this position, the computer is just

the latest in a long series of technological innovations that have failed to have any truly significant, *lasting* impact on schools. To this group, the future of computers in schools will involve an elective course or two in computer programming and some continued use of the computer as a device for providing guided drill and practice in certain highly structured content areas.

At the other extreme stand the visionaries and revolutionaries, who see this new interactive technology as qualitatively different from previous technologies and as certain to have a major transformative effect on the process of education in our country. In one version of this vision, exemplified in the remarks of Bork and Suppes quoted earlier, the computer is seen as an instructional tool that will strengthen and enhance the effectiveness of our schools. In other versions of this general vision, the computer might even supplant schools altogether. Seymour Papert (1980) has presented the following argument:

> I believe that the computer presence will enable us to modify the learning environment outside the classroom so that much, if not all, the knowledge schools presently try to teach with such pain and expense and such limited success will be learned as the child learns to talk, painlessly, successfully, and without organized instruction. This obviously implies that schools as we know them today will have no place in the future. But it is an open question whether they will adapt by transforming themselves into something new altogether or wither away and be replaced. (pp. 8–9)

In between these two extremes fall advocates of a variety of more moderate, evolutionary positions, including those who believe that initially very limited uses of the computer in schools—for tasks such as simple programming and straightforward drill and practice—will eventually be expanded to the point where the computer becomes as much a standard tool of education as the book or the pencil.

Research Opportunities

For each of these larger issues, current debates pose three related sorts of research questions (Lepper, in press; Walker, 1983). First, to the psychologist, each of these controversies should emphasize the need for basic research on motivation and learning of the sort outlined at the outset of this chapter. That is, the outcome of each of these general policy debates should depend on the actual instructional effectiveness and motivational appeal of different educational uses of the computer for different groups of children.

Even a demonstrably unequal distribution of computer experiences will not necessarily increase, or decrease, the eventual inequality of educational attainments by different segments of society. What we need to know is the effectiveness of each use for students of different backgrounds or of different abilities—who learns most, or most efficiently, from each different instructional use of the computer. Similarly, whether word processors should (or are likely to) be used in the classroom to teach higher level skills of composition and rhetoric will depend on their demonstrable effectiveness in achieving this end. Or, whether spelling checkers will produce a need for more, or possibly less, direct instruction remains an empirical issue.

Second, to the sociologist, issues would arise regarding the extent to which different segments of the population have different exposure to computer technology and the reasons behind any such differential experiences. The question of how institutional uses of computers relate to more general, and classic, problems such as the diffusion of technological innovations or the reform of education must also be considered.

Finally, to the policy analyst, each of these

areas poses pragmatic questions about techniques for producing change in social systems and institutions. What sorts of interventions—public or private, national or local, centralized or decentralized—might be necessary to influence the process whereby computers, and appropriate educational programs, are introduced into schools, homes, and other learning settings?

EPILOGUE

In attempting to characterize and highlight the significant research issues raised by the incursion of personal computers into the domain of education, we have selectively focused on the variety of controversies that current conditions stimulate. In view of these highly divergent perspectives and the complexity of the issues, it is hard not be persuaded to seek some middle ground. In this, as in other social issues, the eventual outcome seems likely to bear equally vague resemblance to the dreams of current educational visionaries and the nightmares of present computer critics.

It is easy to be swayed by promises of further improvements in technology "just around the corner" and preliminary results of dramatic demonstration projects staffed with enthusiastic crusaders. Let us reemphasize our earlier comments regarding the sobering history of past technological advances that proved successful in general societal terms, but remained unsuccessful in altering the course of education in this country, by quoting the following ringing, and eerily familiar, endorsement of technological solutions to educational problems:

> Books will soon be obsolete in our schools. Scholars will soon be instructed through the eye. It is possible to teach every branch of human knowledge with the [new technology]. Our

school system will be completely changed in ten years.

The time: 1913. The author: Thomas Alva Edison. The technology: the motion picture.

REFERENCES

Atkinson, R. C. (1972). Ingredients for a theory of instruction. *American Psychologist, 27,* 921–931.

Berlyne, D. E. (1960). *Conflict, arousal, and curiosity.* New York: McGraw-Hill.

Berlyne, D. E. (1966). Curiosity and exploration. *Science, 153,* 25–33.

Bork, A. (1980). Preparing student-computer dialogs: Advice to teachers. In R. P. Taylor (Ed.), *The computer in the school: Tutor, tool, tutee* (pp. 15–52). New York: Teachers College Press.

Brown, J. S. (1983). Learning-by-doing revisited for electronic learning environments. In M. A. White (Ed.), *The future of electronic learning* (pp. 13–32). Hillsdale, NJ: Erlbaum.

Bruner, J. S. (1966). *Toward a theory of instruction.* Cambridge, MA: Harvard University Press.

Condry, J. C. (1977). Enemies of exploration: Self-initiated versus other-initiated learning. *Journal of Personality and Social Psychology, 35,* 459–477.

Condry, J., & Chambers, J. (1978). Intrinsic motivation and the process of learning. In M. R. Lepper & D. Greene (Eds.), *The hidden costs of reward* (pp. 61–84). Hillsdale, NJ: Erlbaum.

Condry, J., & Keith, D. (1983). Educational and recreational uses of computer technology. *Youth and Society, 15,* 87–112.

Cronbach, L. J., & Snow, R. E. (1977). *Aptitudes and instructional methods: Handbook for research on interactions.* New York: Irvington.

Csikszentmihalyi, M. (1975). *Beyond boredom and anxiety.* San Francisco: Jossey-Bass.

deCharms, R. (1968). *Personal causation.* New York: Academic Press.

Deci, E. L. (1975). *Intrinsic motivation.* New York: Plenum.

Deci, E. L. (1981). *The psychology of self-determination.* Lexington, MA: Heath.

Harter, S. (1978). Effectance motivation reconsidered: Toward a developmental model. *Human Development, 1,* 34–64.

Hornik, R. (1981). Out-of-school television and schooling: Hypotheses and methods. *Review of Educational Research, 51,* 193–214.

Hunt, J. McV. (1965). Intrinsic motivation and its role in psychological development. In D. Levine (Ed.), *Nebraska Symposium on Motivation,* (Vol. 13, pp. 189–283). Lincoln, NE: University of Nebraska Press.

Lawler, R. W. (1982). Designing computer microworlds. *Byte, 7,* 138–160.

Lepper, M. R. (in press). Microcomputers in education: Motivational and social issues. *American Psychologist.*

Lepper, M. R., & Greene, D. (Eds.). (1978). *The hidden costs of reward.* Hillsdale, NJ: Erlbaum.

Lepper, M. R., & Malone, T. W. (in press). Intrinsic motivation and instructional effectiveness in computer-based education. In R. E. Snow & M. C. Farr (Eds.), *Aptitude, learning, and instruction: III. Conative and affective process analyses.* Hillsdale, NJ: Erlbaum.

Malone, T. W. (1981a). Toward a theory of intrinsically motivating instruction. *Cognitive Science, 4,* 333–369.

Malone, T. W. (1981b). What makes computer games fun? *Byte, 6,* 258–277.

Malone, T. W., & Lepper, M. R. (in press). Making learning fun: A taxonomy of intrinsic motivation for learning. In R. E. Snow & M. C. Farr (Eds.), *Aptitude, learning, and instruction: III. Conative and affective process analyses.* Hillsdale, NJ: Erlbaum.

Moore, O. K., & Anderson, A. R. (1969). Some principles for the design of clarifying educational environments. In D. Goslin (Ed.), *Handbook of socialization theory and research* (pp. 571–613). Chicago: Rand McNally.

Papert, S. (1980). *Mindstorms: Children, computers, and powerful ideas.* New York: Basic Books.

Piaget, J. (1952). *The origins of intelligence in children.* New York: International University Press.

Salomon, G. (1979). *Interaction of media, cognition, and learning.* San Francisco: Jossey-Bass.

Salomon, G. (1983). The differential investment of mutual effort in learning from different sources. *Educational Psychologist, 18,* 42–50.

Shulman, L. S., & Keislar, E. R. (Eds.). (1966). *Learning by discovery: A critical appraisal.* Chicago: Rand-McNally.

Singer, J. L. (1973). *The child's world of make-believe.* New York: Academic Press.

Sleeman, D., & Brown, J. S. (Eds.). (1982). *Intelligent tutoring systems.* New York: Academic Press.

Suppes, P. (1966). The uses of computers in education. *Scientific American, 215*(3), 206–221.

Taylor, R. P. (Ed.). (1980). *The computer in the school: Tutor, tool, tutee.* New York: Teachers College Press.

Walker, D. F. (1983). Reflections on the educational potential and limitations of microcomputers. *Phi Delta Kappan, 65,* 103–107.

White, R. W. (1959). Motivation reconsidered: The concept of competence. *Psychological Review, 66,* 297–333.

CHAPTER 3

THE MICROCOMPUTER AS A SYMBOLIC MEDIUM

Karen Sheingold
Center for Children and Technology
Bank Street College of Education
New York, New York 10025

Picture a classroom of young children. There is a young boy in a smock, paintbrush in hand, excitedly putting brush to paper, creating his own work. The smell of the paint and the feel of the brush on paper are an integral part of his experience. Two young girls are building a farm in the block corner, discovering that their stable is not sufficiently large for 12 plastic horses to be housed there. In the book corner, a group of young children are creating a story together, which their teacher commits to writing.

What role could or should a microcomputer possibly play in such a lively environment where children are actively working with materials and inventing their own worlds? The computer, a piece of electronic "adult" technology, certainly doesn't smell like paint or feel like blocks. It is not an object in the world the way the class guinea pig is. Does it have a legitimate place in a classroom for young children, or, once it arrives, will it supplant these more important activities?

These are the kinds of questions on the minds of many educators of young children. They want to know whether children younger than 8 years of age should use microcomputers. I have been a witness to and a participant in many lively debates on this topic in the last few years. The intensity and passion with which views are expressed has led me to reflect on what underlies both the questions and their intensity. It is important to "unpack" these general questions to discover what the real issues are and how they can be addressed. The purpose of this chapter is to provide such an analysis.

In the absence of a substantial base of theory and research relating to young children's use of microcomputers, this analysis is difficult to accomplish. That no one knows much about what it means for young children to use microcomputers, however, provides an arena ripe for reflection, experimentation, debate, and cooperation among educators and researchers. Examining educators' questions about microcomputers leads inevitably and fruitfully into research questions, which then lead back into questions about educational practice. In the following pages I will suggest some reasons for the deep concerns I hear about using microcomputers with young children, and relate these to ideas about development, about what the microcomputer is or could be, and to how the power of this educational innovation is interpreted. Wherever possible, I will point to important research issues.

SYMBOLS AND REALITY

It is not possible to talk about young children or microcomputers without first talking about symbols. By a *symbol* I mean anything that represents some kind of information. A word is a symbol because it refers to or denotes a thing, idea, or feeling. Symbols—pictures, numbers, words, gestures—convey meanings. *Symbol systems*, such as language, mathematics, and dance, are organized, complex, and related patterns of symbols that, taken together, comprise broad cultural systems of meaning. *Symbolic products*—stories, poems, songs, symphonies, scientific experiments—are the results of our active engagement with these systems. Symbolic products are created in particular media or materials.

There is a sense in which symbols are not "real." A picture of a tree, or the word *tree*, are not the same as the tree. Looking at a real tree is a different experience from looking at a picture of one or reading a story about one. Symbols are *about* the world and how we give meaning to it.

What does this have to do with young children and microcomputers? First among the concerns that I hear about young children's use of microcomputers is that this new technology is not real in the way other classroom materials are—such as paint, clay, crayons, or rhythm instruments. The microcomputer is fundamentally a symbolic machine. We use it to represent and manipulate symbol systems—language, mathematics, music—and to create symbolic products—poems, mathematical proofs, compositions. In this sense it is *about* the world and not *of* it.

But is a symbolic machine incompatible in some fundamental way with young children—with what they know, what they do, and how they learn and develop in the early years? What we know about early development, about how and in what realms children learn and develop during these years can help answer this question.

Early Symbolic Development

While for many years it was difficult to characterize development between infancy and the school years except in negative terms (the child is preoperational, illogical, and so forth), research in the last decade has modified this view in two significant ways. First, it has become clear that the young child is capable of many cognitive activities at first thought accessible only to older children. Researchers (Gelman & Baillargeon, 1983; Siegler, 1981) have shown that the ways in which tasks are structured for young children dramatically affect what they can demonstrate about what they know. In carefully designed situations, for example, young children reveal that they are not entirely egocentric or perception-bound (Gelman, 1978; Lempers, Flavell & Flavell, 1977), and they can achieve some success on many tests of concrete operations (Donaldson, 1978; Siegel & Brainerd, 1978). What young children know, however, tends to be implicit rather than explicit. That is, these children demonstrate skills and knowledge that they are not aware of and cannot tell us about except by their actions in tasks of the psychologist's design.

The second way in which our views of early childhood have been modified is that there has emerged a more positive characterization of early childhood as a time of accomplishments in the development of symbolization (Gardner, 1983; Gardner & Wolf,

1979). During this period there is a genuine flowering of symbolic capacities and activities, such that by age 5 the child has "first draft knowledge" (Gardner, 1983, p. 305) of symbolization in language, pictures, three-dimensional objects (blocks, clay), dance, music, and pretend play, as well as some number and logical knowledge. Between the ages of 5 and 7, children acquire the rudiments of notational systems—systems which themselves refer to symbol systems. So the child begins to learn a written language, which itself refers to a spoken language.

Symbolic Machine

The lack of "realness" that is attributed to the microcomputer derives, I believe, from the fact that the microcomputer is a symbolic machine. When children use a microcomputer they are interacting with symbols—words, numbers, pictures, graphic representations. But much of the activity young children naturally engage in is also symbolic—communicating with gestures, speaking, pretend play, counting, tapping a rhythm, singing, making a picture or a clay object. In the classroom described at the beginning of this paper, the children were all making symbolic products—a painting, a block scene, a story. The symbolic nature of the microcomputer per se does not make it incompatible with or inappropriate for use by young children. One could, in fact, make just the opposite argument. To do so out of hand, however, would be to ignore the critical issue of *how* the child engages with a particular symbol system via the microcomputer.

There is a direct, active involvement of children with crayons and blocks that is assumed to be absent with the microcomputer. But is this absence intrinsic to working with a microcomputer? The image many people have of microcomputer use in schools reflects the drill-and-practice software that has dominated the educational software marketplace. Used this way, the microcomputer gives children questions to answer or problems to solve, and then tells them whether or not their answers are correct. In some cases, the drill and practice is "dressed up" to look more like a game, but the basic format is the same. For young children, a very large proportion of existing software is devoted to letter and number recognition.

This type of activity is relatively passive. Children respond to questions. Answers are correct or incorrect. There are few degrees of freedom in what they do, and no opportunities for invention, for shaping the medium to make their own products or achieve their own goals. This type of activity, however, is an extremely small and limited subset of the ways in which children can interact with the machine.

Within any given symbol system represented on the microcomputer, there are many different kinds of activities a child can do, some of which are more and some less constrained by the software itself. Take graphics, for example. A program can ask a child to do one of several things. One program might ask the child simply to detect correspondence among specific shapes. Another might provide an array of shapes and objects that the child can arrange in a design of his or her choosing. A third might provide the equivalent of paint and brushes and permit the child to create pictures or designs from scratch. Not only are these all different kinds of tasks requiring different skills, but the options open to the child increase as we move from the first program to the third. In both the second and third examples, the child can make something, rather than simply respond. At least in principle, the microcomputer is a medium that the child can use for making, doing, and creating.

Moreover, there are many different ways of giving information to the microcomputer, the keyboard being the most familiar as well as the most indirect. Mice, paddles, and joysticks, for example, are analog devices that make possible a direct mapping between the child's hand and finger movements and what happens on the screen. Many games make

use of paddles and joysticks for controlling moves on the screen. Children can even manipulate directly what happens on the screen by touching it with a light pen. Special keypads have been developed for young children, and others could be, which have larger, fewer, and/or different symbols from what is on the keyboard. So, not only can the microcomputer be a medium for making and doing, but it can be more or less similar to other media with which the child is familiar.

The microcomputer is not one thing or one kind of experience, for young children or anyone else. Its flexibility presents a great challenge to our imaginations. The challenge is to determine whether and how the microcomputer can be made interesting, appropriate, and useful for young children.

POSSIBILITIES FOR MICROCOMPUTER USE WITH YOUNG CHILDREN

What would we have this technology be for the young child? What would we use it for? Such questions are difficult to answer in the absence of careful research and development work, but there are four possibilities that come to mind. Not an exhaustive list, these are examples of how we might think about using microcomputers with young children. I propose these as hypotheses to be tested, not as answers. First, we could use the microcomputer to acquaint the child with properties that are unique to it, such as dynamic movement and programmability, and thus provide experiences not possible with other classroom media. Second, we could use the microcomputer to support learning so that children can explore aspects of experience that would normally require skills they do not yet have. Third, we could use the microcomputer as a way for children to better understand what they do in other media. Fourth, we could use the microcomputer to help children gain a broader view of what the computer is as an important piece of technology in the world.

Exploring Unique Properties of the Microcomputer

There is no doubt that young children will approach the microcomputer as they do other new objects—with curiosity and excitement—and subject it to whatever means of exploration they have at their disposal so that it reveals its properties and "secrets" to them. But since the microcomputer is not just one thing, teachers must decide which software to use, which properties children might profitably explore.

One question that many educators ask themselves is whether or not microcomputer-based activity offers anything that is substantially different from what can be obtained in the classroom by other means. In its programmable and dynamic properties the microcomputer is different from most other media with which children interact. Introducing young children in simple ways to these properties may provide interesting learning opportunities. For example, children could explore the dynamic properties of movement by having a set of objects that they could cause to move on the screen in ways that they would specify. Children could convey their instructions via simple, specially designed input devices (e.g., keypads, mice, light pens). With a dynamic toolkit of shapes and movements, children could construct their own moving pictures and scenes. In this new medium, children could make something interesting to look at, play with, share with others, and redesign at will.

Programmability is another property unique to computers, and one to which I believe young children can be exposed in simple form. What might a young child learn about programmability? First, that a person can make a choice or give an instruction to the microcomputer to make something happen, and, second, that instructions can be combined to make a sequence of events occur. Programmability could be taught with respect to a number of different symbol systems, but graphics and music come to mind as ones that are likely to be particularly in-teresting for young children. These "simple ideas" about instructions and sequence could be introduced to young children without using programming languages per se.

These ideas that I refer to as *simple* are not necessarily so, and it will be important to discover whether or not young children are able to comprehend and use them with fluency. I have no doubt that young children will find it easy and interesting to give instructions to the microcomputer that result in events occurring on the screen. Many older children do. But there may be a problem in our interpretation of what is understood by the child. In working with older children, we find that they are capable of producing impressive arrays on the screen without having a flexible or deep understanding of the program that resulted in that array (Mawby, 1984; Pea, 1983). Programming languages are, it turns out, very complex symbol systems, the mastery of which takes much time and intensive effort (Kurland & Cahir, 1984; Pea & Kurland, 1984b). So, while I think it worthwhile to introduce young children to ideas about programmability, it is equally important for educators and researchers to look carefully at what is actually learned and understood. We cannot assume that if a child can create some sequenced instructions on the microcomputer he or she "knows how to program."

Microcomputer as Cognitive Support

The second way in which it might be beneficial to use the microcomputer is as a support for or facilitator of activities that young children would not normally be able to do. It is widely assumed that there are sequences of skills that must be learned before being able to produce a symbolic product. So, in most cases one learns a musical instrument and musical notation before attempting to compose. Yet it is not clear that such skills are prerequisite to composing. While composing is generally reserved for a small segment of skilled musicians, we know that children as young as 2 years of age make up their own songs (McKernon, 1979). In a similar vein, one must be able to put letters and words on paper before being able to write a story. Again, it is not clear that composing with language depends on being able to form those letters and words. Young children are good at telling stories (Sutton-Smith, 1972), yet writing them down poses difficulties of many kinds. Can young children create these complex symbolic products without having mastered the notational systems and all of the cognitive skills an adult or older child would bring to the enterprise?

A microcomputer might afford such opportunities. To begin with, much-simplified versions of existing word processors and music editors are required. Making such software simple enough and simple in the right ways is a significant design challenge. By allowing children to bypass some of the physical and cognitive obstacles in a particular arena, we may make it possible for them to enjoy creative experiences that would be difficult, if not impossible, to obtain without such support.

There is, however, another sense in which microcomputer-based work may serve to support and extend children's cognitive activities. It turns out that, for older children, microcomputer-based work in classrooms tends to be collaborative (Hawkins, Sheingold, Gearhart & Berger, 1982; Levin & Boruta, 1983). Children work together and use each other as resources while they do such varied activities as programming, writing stories and articles, engaging in games and simulations, or simply figuring out how to get the microcomputer to work. This kind of joint activity provides a kind of "scaffolding" of the social environment for children to accomplish what they might not be able to on their own. Here we have the intriguing possibility that the microcomputer may serve as a kind of cognitive support, not by itself, but because of its impact on the social life of the classroom. When teachers allow it,

microcomputer-based activities "invite" collaboration, which can assist accomplishments for children both as individuals and groups.

Reflecting on Other Activities

"The computer, rather than being a super-brain, teaching us with its consistent and logical 'thinking,' is instead a fantasy world which, like a hall of mirrors, reflects back to us images of our commonsense ways of making *things* and making *sense*" (Bamberger, 1983, p. 1). In these words Jeanne Bamberger proposed that we think about the microcomputer in yet another way—as a medium that can help us discover and reflect on what we already know intuitively. By playing with what we make in the microcomputer world, she suggested, we come to see familiar actions and objects in new ways.

She described, for example, how, in translating a drummed rhythm into a simple program for the microcomputer, we discover new properties of the rhythmic structure. Her general argument was that we have implicit knowledge about many things—how to clap a rhythm, build a block tower, draw a picture. Having to program that same activity on the microcomputer requires making explicit the knowledge that we have "in our muscles." In so doing, we know differently and better what we knew before.

Does this argument apply to young children? I think it does, if made more broadly. Since there is more than one way of knowing, giving children access to multiple ways of knowing may lead to better understanding in a particular domain (Dewey & Bentley, 1960). If some kinds of microcomputer experience offer ways of knowing that differ from what the child does with other media in the classroom, then it is precisely through the *connecting* of these related, but different, kinds of experience that new learning may be possible.

To try but one example, let's give the child

an opportunity to paint with a microcomputer. With a typical paint program, the child chooses a brush thickness and can even choose the type of pattern the brush will make as it moves around on the screen. Colors can be selected, mixed, and tried out. Shapes can be created and made smaller or larger. Many possibilities can be explored alone or in combination, erased, changed, or moved. Painting with the microcomputer could make children aware of choices and possibilities that they would otherwise accept as givens when they use paint and paper. With such rapid experimentation the child may make discoveries in microcomputer painting that enable him or her to attempt new things with paint and paper.

The flaw in this argument rests on *how* the child makes connections from one medium to another. Research conducted with older children at the Center for Children and Technology leads me to doubt that such connections will come naturally or easily. For example, children learning to program were often unable to apply a command or concept they had used successfully in one program to another program (Pea, 1983). That is, making connections *within* programming was difficult. Moreover, there was no general transfer of planning and problem-solving skills to a noncomputer task by children who had learned programming for a year, compared with those who had not (Pea & Kurland, 1984a). It follows, then, that if we are to use the microcomputer to help children see and reflect on connections from one medium to another, teachers will need to structure children's experiences and provide support to make this possible.

Microcomputer as Object

I want to conclude by going back to the original assumption about the microcomputer as something that is not truly real because it is a symbolic medium. There is, of course, a sense in which it is very real, and will become increasingly so for the young child. It is an object in the world, with its own physical and tactile properties. It is also a very powerful tool with which people can do many important and interesting symbolic tasks, from writing a book to designing a house to constructing a budget to communicating with people on another continent.

As children use microcomputers at home and in classrooms they will develop their own ideas about what this machine is and what it is for (Mawby, Clement, Pea, & Hawkins, 1984). It will require serious and clever research to find out just how it is that young minds comprehend this peculiar and flexible object. There is no doubt, however, that children's notions will be influenced by the kinds of experiences they have had with the machine and the kinds of interpretations of it offered by teachers and peers. What they think it is and what they think it is for, will, at least in part, reflect what they do with it and what they see others doing. Therefore, educational choices about how children use microcomputers in classrooms have implications for children's initial understanding of a significant piece of cultural technology.

My personal view is that I would like children to approach this machine matter-of-factly. I would want them to understand at some level that this is a tool that does more than one thing, that people use it for their own purposes, and that children, too, have a variety of purposes for which its use is appropriate. Such a view would be fostered in a classroom where the technology was treated matter-of-factly, where children were helped to use the machine in a number of ways, and where they could make use of it when they were interested or had something to do with which they thought the microcomputer could be of help.

In such a classroom the functionality and purposes of the microcomputer—the ways in which it helped teachers and students do things, its connections to other classroom activities—would get worked out over time as uses were discovered, tried, and found to be productive. The microcomputer, then, would not be a thing apart. It would simply be another material for the classroom. As with other media, some children would find it more interesting than would other children. And there would be individual differences in the ways children chose to use the machine. In their imaginative play, children wouldn't "play computer," just as they don't "play telephone." Rather, they would incorporate the microcomputer into their play about other things.

SHAPING AN INNOVATION

I believe that the greatest source of concern about having microcomputers in classrooms for young children is that the microcomputer activities will *supplant* the many activities children do with "real" materials. Having a microcomputer in a classroom means, it is feared, these other activities will disappear in the face of their computerized versions. There is no doubt that working with materials is important for young children, and it would be unimaginable, not to say absurd, to have a microcomputer replace the water table, block corner, or pet rabbit.

What seems to underlie this concern is a sense that the microcomputer innovation has a life of its own proceeding at an intense, unstoppable pace. Such a fear is understandable when schools are acquiring microcomputers at an ever-accelerating rate, when parents are playing an active role in urging schools to buy microcomputers, and when advertisements for microcomputer hardware and software attempt to make us believe that serious cognitive deprivation and/or failure to get ahead in life will result if children do not have access to microcomputers at an early age.

On the other hand, this view implies that the technology will take over, that what teachers do or believe will not matter. What-

ever research knowledge we have on this issue suggests quite the opposite—that what school systems and teachers do with computers—what they use them for, how they interpret them, how they present them to children—has an enormous effect on what happens in a particular system or classroom (Char, Hawkins, Wooten, Sheingold, & Roberts, 1983; Sheingold, Hawkins, & Char, 1984; Sheingold, Kane, & Endreweit, 1983). The technology does not have a life of its own, nor does it stand on its own. It is always used by people in a social context. Because it is such a flexible tool, people make choices in using it and thus shape its use in important ways. What teachers do *does* matter and will continue to matter. Teachers will help to shape this innovation by their decisions about how to use this new technology, by their willingness to experiment with it and to share what they learn, and by their involvement in research and software development efforts. Finally, they will have an impact on this innovation by their willingness to say "no" to uses of technology that they believe are not in the best interests of young children.

As I see it, questions about whether and how microcomputers can be used by young children cannot be answered in the abstract. Nor can these questions be answered simply by putting currently available software into classrooms and "seeing what happens." There is a complex, cooperative enterprise called for among teachers, researchers, and developers. We need software that is well-designed for the young child, teachers who are willing to experiment with interesting uses for it in their classrooms, and researchers who can ask insightful questions about the learning that the technology affords. With endeavors in place that are interactive among teachers, researchers, and developers, we will gradually be able to answer some of our questions about the use of microcomputers by young children. We will also discover new questions, which will require new research, development, and classroom implementation to answer. At each stage of this recursive process, we may learn more about questions that have always intrigued us—how it is that children learn and develop, how new technologies transform and support such learning, and how sensitive practitioners create effective learning environments for young children.

REFERENCES

Bamberger, J. (1983, April). The computer as sandcastle. In K. Sheingold (Chair), *Chameleon in the classroom: Developing roles for computers.* Symposium conducted at the American Educational Research Association, Montreal, Canada.

Char, C., Hawkins, J., Wooten, J., Sheingold, K., & Roberts, T. (1983). *"The Voyage of the Mimi": Classroom case studies of software, video, and print materials* (Contract No. 300–81–0375). Washington, DC: U.S. Department of Education.

Dewey, J., & Bentley, A. F. (1960). *Knowing and the known.* Boston: Beacon Press. (Original work published 1949)

Donaldson, M. (1978). *Children's minds.* London: Croom Helm.

Gardner, H. (1983). *Frames of mind.* New York: Basic Books.

Gardner, H., & Wolf, D. (Eds.). (1979). *New directions for child development: Early symbolization.* San Francisco: Jossey-Bass.

Gelman, R. (1978). Cognitive development. *Annual Review of Psychology, 29,* 297–332.

Gelman, R., & Baillargeon, R. (1983). A review of some Piagetian concepts. In P. H. Mussen (Ed.), *Handbook of child psychology* (4th ed., Vol. 3, pp. 167–230). New York: Wiley.

Hawkins, J., Sheingold, K., Gearhart, M., & Berger, C. (1982). Microcomputers in schools: Impact on the social life of elementary class-rooms. *Journal of Applied Developmental Psychology, 3,* 361–373.

Kurland, D. M., & Cahir, N. (1984). *The development of computer programming expertise: An interview study of expert adult programmers* (Technical Report No. 17). New York: Bank Street College of Education, Center for Children and Technology.

Lempers, J. D., Flavell, E. R., & Flavell, J. H. (1977). The development in very young children of tacit knowledge concerning visual perception. *Genetic Psychology Monographs, 95,* 3–53.

Levin, J. A., & Boruta, M. J. (1983). Writing with computers in classrooms: "You get EXACTLY the right amount of space!" *Theory into Practice, 22,* 291–295.

Mawby, R. (1984, April). *Determining students' understanding of programming concepts.* Paper presented at the meeting of the American Educational Research Association, New Orleans, LA.

Mawby, R., Clement, C., Pea, R. D., & Hawkins, J. (1984). *Structured interviews on children's conceptions of computers* (Technical Report No. 19). New York: Bank Street College of Education, Center for Children and Technology.

McKernon, P. E. (1979). The development of first songs in young children. In H. Gardner & D. Wolf (Eds.), *New directions for child development: Early symbolization* (pp. 43–58). San Francisco: Jossey-Bass.

Pea, R. D. (1983, April). Logo programming and problem solving. In K. Sheingold (Chair), *Chameleon in the classroom: Developing roles for computers.* Symposium conducted at the meeting of the American Educational Research Association, Montreal, Canada.

Pea, R. D., & Kurland, D. M. (1984a). *Logo programming and the development of planning skills* (Technical Report No. 16). New York: Bank Street College of Education, Center for Children and Technology.

Pea, R. D., & Kurland, D. M. (1984b). On the cognitive effects of learning computer programming. *New Ideas in Psychology, 2,* 137–168.

Sheingold, K., Hawkins, J., & Char, C. (1984). *"I'm the thinkist, you're the typist": The interaction of technology and the social life of classrooms.* Manuscript submitted for publication.

Sheingold, K., Kane, J. H., & Endreweit, M. E. (1983). Microcomputer use in schools: Developing a research agenda. *Harvard Educational Review, 53,* 412–432.

Siegel, L. S., & Brainerd, C. J. (Eds.). (1978). *Alternatives to Piaget.* New York: Academic Press.

Siegler, R. S. (1981). Developmental sequences within and between concepts. *Monographs of the Society for Research in Child Development, 46* (2, Serial No. 189).

Sutton-Smith, B. (1972). *The folkgames of children.* Austin: University of Texas Press.

PART II

CONCERNS

CHAPTER 4

TWO PRESCHOOLERS SHARING ONE MICROCOMPUTER: CREATING PROSOCIAL BEHAVIOR WITH HARDWARE AND SOFTWARE

Karin Borgh
W. Patrick Dickson
Child and Family Studies
University of Wisconsin
Madison, Wisconsin 53706

During the past year and a half preschool children at the University of Wisconsin Laboratory Preschool have been using a microcomputer with a wide variety of software and peripherals. During this period we have continually explored various ways of integrating the microcomputer into the overall curriculum of the preschool. Although we have gathered some observational data on the patterns of social interaction among the preschoolers using the computer, our primary orientation has been to try out many different approaches for using the microcomputer rather than to pursue tightly framed hypotheses. Nevertheless, our explorations have been guided by four themes.

THEMES

When we first began mulling over the idea of introducing a microcomputer into the preschool, several issues were prominent in the media and in our discussions with preschool teachers. A recurring theme was simply whether 3- and 4-year-old children could use a microcomputer, especially if it required them to cope with the standard keyboard. Some of the earliest researchers (Rothenberg, 1984) seemed to make the assumption that they could not and devised special-purpose devices to simplify input. We felt that this assumption needed to be examined more closely.

A second theme dealt with concerns about potentially negative effects of the microcomputer on social interactions among young children. One concern was whether individual children would become so absorbed with the microcomputer that they would spend inadequate time playing with other children. Another concern was that the microcomputer would become a male-dominated activity, thereby fostering sex role stereotyping. Some teachers, familiar with the violence and aggression dominating arcade games and

much microcomputer software, questioned the wisdom of introducing such experiences into the preschool. Some early reports lent support to these concerns. Because we shared some of these worries, we sought from the outset to use the microcomputer in ways that would foster prosocial interaction, equal access by males and females, and constructive rather than destructive activities.

A third theme guiding our activities was the identification of software characteristics that seemed to facilitate use of the microcomputer by young children, especially in group settings such as preschools. We obtained a large collection of software advertised as appropriate for very young children. This software ranged from good to intriguing, from promising but flawed to abysmal. From this collection we selected a small number of software packages to use in our more extensive observations.

The fourth theme dealt with use of the microcomputer in the classroom context. We placed the microcomputer in different places in the room, tried different ways of displaying the software, and varied the degree to which children's use of the microcomputer was teacher-directed or self-directed. We have arrived at what appears to be one satisfactory approach.

THE LABORATORY PRESCHOOL

The variations we explored and the conclusions we reached are affected necessarily by the context in which we conducted our observations. The University of Wisconsin Laboratory Preschool serves approximately 20 children between the ages of 3 and 5. These children come from diverse backgrounds, many being the children of faculty and graduate students. The children are predominantly middle class and include a substantial number whose native language is not

English. The preschool follows a curriculum based on the theories of Ausubel (1963), emphasizing use of advanced organizers and the presentation of concepts in a structured manner.

Our observations are based primarily on one Apple® II Plus microcomputer, although we did occasionally have a Commodore 64® and a VIC–20® microcomputer in the classroom. The Apple was equipped with a color monitor, a joystick, and later a touch pad (KoalaPad™).

WHAT WE OBSERVED

Can They Use It?

Observation has shown that the answer to this is "Yes." Children as young as 3 are quite able to use a standard keyboard. Indeed, given that a 6-month-old infant can pick up a raisin, it is surprising that we ever doubted that preschoolers could cope with the keyboard. After a brief period of instruction, a 3-year-old child can be taught to pick up a disk without touching the magnetic surface, insert it into a disk drive, close the disk drive, and turn on the computer. Again, with the benefit of hindsight after hours of observing preschoolers using the microcomputer, this is not remarkable. Many construction toys require greater dexterity, and eating a banana requires as much care. But we ought to keep in mind how remarkable this appears to adults when they first see it. Parents of the children in our school would gasp with astonishment and pride when they saw their children perform this act. A reporter doing a news story on our preschool expressed inordinate amazement at the sight. This astonishment reveals more about adult mystification and ignorance of the microcomputer than it does about the apparent precocity of preschoolers using microcomputers.

We have also found that 3- and 4-year-olds can, with approximately 15 minutes of practice, learn to use a joystick or a touch pad. The touch pad appears to be slightly easier for them to control. Again, adult presumptions tend to be askew. Several preschool teachers and parents, when shown the touch pad, wondered whether preschoolers could make the appropriate connection between their fingers moving on the touch pad and the cursor moving on the screen. A common question was, "Why don't you get a touch screen so they can touch it directly?" Although a touch screen may be useful and eventually economically feasible, what is significant is the predisposition of many adults to imagine problems for children that simply do not occur.

Finally, the microcomputer is a very attractive activity for most children in the preschool. With only one microcomputer for approximately 20 children, many of the children in our class would have liked more access time than these resources permitted. The children did differ, however, in their interest in the microcomputer. Older children tended to be more interested in the microcomputer than younger children, although most of the children spent some time at it. We did not notice much difference between boys and girls in their interest, perhaps because of the steps we took to encourage equal access for boys and girls.

Sharing One Microcomputer

Our interest in avoiding social isolation and competitive interactions led us to establish the rule that the microcomputer was to be shared by two children at a time. This rule was initially presented to the group at "line time." During their first exposure to the microcomputer, the children were paired with partners whom we thought would work well together. At this time an adult encouraged the children to take turns and sat with them to provide support for turntaking. Having two children share the microcomputer not only doubles access time for children but it also promotes quite high levels of prosocial interaction (Dickson & Vereen, 1983).

Two Software Packages

During the first semester of microcomputer use we gathered systematic data on nine pairs of children using two different programs: Hodge Podge™ (Dynacomp) and Counting Bee (EduWare®). Hodge Podge displays graphics and sometimes plays music for each key press. For example, when you press "F," a farm appears on the screen, a few bars of "Old McDonald Had a Farm" are played, and then a farm animal appears. Hodge Podge has no "right" answers and is virtually failure proof: No matter which key the child presses, something interesting happens.

Counting Bee, on the other hand, is a more structured, task-oriented program. It represents several relatively simple counting tasks, as well as more difficult problems involving weight and seriation. Right and wrong answers are identified by smiling and frowning faces, and a running total is displayed of right and wrong answers. When a mistake is made, a buzzer sounds and the correct solution is shown. We configured Counting Bee so that only three of the six tasks were used: one in which the child counted balls and pressed the number from 1 to 9; one in which the child counted the number of triangles, squares, or circles in an array; and one in which the child counted the number of units of liquid in a graduated cylinder.

PROCEDURE

The pairs of children were randomly assigned to begin with either Hodge Podge or Counting Bee. The sessions ranged from 10 to 17 minutes in length, and each pair had one session with each program. An office across the hall from the regular classroom was used for all sessions. Six of the children had had some exposure to the microcomputer during the summer and were paired with each other. The children varied greatly in their reaction to the microcomputer. Some needed to be told, "Be gentle. You don't need to press the keys so hard." Others needed encouragement: "Go ahead. Try it. . . . Try pressing the 'J' for your name." Generally, the children were eager to use the microcomputer and wanted to continue with the programs.

The sessions were tape-recorded. The recordings were transcribed, divided into message units corresponding to simple clauses, and coded. The coding system divided each child's utterances into social and nonsocial comments, reflecting our primary interest in the impact of the microcomputer on social interaction. Within these major categories, we identified subcategories indicative of turntaking, awareness of right and wrong answers, teaching, hypothesizing, and verbally interacting with the microcomputer itself. The number of message units was approximately the same in each activity (186 for Counting Bee and 209 for Hodge Podge). In order to analyze the data, we converted all counts into percentages of total message units.

RESULTS

Turntaking

As expected, when two children share a microcomputer, a substantial portion of their verbal interaction reflects the management of turntaking. About 12% of all messages across both games involved turntaking. About 8% of these were children's messages, and about 4% were those of the experimenter. The need for adult intervention decreased over the course of the two sessions as the children learned to manage turntaking themselves. There were no significant differences between the two programs in the number of messages explicitly dealing with turntaking. The following transcript of a pair of 3-year-olds using Hodge Podge illustrates turntaking:

Andy:	Now your turn, Susan. Ah! [Laughing] Your turn, Susan. Oh, you turn the bear.
Susan:	Oh, your turn to do it.
Andy:	[Laughing] Your turn.
Susan:	Oh, oh, you started the "L"! "L" "U" "M" "P". [It actually wrote "JUMP".]

Sometimes the children accidentally pressed two keys and, as the following anecdote shows, kept track of their turns.

Carol:	I like ziggies [laughing].
Anne:	I don't like ziggies. I like J's. [Talking to the microcomputer:] What's wrong with you? Stop! Carol's turn. . . . She gets two turns 'cause I took two turns.
Carol:	Ah, I zig [laughs].

Verbal Interactions

Software characteristics exert considerable influence on children's verbal interactions. There were almost five times as many messages talking about whether the responses were right or wrong in Counting Bee as there were for Hodge Podge (1.3% vs. 0.3%, $p < .01$). Although these percentages are small, they are of considerable interest, given the importance attached by parents, teachers, and educational theorists to this issue. For example, some preschool teachers have expressed disapproval of Counting Bee because it uses smiling and frowning faces as well as sounds to emphasize correctness. Consider the following example from a transcript of 3-year-old children using Counting Bee.

Sam:	Three, four, five. Five. Got five.
Jeff:	No. That has to be all the way up here if it's five. It's three.
Sam:	One, two, three . . . one, two, three, four, five. [He presses '5' and the computer buzzes.]
Jeff:	See. That's four. See? I'm right, you're wrong.
Sam:	No, I'm right and you're wrong.
Jeff:	No.

Some, but not all, early childhood educators would view this emphasis on correctness and who was right as undesirable. On the other hand, many, perhaps most, of these same educators would be pleased by the kind of peer teaching we observed. Peer teaching occurred with greater frequency with Counting Bee than with Hodge Podge (5% vs. 2%, $p = .06$). Consider the following excerpt from another transcript:

Chris:	It's your turn.
Pat:	All right. I'll push a "U." Eight [guessing at random].
Chris:	Count. . . . Count it first.
Pat:	[Whispering] One, two, three, four.
Chris:	[Cueing Pat for the answer] Four! It's after three [guiding Pat's finger to the key].
Pat:	[Presses the correct key: 4]

Both of these children were learning more from this interaction than either would have learned alone. Perhaps software could be designed with a clear goal that encouraged this type of tutorial, prosocial interaction while deemphasizing the competitive notion of who got it right. Perhaps most important, given the concern that microcomputers would foster antisocial or asocial behavior, is the fact that we found substantial amounts of such supportive, cooperative interaction between children in the context created by the microcomputer.

Nonsocial Verbalization

From an educational standpoint, the nonsocial verbalization that occurred was also interesting. Nonsocial comments (that is, comments not directed at another person) accounted for 22% of all messages in Counting Bee and 16% in Hodge Podge. In Counting Bee most of these nonsocial messages consisted of counting out loud. In Hodge Podge the most common type of nonsocial message consisted of labeling a key before pressing it.

Within the nonsocial category, we were especially interested in whether or not the microcomputer spurred children's imagination, so we created a category called "hypothesizing." For example, hypothesizing included all comments indicative of wondering how the program worked, remembering what happened with specific key presses, or thinking about how the microcomputer worked. Although infrequent (1.7% in Hodge Podge and 0.6% in Counting Bee), the instances reflected children's keen interest in the microcomputer. In the following example, 4-year-old Carol is checking back and forth between the screen and the keyboard.

Carol:	Mm. Mm. What does that? What is this? Ah, melt. Ah, bear. Ah, volcano.

Questions about the microcomputer were common.

Nicole:	[Noticing the power light] Can I push that one? What is it?
E:	That's a light to tell you the computer's on.
Lucas:	Oh?
E:	Yes.
Lucas:	You push it. No, you push it. Oh, it's hot. Look.
Nicole:	It's warm?
Lucas:	Press it.
Nicole:	It's hot.

Many of the children talked to the microcomputer as if it were alive (3% of messages in Hodge Podge, 0.2% in Counting Bee, $p < .05$). They often sang or hummed along with the microcomputer. When the changes on the monitor screen did not seem to be keeping pace with their key presses, they talked to it.

Lucas:	[Speaking to the picture on the screen] Come on! When are you going away?
Nicole:	When are you going away?

CONCLUSIONS

Our informal observations subsequent to the period when we collected these transcripts support the view that the microcomputer need not have negative effects on social interactions among children. Given appropriate software and a classroom policy emphasizing sharing, the microcomputer can be used to increase the amount of cooperative, collaborative interaction in preschool classrooms. We feel that the social interactions that take place among children using the microcomputer may be of greater educational significance than the interactions that take place between children and the microcomputer itself, at least with current software. This conclusion is consonant with findings involving older children (Hawkins, Sheingold, Gearhart, & Berger, 1982).

Importance of Software

Our conclusions concerning software characteristics and their effects on the use of microcomputers by young children are beyond the scope of this chapter (see Dickson & Borgh, 1983). However, several points deserve mention. First, software is of utmost importance. Preschool children do not interact with a microcomputer, they interact with the software on the microcomputer. Second, the amount of software available for young children is growing at a rapid rate. Unfortunately, the quality of software is not improving at nearly so rapid a rate as the quality of packaging and advertising. Initially we were surprised by the poor quality of much of the software we reviewed. The more we have looked at the problem, the more aware we have become of how difficult it is to write good software. There are many factors that converge to make it remarkably difficult to create and market good software. Nevertheless, we are cautiously optimistic that over the next few years better and better software will be available.

Fortunately, and somewhat surprisingly, the limited availability of software is not of great importance to the use of microcomputers in preschools. Currently, few preschools have more than one microcomputer. It appears likely that most preschools, perhaps largely due to parent pressure, will buy one microcomputer in the next year or so. But in settings where there are 20 or more children per microcomputer, a school may not need much software. A small selection of high quality disks is adequate. Again, the effect of the microcomputer on the classroom and on children depends heavily on how the teachers conceptualize it. If the focus is on sharing and using the computer to create social interactions between children, as op-

posed to, for example, using it to teach counting, then a few good programs are sufficient.

The Classroom Context: Practical Considerations

This brings us to the final theme that guided our observations. Preschool teachers must make many decisions regarding use of the microcomputer. These include where to locate it, which software to provide, how much access time to allow individual children, and how to set up the microcomputer so that it does not require continual adult supervision. The reality of most preschool classrooms is that teachers do not have the luxury of spending much time supervising a few children at any one activity.

During the first year that the microcomputer was introduced into our classroom, the first author was supported by an assistantship that allowed her to devote considerable time to working with the children and the microcomputer. Since then, she has had to assume regular duties as a teacher in the preschool while continuing to oversee the use of the microcomputer. Currently, the microcomputer is set up next to an art area in a room used for small-group learning activities. The children have all been taught the basics of operating the microcomputer, as well as the general rule that they should work together when using it.

Approximately six disks are available for the children to choose from at all times. These disks are labeled with pictures that the children can recognize and are kept in envelopes taped to the wall next to the microcomputer. Basic instructions for using each disk are taped to the envelope. This apparently simple decision, to display the disks and to allow the children to choose, turns out to have several important consequences. First, children appear to like choices. Second, children know which programs they like and know how to use, so they individualize their own curriculum. This has practical benefits as well. If the microcomputer is set up with only one program and a child does not know how to run it, the child wants the teacher's attention immediately. But if the child is free to choose a familiar program, teacher supervision is not needed. Third, children learn how to use new programs by looking over the shoulders of other children or by peer teaching, thereby reducing the need for adult instruction.

Finally, we have encouraged parents to drop by and use the microcomputer with the children. This relieves the demand for teacher supervision and provides an avenue to encourage parental involvement in the preschool.

Attention to practical considerations such as where to put the microcomputer, what software to buy, and how to provide adequate supervision for children is not a trivial matter. The second author is a member of the parent board of another preschool that his children attend. The school has purchased a microcomputer and is in the process of introducing it into the curriculum. Although the teachers are interested in using the microcomputer, they have little free time during the day to work with children at the microcomputer. Preschools are busy places. An enigmatic error message or a child's demand for instruction on an unfamiliar piece of software cannot be addressed with leisure. Furthermore, software that cannot be deterred from making noxious (or even melodic) noises becomes an irritant during quiet times in classrooms. We have now begun using parent volunteers to help with the introduction of the microcomputer into the classrooms at the school. This experience has made us more cautious about the generalizability to other preschools of our success at the Laboratory Preschool, where we have had unusual resources. Perhaps the most essential resource is a teacher who is enthusiastic about the microcomputer and who is given time and support for work with it.

SUMMARY

We end, then, with cautious optimism. Children can do many interesting and educationally valuable things with a standard microcomputer. Rich social and verbal interactions tend to take place between children when using the microcomputer in pairs. Although current software leaves much to be desired, it is getting better. Most preschools in the next few years need only to find a few programs to make good use of a microcomputer. Perhaps the greatest challenge for the immediate future is to find ways of integrating the microcomputer into the regular functioning of a typical busy preschool. Properly used, the microcomputer can enrich children's experiences and lighten enormous demands on teachers' time and attention.

REFERENCES

Ausubel, D. P. (1963). *The psychology of meaningful verbal learning.* New York: Grune & Stratton.

Dickson, W. P., & Borgh, K. (1983). Software for preschoolers. *Family Computing, 1*(3), 64–65.

Dickson, W. P., & Vereen, M. A. (1983). Two students at one microcomputer. *Theory into Practice, 22,* 296–300.

Hawkins, J., Sheingold, K., Gearhart, M., & Berger, C. (1982). Microcomputers in schools: Impact on the social life of elementary school classrooms. *Journal of Applied Developmental Psychology, 3,* 361–373.

Rothenberg, D. (1984). Research on young children's keyboarding. *Micro Notes on Children and Computers, 1*(5), 1–4. Urbana, IL: ERIC Clearinghouse on Elementary and Early Childhood Education.

CHAPTER 5

MICROCOMPUTERS IN THE PRESCHOOL: CHILDREN, PARENTS, AND TEACHERS

Patricia F. Campbell
Shirley S. Schwartz
Department of Curriculum and Instruction
University of Maryland
College Park, Maryland 20742

Shaing:	There are roads and water all around. My [fishing] line in the water. [Laughter]
Esben:	Oh, no! You fell in the water.
Shaing:	Help me!
Esben:	OK.
Shaing:	I'm out on the road now.
Esben:	I'm on the road in my truck.
Shaing:	I'm gonna wash your car [truck].
Esben:	It's already clean. See, look here I'm under the bridge.

This verbal interaction records a cooperative pretend activity between two 4-year-olds. They are using one of the materials found in an activity center at their nursery school. But this material—a microcomputer equipped with a graphics program—responds to their 4-year-old ideas in a unique way. Not only does it depict their pretend world, but it also permits them to transform their fantasies and ideas into visual objects. These 4-year-olds are among the growing number of children exposed to the technology of computers in their classroom. In a recent survey of over 2,000 elementary and secondary schools in the United States (Becker, 1983), approximately one-half indicated that they had obtained a microcomputer for instructional purposes. No longer confined to the intermediate or secondary level, the use of microcomputers is rapidly expanding into primary and preschool programs.

QUESTIONS REGARDING THE USE OF MICROCOMPUTERS IN THE PRESCHOOL

The addition of this new technology into an established curriculum for young children provokes debate among educators. The traditional preschool curriculum provides an assortment of offerings—sharing or group time, art, blocks, manipulative materials, the housekeeping corner, books, the water/sand table, and outdoor play—designed to promote a balance of social, emotional, physical, and intellectual stimulation for the young child. Now, into this carefully balanced environment, comes the microcomputer, and with it a score of unanswered questions concerning its role in the preschool. How will this technology be used? How will it affect young children's development?

Unabashed supporters of the microcomputer speak glowingly of its potential for developing thinking skills such as planning, problem solving, evaluation, and reflection. They hypothesize that not only will these skills develop, but they will also transfer and be applied by children to other aspects of their lives (Feurzeig, Horwitz, & Nickerson, 1981; Papert, 1980).

Other educators however, oppose the use of the new technology, particularly in the preschool. Noting the social and emotional development that occurs during the preschool and primary grades, the opposition questions whether the microcomputer will discourage or distort this growth in some children. Tittnick and Brown (1982) have been particularly apprehensive about this possibility, noting that children "are extremely gratified by the responsiveness of a machine when they touch a button or turn a knob. It heightens the sense of being in control and comforts the child with its predictability" (p. 20). Children experiencing troubled human interactions may be especially attracted to the microcomputer, preferring its responsiveness and predictability to less satisfying interchanges with peers and adults. This never critical, always patient, immediately responsive machine may also become a friend-in-need to the young child who is experiencing a lag in social development (Burg, 1984; Hofmann, 1983).

The cognitive limitations of the young child led Barnes and Hill (1983) to question the use of the microcomputer with children who have not yet, in Piagetian terms, reached the concrete operational level of thinking. Before the age of 6 or 7 years, children's thought is dominated by sensorimotor knowledge, not abstractions. These critics question whether a young child is able to think and act in a precise, sequential manner without frustration. Primarily, however, they are apprehensive that well-intentioned parents and teachers will allow the microcomputer to replace active manipulation, imaginary play, and experiential learning.

Social Issues

Will the microcomputer disrupt the environmental balance in the preschool classroom? Will it diminish the young child's involvement with other materials and learning tools? Does the presence of a microcomputer influence social participation patterns in the preschool classroom? How do teachers influence the use of microcomputers by young children? What are the parental values and attitudes regarding use of microcomputers by young children? Do boys and girls differ in their use of the microcomputer? Much of the research conducted thus far has not addressed these social issues. Rather, it has focused on understanding the intellectual aspects of microcomputer use by individual children in a solitary context (e.g., Solomon & Papert, 1976). Gradually, however, this solitary cognitive model is being expanded. Aware of the multidimensional nature of the environment in which young children live and play (Darvill, 1982; Krasnor & Pepler, 1980), researchers are beginning to investigate other aspects of children's use of the microcomputer in the regular classroom setting (Fein, Campbell, & Schwartz, 1984; Hawkins, Sheingold, Gearhart, & Berger, 1982; Piestrup, 1981). Microcomputer use is being investigated in naturalistic settings where many activities and a number of children are present. This type of setting may

allow the child to interact with peers while exploring and experiencing the microcomputer.

THE NOVELTY EFFECT

With the introduction of any new object into an established setting, the natural response is one of curiosity and excitement. This is true for children and for adults. The initial introduction of a microcomputer into a preschool classroom may cause disruption of routine. For example, Piestrup (1981) noted that a crowd formed when a microcomputer was brought into Stanford's Bing Nursery School during the free-play period. During the first week, as many as 20 observers clustered around the microcomputer. This was not simply a function of age. Parents, teachers, and administrators were among the group observing a 3- or 4-year-old's operation of the microcomputer. However, by the second week, the classroom routine returned to prior patterns as both adults and children integrated the microcomputer into their classroom life. When the children learned that they would each have an opportunity at the microcomputer, they resumed their established play activities, taking turns at the microcomputer. In a short time, with repeated contact assured, the microcomputer lost its strong novelty effect.

Questions for Research

Even after the initial novelty of the machine diminishes, the microcomputer has potential for disruption in the classroom. Because it is not a large-group activity, children must take turns for individual or paired access. How involved in their tasks or play will the children be if they know that it is "almost" their turn? How should teachers provide for equity of access? What happens when a new software program is made available? Does the novelty effect reassert itself?

Research Procedure

To answer these questions, thirty 4-year-olds from two different nursery school classrooms were observed during the free-play period for 8 weeks, spread over a 12-week period (Fein et al., 1984). We observed children for 4 days each week. On 2 days, two microcomputers were present in the classroom; the other 2 days, they were not present. During the first 5 weeks, two different graphics programs (Scribbling® and Creative Crayon®) were available. By manipulating a joystick, a knob, and some buttons, the children were able to control the width, direction, and color of a drawing line; the background color of the monitor screen; and the movements of line segments across the screen. During the last 3 weeks of observation, a different microcomputer characterized by a keyboard and new programs was available.

Observations

Over the 12-week play period, observers coded whether each child's vision and physical movement was on- or off-task, no matter what activity the child was engaged in during the free-play period. The presence of the microcomputer did not affect the children's degree of involvement in noncomputer tasks. Similarly, changing the type of microcomputer program available did not have an effect. Contrary to Berlyne's theory of novelty and exploration (Berlyne, 1966; Hutt, 1970), there was no relationship between the children's preoccupation with the microcomputers and the number of weeks during which the microcomputers had been available. However, the novelty effect in this study may have been suppressed. Each child had the

opportunity to use the machine before it was brought into the classroom. Therefore, although the microcomputer activity center was new to the children, the microcomputers were not. Thus this study may indicate that brief prior contact with the microcomputer (for example, in a library or a computer room) may prevent the disruption observed by Piestrup.

Classrooms differ from each other, and children's behavior changes from week to week. In our study, we noted several classroom differences. In one class, the introduction of the microcomputers was accompanied by a significant increase of on-task behavior and a trend toward less distractibility. In the other classroom, there was no significant change in the occurrence of on-task behavior; however, the children did exhibit significantly more distractibility. These two classrooms also differed in terms of children's observed involvement on tasks when the microcomputers were not present. These established differences between the two classrooms may have been more influential than the presence or absence of the microcomputers.

EFFECT OF THE MICROCOMPUTER ON FREE-PLAY ACTIVITIES

The preschool classroom contains a myriad of activities to stimulate the developing social and cognitive skills of the young child. During the free-play period, children may choose activities from this assortment. Generally, constraints on children's choices arise from the teacher's desire to ensure the involvement of each child in an activity, to discourage conflict between children, and to encourage the children to try different activities. From a developmental point of view, varied experiences are needed to promote a balance of social and cognitive outcomes. The addition of a microcomputer into the free-play period raises questions regarding the possible disruption of this balance.

Sex-Related Differences in Microcomputer Use

If a child uses the microcomputer during the free-play period, then some other activity in the classroom has one less participant. Will the microcomputer uniformly attract children away from other available activities? Will boys and girls exhibit the same interest in the microcomputer? With older elementary and secondary school age children, there seems to be a tendency to perceive optional use of the microcomputer as an activity for boys rather than girls (Campbell, 1983; Pea, 1983; Sheingold, Kane, & Endreweit, 1983). It is hypothesized that this may be due to a hesitancy on the part of the girls to try something new or to compete with the boys for access to the machines (Kiesler, Sproull, & Eccles, 1983; Kolata, 1984). Will this pattern of sex differences for microcomputer use manifest itself in the preschool classroom as well? There is a sex-related preference associated with other activities such as blocks and arts. Can the microcomputer be "neutral"?

By the time children enter preschool, they have begun to associate particular toys and types of play as activities for either boys or girls (Johnson & Roopnarine, 1983; Maccoby & Jacklin, 1974; O'Brien, Huston, & Risley, 1983). As noted by Carpenter (1983), this assignment of patterns of behavior—which may then be classified by sex—is not inherent in the physical attributes of the toy or activity. Rather, social conventions and expectations are defined by parents (Giddings & Halverson, 1981), peers (Lamb & Roopnarine, 1979), older siblings (Sutton-Smith & Rosenberg, 1970), and teachers (Johnson & Ershler, 1981) and then communicated to the child. In the nursery school, girls are more likely to play with smaller objects and constructive materials such as magnetic numerals and letters, felt boards, and beads. Girls also seem to prefer art activities and the housekeeping corner, particularly if it includes support materials for dolls such as cradles or strollers. Boys prefer physically stimulating activities such as large blocks and trucks that encourage active and exploratory play (Connor & Serbin, 1977; Eisenberg-Berg, Boothby, & Matson, 1979; Johnson & Ershler, 1981).

Research Procedure and Results

To assess whether these sex-related activity patterns were influenced by the presence of a microcomputer, thirty 4-year-old children in two preschool classrooms were observed during free play over a 4-week period (Campbell, Fein, & Schwartz, 1985). The children's free-play activities were categorized as art-related, blocks, the housekeeping corner, manipulative materials, microcomputers, and other activities. After adjustments were made for the presence of one additional choice (the microcomputer) during one-half of the observed periods, the activity patterns were reviewed. Analysis revealed that the children's participation in nonmicrocomputer activities was not influenced by the presence or absence of microcomputers. Established sex-related patterns of activity preference were unchanged by the presence of the microcomputer. The girls selected art-related tasks approximately 28% of the time, while the boys participated in art during approximately 15% of the free play. Only 3% of the girls' free play was spent in large block play, while the blocks constituted 15% of the boys' free play. For a comparison of the observed activity choice broken down by sex and microcomputer presence, see Table 5–1.

No significant sex-related difference in microcomputer use was noted (5% of the girls' free play; 7% of the boys' free play). For

TABLE 5–1.
Adjusted Percentage of Free Play Time

	Microcomputer Present	Microcomputer Absent
Girls		
Art	25.4	29.7
Blocks	5.0	1.6
Housekeeping	10.6	10.3
Manipulative Materials	10.9	12.4
Other Activities	48.1	46.0
Boys		
Art	16.1	14.7
Blocks	17.6	12.8
Housekeeping	8.6	11.2
Manipulative Materials	16.1	11.6
Other Activities	41.6	49.7

these young children, the microcomputer seemed to have no identification as either a male or female activity. Beeson and Williams (1983) also found that preschool boys and girls showed no significant differences in their use of the microcomputers during free-choice periods.

Thus, while children show sex-related preferences for other preschool activities, these were not found for the microcomputers. One explanation might be that the carefully chosen graphics programs used in this study had no identifiable sex-related content. Commercial home computer software or arcade games, on the other hand, typically portray violent or aggressive settings involving missiles or objects being propelled through space. Generally, these fantasy settings are more appealing to males than to females (Kolata, 1984; Lepper, 1982; Malone, 1981; Pulaski, 1973), which may account for sex-related differences associated with microcomputer use by older children or adolescents (Sheingold et al., 1983). These dif-

ferences may also be a manifestation of the implicit encouragement given to males to attempt microcomputer use. If both boys and girls are encouraged to use microcomputers in cooperative, nonsexist settings at an early age, perhaps the perception of computers as a male-dominated domain will diminish.

EFFECTS ON SOCIAL AND COGNITIVE BEHAVIOR

Social Components of Play

The observed free-play behaviors of young children may be categorized along both social and cognitive dimensions. The social components of play that have been investigated stem from Parten's (1932) classic study of age differences in interactive behaviors. Parten defined six sequential social participation categories. *Unoccupied behavior* occurs when the child does not seem to be playing, but rather occupies himself or herself by watching activities of momentary interest. If a child is walking about or sitting preoccupied with personal thoughts or body, the behavior is considered unoccupied. *Solitary play* is defined as a child playing alone with materials. Others may be near, but no attempt is made to speak to them or to join play activities. If a child is intent on watching other children play but makes no overt effort to join in the activity, the child's behavior would be termed that of an *onlooker*. *Parallel play* occurs when the child plays independently with toys and materials in close proximity to other children but with no effort to organize their play together. *Associative* and *cooperative play* are characterized by children playing together. In associative play, as opposed to cooperative play, there is no assignment of roles nor is there evidence of organization in the play. The distinction between these two categories is a fine one, and for coding purposes many researchers (e.g., Rubin, Maioni, & Hornung, 1976) have combined these two categories to form one category, associative-cooperative. Parten concluded that with increasing age children engage in more social and cooperative play, with less solitary, onlooker, and parallel play behaviors.

Cognitive Components of Play

Cognitively, the components of play that have been studied are based on Piaget's (1962) studies of sensorimotor and preoperational intelligence. Smilansky (1968) adapted Piaget's formulations and identified four types of play prevalent during the early years: functional (simple, often repetitive, motions involving materials and objects as they are meant to be used); constructive (creating or constructing something that results in an end product); dramatic (activities that have an "as if" quality; play within an imaginary set-

ting); and games with rules (play in which the child accepts prearranged rules).

Social and Cognitive Interactions

A number of recent studies have used a coding system that combines a scoring of the social level of the child's behavior with a scoring of the cognitive components of play (Fein, Moorin, & Enslein, 1982; Johnson, Ershler, & Bell, 1980; Rubin et al., 1976; Rubin, Watson, & Jambor, 1978) to produce a code representing the social and cognitive levels of play a child is engaged in.

The play materials and available activity choices in the classroom facilitate differing social and cognitive interactions (Johnson et al., 1980; Quilitch & Risley, 1973; Rubin, 1977; Rubin & Seibel, 1979; Shure, 1963; Stoneman, Cantrell, & Hoover-Dempsey, 1983; Vandenberg, 1981). For example, library books and art materials promote solitary or parallel play that is functional (in the case of the books) or constructive (in the case of the art materials). Other activity centers such as the housekeeping corner and block areas promote more cooperative, interactive play within a dramatic setting (Johnson et al., 1980; Tizard, Philips, & Plewis, 1976).

The microcomputer is something of an unknown within these dimensions. A first reaction may be to assume that the microcomputer would facilitate solitary functional play with a child pressing the keyboard in order to react to the situations portrayed on the monitor screen. However, recent surveys have not supported this image. In elementary and secondary schools, teachers have noted that the presence of the microcomputer has stimulated collaborative work between students with peers serving as sources of information (Becker, 1983; Hawkins et al., 1982). If the microcomputer is loaded with a software package that permits student control or if students are learning to program the microcomputer, then both constructive and dramatic play behavior may be observed.

Research Procedure and Analysis

During our observations of 4-year-olds' use of microcomputers (Fein et al., 1984, described earlier in this chapter), we coded the play and social behavior of the children during the free-play period using the nested hierarchy devised by Rubin and colleagues (1976). This system consisted of the three cognitive categories (functional, constructive, and dramatic play) adapted from Piaget (1962) and Smilansky (1968), crossed with Parten's (1932, 1933) indices of social participation. The social categories used in this study were unoccupied, onlooker, solitary, parallel, and interactive, which combined Parten's associative and cooperative categories. Three additional behaviors were coded: conflict, nonplay and adult-directed/oriented play. In particular, we were interested in determining whether or not the microcomputer did encourage any one type of social or cognitive play. If so, a further question was whether or not such behavior would be transferred by the children to their play with other materials.

Analysis of the data revealed that constructive play was the predominant cognitive activity, regardless of the presence or absence of the microcomputer in the classroom. Parallel play was the most frequently observed category of social interaction, with a slight but insignificant increase in parallel play when the microcomputer was removed from the classroom. Overall, the patterns of social and cognitive behavior in the observed classrooms were not influenced by the presence of the microcomputer.

However, the observational instrument used in this study was designed to assess only overt cognitive behavior. Thus, instances of covert dramatic or constructive

behavior at the microcomputer may have been coded as functional. For example, suppose a child is seated at the microcomputer. He is working silently and very intently. The monitor displays an elaborate graphic representation of a rocket ship. This child may have defined an imaginary setting for his rocket ship. In his mind he may be planning a trip to outer space. An equally reasonable explanation is that this child may be testing out his growing command of computer graphic skills to create a satisfying pictorial structure, much in the same way as he would experiment with blocks to create a three-dimensional structure. However, if the child's overt behavior is nonverbal, nongestural, and solitary, his cognitive play would be coded by observers as constructive or functional, rather than as dramatic. Without an awareness of the basis of a child's movement of graphic lines on the screen, the interpretation would be either that random lines were being placed on the screen (functional) or that the lines were similar to a crayoned picture (constructive).

Although we did not note microcomputer-related effects on cognitive and social behavior, both sex and classroom differences with respect to play and social participation were noted. In particular, when the microcomputer was initially placed in the classroom, girls were likely to be engaged in more constructive parallel play and less dramatic/interactive play than were the boys. This finding supports established patterns of play reported in the literature (e.g., Johnson & Ershler, 1981). With time, however, this pattern dissipated. One classroom in this study had children who were, on the average, 4 months younger than the children in the other class. As might be expected (Fein et al., 1982; Johnson and Ershler, 1981; Rubin, 1982), the children in this younger class engaged in more constructive and adult-directed behavior with less interactive play than did the class of older children.

Teacher Variables

This analysis indicates that microcomputers are unlikely to have a uniform effect on children's social and cognitive behavior in the preschool. A variety of factors influence children's behavior in the classroom; the influence of these factors is not diminished by the introduction of the microcomputer. In particular, the teacher is a critical variable (Amarel, 1983). We noted that whenever the microcomputer was present in one classroom, the adults were more involved in directing activities that promoted functional and constructive behavior, with little or no adult direction at the centers that encouraged dramatic play. In the other classroom, a similar but reversed reaction was noted. The teaching style and strategies of the adult computer facilitator (not the regular classroom teacher) also had an effect on the children's participation at the microcomputer activity center. In one classroom, the facilitator's approach was open-ended and nondirective, in the other a more structured approach was employed. In the classroom with the open-ended facilitator, more microcomputer use was noted.

THE PARENTS' VIEW

Educational innovations reach beyond the school setting to the home and family. Parents of preschool children are particularly interested in what their children are being exposed to in school. At the same time, parents have a great influence on the early development of sex-differentiated play behaviors (Langlois & Downs, 1980); motivation (Maccoby, 1980); intellectual and academic achievement (Seginer, 1983); and the development of attitudes, opinions, and interests (Caldwell & Bradley, 1979; Moore, 1982). The kinds of experiences parents provide at home as well as their expectations and values concerning the use of technology will affect the child's willingness to venture into new ways of learning.

Questions for Research

What kinds of experiences with technology are children having outside the school setting? In particular, is there a microcomputer in the home that children may use? Do older siblings play home or commercial video games and share this activity with their younger brothers and sisters? Are young children playing with electronic learning devices (e.g., Speak and Spell,™ Little Professor™)? How do parents feel about the experiences their children may be having with electronic media?

Research Procedure and Results

To help investigate these questions a questionnaire was sent to the parents of 4-year-old children participating in the study of computer use in the preschool classroom (Center for Young Children, 1983). Analysis revealed that 45% of the questionnaires were completed by the children's mothers, 43% by fathers, and 12% by both parents. The questionnaire was designed to elicit information regarding the children's exposure to and use of electronic media outside the school setting; parental views concerning children's use of computer technologies; and parental expectations for the children's continued use of technology in subsequent school settings as well as in adulthood.

Parents reported that their children had limited experience across a variety of technologies. Only 5% of the children used microcomputers outside of the school setting. The children had some experience with video games, either at home (20%) or in an arcade (15%). However, 40% of the children had experiences with electronic learning aids such as Speak and Spell or Little Professor. Summed over all categories, the amount of time children spent in these activities was limited to less than 1 hour per week.

Thompson and Cloer (1982) have reported that the "primary goal of electronic learning aids is to use available technologies in the fulfillment of educational objectives" (p. 84). These authors are enthusiastic about the potential of these devices to help children learn in an interactive manner. The parents in this sample echoed this enthusiasm. However, their enthusiasm was tempered with the caution that the learning aid must be educationally sound and age-appropriate. The parents also felt that while these devices were somewhat limited in function, they were encouraging, motivating, and useful reinforcers of young children's growing intellectual skills.

Video games, whether at home or in arcades, elicited the most negative comments. Parents felt that video arcade games were too costly, too noisy, and provided an inappropriate atmosphere for young children. Although there is little empirical evidence that video games are addictive, the parents expressed concerns about the captivating allure of these fast-paced electronic games. Parents feared that their children would become overly involved in these games, thus lessening their participation in other, more physically and socially appropriate activities. A concomitant issue for parents was the effects that video games might have on their children's behavior. For example, would children become more aggressive and be less prosocial as a result of being exposed to violent software? Approximately 25% of the parents in this sample reported that their children enjoyed playing some type of computer game with older siblings. In their view, the chief benefits of video game playing, especially in the home, was the opportunity it provided for family interaction.

When questioned about the advantages and disadvantages of microcomputer use in the preschool setting, parents repeatedly expressed a desire for their children to be "computer comfortable." They viewed the preschool microcomputer experience as an opportunity to experience new ways of learning and communicating. A few parents (11%) expressed some reservations. These concerned the potential availability of microcomputers at the primary level as well as the possibility of negative consequences in the areas of social and intellectual development. Of the parents surveyed, 82% believed that their children would be using microcomputers in subsequent school settings. They envisioned the computer being integrated into all content areas of the curriculum. The remaining parents cited the lack of equipment and untrained teachers as the reason for nonuse.

Viewing their children as part of the new "information age," these parents saw microcomputers as an integral part of their children's lives as adults, influencing career choice, home life, and recreational pursuits. As microcomputers become more common in homes, as indeed they are, parents will be assuming a more active role in integrating this technological innovation in their children's lives.

CONCLUSIONS

A rationale is developing for the use of microcomputers by young children in preschool settings. Observers of young children using microcomputers uniformly report the high level of motivation, long attention span, and obvious enjoyment children display while actively engaging this powerful machine. Evidence from our research suggests that microcomputers in the classroom are unlikely to have a uniform impact on the cognitive and social aspects of children's play and activity choices. A variety of factors need to be investigated when the preschool classroom and curriculum are modified by technological innovations. Changes seem to stem from a complex set of variables that differ across preschool classrooms.

Mediating Variables in Computer Use

How the microcomputer is used and its effects (social, emotional, cognitive) depend on interactions among teachers, materials, and peers. The different ways teachers encourage preschoolers to perceive and interact with the microcomputer and with each other in the microcomputer's presence are likely to mediate different behavioral outcomes. In part, the child's mastery and competence at the microcomputer will depend on developmental level and individual personality characteristics. Parental expectations and values concerning the use of new technological innovations will affect the child's willingness to venture into this new area of learning and communicating. The choice of microcomputer software programs will also affect educational outcomes. In sum, understanding microcomputer effects on children's behavior requires identifying the mediating variables and mechanisms responsible for them—the content, structure, and timing of events within the classroom environment, as well as the relationship these variables have to developmental and personality characteristics.

Classrooms are complex organizations. It may be that they absorb new innovations into their already existing structures (Amarel, 1983). Analysis of our data revealed that established patterns of teacher and child behavior were not influenced by the presence or absence of the microcomputer. Further the data indicated that in a rich and stimulating preschool setting children continue to participate in activities providing concrete as well as symbolic experiences. The quality of classroom experiences and the quality of

the microcomputer curricula to which young children are exposed are important variables in assessing the effects microcomputers will have on behavior and activity patterns within classrooms. In the classrooms in our study, the microcomputer was integrated into the established curriculum, it was not an unrelated, separate entity. Thus, the microcomputer became a vehicle for providing more and varied experiences. Established activity patterns remained stable and microcomputer use caused no disruption of traditional activities.

Issues for Teachers

This additional resource enriches the classroom at the same time that it raises a host of complex issues for teachers. In structuring their classrooms, preschool teachers must make decisions in managing time and space and in sequencing and organizing daily activities (Phyfe-Perkins, 1980). Since the ratio of children to available microcomputers is high, teachers confront issues of equal access. Teachers are faced with decisions about the ways the microcomputer will be used in the classroom: whether as rewards or as an integral part of the instructional program; by whom—"gifted" children or children with special needs; and by how many at a time—individuals, pairs, or small groups. In addition to these considerations, teachers must also develop appropriate teaching strategies for the microcomputer. The teachers' approaches and attitudes to microcomptuer learning will influence microcomputer use in the classroom. Whether these decisions are carefully considered or reached by inaction, young children's educational experiences will have been affected.

Potential for Modifying the Gender Gap

The implementation of microcomputers in classrooms has the potential to counteract the trend of girls losing interest in science and technology as they grow older. In our study, the microcomputer activity center proved to be an equally attractive activity for males and females. This may have been due to two factors: Software programs were carefully chosen to appeal equally to males and females, and the microcomputer facilitators and teachers actively encouraged *all* children to explore and interact with this new medium. Research indicates that there are sex-related preferences associated with the activities in the preschool classroom. At the very least, the microcomputer has the potential to be equally attractive to boys and girls. At best, early exposure and mastery of microcomputer technology offers the possibility of modifying male dominance in the areas of mathematics and science.

Need for Further Research

At present, we are in a state of uncertainty concerning the impact of microcomputers in the education of young children. There is a need for theoretical frameworks within which to investigate the role and value of microcomputers in this area. Many important questions need to be framed and investigated regarding the match between goals for children and computer education. Microcomputers may be an important bridge to abstraction for the child.

It should be clear that microcomputers are not being proposed as a replacement for those activities and materials that are already effectively used in preschools for children's social, cognitive, and affective development. Instead, the microcomputer should be used as another potential activity for young children to experience and explore in their world.

REFERENCES

Amarel, M. (1983). The classroom: An instructional setting for teachers, students and the computer. In A. C. Wilkinson (Ed.), *Classroom computers and cognitive science* (pp. 15–29). New York: Academic Press.

Barnes, B. J., & Hill, S. (1983). Should young children work with microcomputers—Logo before Lego? *The Computing Teacher, 10*(9), 11–14.

Becker, H. J. (1983). *School uses of microcomputers: Reports from a national survey* (Vol. 1, p. 7). Baltimore: The Johns Hopkins University, Center for Social Organization of Schools.

Beeson, B. S., & Williams, R. A. (1983). *The effect of gender and age in pre-school children's choice of the computer as a child selected activity.* Unpublished manuscript, Ball State University, Muncie, IN.

Berlyne, D. E. (1966). Curiosity and exploration. *Science, 153*, 25–33.

Burg, K. (1984). The microcomputer in the kindergarten. *Young Children, 39*(3), 28–33.

Caldwell, B. M., & Bradley, R. (1979). *Home observation for measurement of the environment.* Little Rock, AR: University of Arkansas.

Campbell, P. F. (1983, April). *The effect of programming instruction in the high school on performance in a university level programming course.* Paper presented at the meeting of the National Council of Teachers of Mathematics, Detroit, MI.

Campbell, P. F., Fein, G. G., & Schwartz, S. S. (1985). *Microcomputers in the preschool: Temporal changes in the activity choices of boys and girls.* Manuscript in preparation.

Carpenter, C. J. (1983). Activity structure and play: Implications for socialization. In M. B. Liss (Ed.), *Social and cognitive skills: Sex roles and children's play* (pp. 117–145). New York: Academic Press.

Center for Young Children. (1983). *Parent Computer Questionnarie.* Unpublished questionnaire, University of Maryland, College Park, MD.

Connor, J. M., & Serbin, L. A. (1977). Behaviorally based masculine- and feminine-activity-preference scales for preschoolers: Correlates with other classroom behaviors and cognitive tests. *Child Development, 48,* 1411–1466.

Darvill, D. (1982). Ecological influences on children's play: Issues and approaches. In D. J. Pepler & K. H. Rubin (Eds.), *The play of children: Current theory and research* (pp. 144–153). Basel, Switzerland: S. Karger.

Eisenberg-Berg, N., Boothby, R., & Matson, T. (1979). Correlates of pre-school girls' feminine and masculine toy preferences. *Developmental Psychology, 15,* 354–355.

Fein, G. G., Campbell, P. F., & Schwartz, S. S. (1984). *Microcomputers in the preschool: Effects on cognitive and social behavior.* Manuscript submitted for publication.

Fein, G. G., Moorin, E. R., & Enslein, J. (1982). Pretense and peer behavior: An intersectional analysis. *Human Development, 25,* 392–406.

Feurzeig, W., Horwitz, P., & Nickerson, R. S. (1981, October). *Microcomputers in education* (Report No. 4798). Prepared for: Department of Health Education and Welfare, National Institute of Education; and Ministry for the Development of Human Intelligence, Republic of Venezuela. Cambridge, MA: Bolt, Beranek, and Newman. (ERIC Document Reproduction Service No. ED 208 901)

Giddings, M., & Halverson, C. (1981). Young children's use of toys in home environments. *Family Relations, 30,* 69–74.

Hawkins, J., Sheingold, K., Gearhart, M., & Berger, C. (1982). Microcomputers in schools: Impact on the social life of elementary school classrooms. *Journal of Applied Developmental Psychology, 3,* 361–373.

Hofmann, R. J. (1983). Would you like a bite of my peanut butter sandwich? *Journal of Learning Disabilities, 16*(3), 174–177.

Hutt, C. (1970). Specific and diversive exploration. In F. W. Reese & L. P. Lipsitt (Eds.),

Advances in child development and behavior (Vol. 5, pp. 231–251). New York: Academic Press.

Johnson, J. E., & Ershler, J. (1981). Developmental trends in preschool play as a function of classroom program and child gender. *Child Development, 52,* 995–1004.

Johnson, J. E., Ershler, J., & Bell, C. (1980). Play behavior in a discovery-based and a formal education preschool program. *Child Development, 51,* 271–274.

Johnson, J. E., & Roopnarine, J. L. (1983). The preschool classroom and sex differences in children's play. In M. B. Liss (Ed.), *Social and cognitive skills: Sex roles and children's play* (pp. 193–218). New York: Academic Press.

Kiesler, S., Sproull, L., & Eccles, J. S. (1983, March). Second class citizen? *Psychology Today, 17*(3). 40–48.

Kolata, G. (1984, January). Equal time for women. *Discover, 5*(1), 24–27.

Krasnor, L. R., & Pepler, D. J. (1980). The study of children's play: Some suggested future directions. In K. Rubin (Ed.), *Children's play* (pp. 85–96). San Francisco: Jossey-Bass.

Lamb, M., & Roopnarine, J. L. (1979). Peer influences on sex-role development in preschoolers. *Child Development, 50,* 1219–1222.

Langlois, J. H., & Downs, A. C. (1980). Mothers, fathers and peers as socialization agents of sex-typed play behaviors in young children. *Child Development, 51,* 1217–1247.

Lepper, M. (1982, August). *Microcomputers in education: Motivational and social issues.* Invited address at the annual meeting of the American Psychological Association, Washington, DC.

Maccoby, E. E. (1980). *Social development: Psychological growth and the parent-child relationship.* New York: Harcourt Brace Jovanovich.

Maccoby, E. E., & Jacklin, C. N. (1974). *The psychology of sex differences.* Palo Alto, CA: Stanford University Press.

Malone, T. W. (1981). Toward a theory of intrinsically motivating instruction. *Cognitive Science, 4,* 333–369.

Moore, S. G. (1982). Prosocial behavior in the early years: Parent and peer influences. In B. Spodek (Ed.), *Handbook of research in early childhood education* (pp. 65–81). New York: The Free Press.

O'Brien, M., Huston, C., & Risley, T. R. (1983). Sex-typed play of toddlers in a day care center. *Journal of Applied Developmental Psychology, 4,* 1–9.

Papert, S. (1980). *Mindstorms: Children, computers and powerful ideas.* New York: Basic Books.

Parten, M. B. (1932). Social participation among preschool children. *Journal of Abnormal and Social Psychology, 27,* 243–269.

Parten, M. B. (1933). Social participation among preschool children. *Journal of Abnormal and Social Psychology, 28,* 136–147.

Pea, R. D. (1983). *Logo programming and problem solving* (Technical Report No. 12). New York: Bank Street College of Education, Center for Children and Technology.

Phyfe-Perkins, E. (1980). Children's behavior in preschool settings: The influence of the physical environment. In L. G. Katz (Ed.), *Current topics in early childhood education* (Vol. 3, pp. 91–125). Norwood, NJ: Ablex Publishing.

Piaget, J. (1962). *Play dreams and imitation in childhood.* New York: Norton.

Piestrup, A. M. (1981, January). *Young children use Apple II to test reading skills program.* Portola Valley, CA: Advanced Learning Technology. (ERIC Document Reproduction Service No. ED 202 476)

Pulaski, M. A. (1973). Toys and imaginative play. In J. L. Singer (Ed.), *The child's world of make believe: Experimental studies of imaginative play* (pp. 74–103). New York: Academic Press.

Quilitch, H. R., & Risley, T. R. (1973). The effects of play materials on social play. *Journal of Applied Behavior Analysis, 6,* 573–578.

Rubin, K. H. (1977). The social and cognitive value of preschool toys and activities. *Canadian Journal of Behavioral Science, 9,* 382–385.

Rubin, K. H. (1982). Nonsocial play in preschoolers: Necessarily evil? *Child Development, 53,* 651–657.

Rubin, K. H., Maioni, T. L., & Hornung, M. (1976). Free play behaviors in preschool and kindergarten children. *Child Development, 49,* 534–536.

Rubin, K. H., & Seibel, C. (1979, April). *The effects of ecological setting on the cognitive and social play behaviors of preschoolers.* Paper presented at the annual meeting of the American Education Research Association, San Francisco.

Rubin, K. H., Watson, K. S., & Jambor, T. W. (1978). Free-play behaviors in preschool and kindergarten children. *Child Development, 49,* 534–536.

Seginer, R. (1983). Parents' educational expectations and children's academic achievement: A literature review. *Merrill Palmer Quarterly, 29,* 1–23.

Sheingold, K., Kane, J., & Endreweit, M. (1983). Microcomputer use in schools: Developing a research agenda. *Harvard Educational Review, 53,* 412–432.

Shure, M. B. (1963). Psychological ecology of a nursery school. *Child Development, 34,* 979–992.

Smilansky, S. (1968). *The effects of sociodramatic play on disadvantaged preschool children.* New York: Wiley.

Solomon, C., & Papert, S. (1976). *A case study of a young child doing Turtle Graphics in Logo* (Artificial Intelligence Laboratory Memo 375). Cambridge, MA: Massachusetts Institute of Technology, Artificial Intelligence Laboratory.

Stoneman, Z., Cantrell, M. L., & Hoover-Dempsey, K. (1983). The association between play materials and social behavior in a mainstreamed preschool: A naturalistic investigation. *Journal of Applied Developmental Psychology, 4,* 163–174.

Sutton-Smith, B., & Rosenberg, B. G. (1970). *The sibling.* New York: Holt, Rinehart & Winston.

Thompson, B., & Cloer, T. (1982). A learning aid: Imaginative electronics applied to education. In M. Frank (Ed.), *Young children in a computerized environment* (pp. 83–87). New York: Haworth Press.

Tittnick, E. M., & Brown, N. (1982). Positive and negative uses of technology in human interactions. In M. Frank (Ed.), *Young children in a computerized environment* (pp. 15–21). New York: Haworth Press.

Tizard, B., Philips, J., & Plewis, I. (1976). Play in preschool centers: Effects on play of the child's social class and of the educational orientation of the centre. *Journal of Child Psychology and Psychiatry, 17,* 265–274.

Vandenberg, B. (1981). Environmental and cognitive factors in social play. *Journal of Experimental Child Psychology, 31,* 169–175.

CHAPTER 6

VIDEO GAMES:
AFFECT, AROUSAL,
AND AGGRESSION

Steven B. Silvern

Department of Curriculum and Teaching
Auburn University
Auburn, Alabama 36849

Walk into a video arcade and listen. What do you hear? If this arcade has my favorites, you might hear the dull heartthrob of Space Invaders®, the wocka-wocka of PAC-MAN* and Ms. PAC-MAN*, the squeaky squinch-squinch and kolioko of DONKEY KONG™, the choink of Q*bert™, the drone of POLE POSITION*, the swish of Alpine Ski, and the drone of FROGGER™. All of these sounds tumble together in a cacophony of stimulation. As you stand there listening to this general rumble one sound might stand out, soon to be overtaken by another. Occasionally, the noise is punctuated by a musical jingle or a shattering crash. The sheer press of noise seems enough to create a state of heightened physical response. The higher the level of play the faster the rhythm of sound, until you feel your heart racing along with PAC-MAN and some other fantasy creature.

Less obvious than the press of sound in the arcade, but equally penetrating, are the sounds associated with home video games. Like their big brothers, these games use pulses, whirrs, and hums that increase in rate and frequency to cue and stimulate the player. While these effects of video game noise are untested, you need only spend a short time in an arcade to note that your heart palpitates, your face seems to be flushed, you might be uncomfortably warm, and your breath seems to be short. Add to the sound the visual stimulation of watching a game. Either the background, foreground, or both background and foreground images are constantly moving. Colors burst on the screen and fade or blur across your vision. Objects and backgrounds move so quickly that it is difficult to keep your head still, and your eyes begin to roll. These visual images seem to have a physical effect similar to those experienced through sound stimulation. Finally, add the tactile and kinesthetic stimulation of actually playing the game. As a player you must react to various events on the screen by pressing buttons, pushing joysticks, spinning tracballs, or turning dials. Again, reacting at an almost instinctual level

excites the sympathetic system so that you may begin to feel a nonspecific emotional effect. Thus, through three of the five sensory systems, video games may provide stimulation that seems to create an emotional response. This response is known as *arousal*.

AROUSAL THEORY

Schachter (1964) traced arousal theory back to Henry James's belief that emotion was the result of secretions in the body. Modern arousal theory is discussed in both physical and cognitive terms. Essentially, the sympathetic system produces a pattern of physical changes (including secretions) in response to certain types of stimulation. A cognitive response to the stimulus allows us to name the resulting physical state or emotion. For example, you may be watching a scary movie on the late show when, suddenly, the house begins to creak and thump. Based on cognitive experience you are able to label the feeling at that moment as fear. Similarly, you may be sharing wine, candlelight, and soft music with someone you find attractive. The sympathetic system will respond in the same way as in the fear condition; however, because of the cognitive experience the emotion is labeled love rather than fear.

When a person is aroused, metabolic rates change; blood pressure goes up, and heart rate, blood sugar, lactic acid concentrations, and respiration rate increase. Under conditions of arousal an individual may experience palpitations, tremors, flushing, and shortness of breath. Such changes may also be brought about by surprise, novelty of stimuli (Berlyne, 1957; Berlyne, Craw, Salapatek, & Lewis, 1963), drugs (Schachter, 1964), and uncertainty (Hanneman, 1971).

Because individuals may be aroused by stimuli of which they are cognizant (e.g., situations that produce feelings of fear, anger, or love) and by stimuli of which they are not cognizant (e.g., stimulation by drugs, novelty, or uncertainty) it appears that there are two kinds of arousal. One kind of arousal is identified with a specific emotion. The second—generalized arousal—occurs in situations that produce physical changes but lack cognitive cues identifying the cause of the arousal; for example, the individual feels irritable but doesn't know why.

When in a state of generalized arousal, the individual tries to label the emotion and is suggestible to specific emotional states. When Schachter (1964) injected subjects with epinephrine to produce a state of generalized arousal, he found that these subjects could be "... readily manipulated into states of euphoria, of anger, and of amusement at a movie" (p. 69). This phenomenon of generalized arousal will be addressed in this chapter. If a person is in a state of generalized arousal, how will the person react? Under what circumstances will the person be aggressive, passive, hostile, or cooperative? What happens when this person has no overt suggestions to aid in the understanding (or misunderstanding) of the aroused state?

AROUSAL AND AGGRESSION

Catharsis and Social Learning Models

Research on the effects of television viewing, which has attempted to answer some of these questions, offers a model upon which further research may be based. Early television research asked the question: Does television viewing increase or decrease aggression? Since this question was too broad, it was redefined as: Does the viewing of violent programming increase or decrease aggression? This question was designed to test two models, the catharsis model and the social learning model.

The catharsis model suggested that individuals have drive states that can be reduced through vicarious experiences, thus decreasing those drives. Watching violence on television may reduce the drive state for aggression, thus decreasing aggressive behavior. The social learning model suggested that individuals produce the behaviors they observe and that appear to be socially sanctioned. According to this theory, if it is acceptable for "national heroes" such as the Lone Ranger, Annie Oakley, Wonder Woman, Superman, the Six-Million Dollar Man, or the Bionic Woman to use violence in place of negotiation, then it must be acceptable for the viewer to use violence also. Therefore, watching violent television programs would increase violent behavior. Research overwhelmingly supports the social learning model, that is, violence on television promotes aggressive behavior (Comstock, Chaffee, Katzman, McCombs, & Roberts, 1978; Singer & Singer, 1981; Stein & Friedrich, 1975).

Effect of Program Form on Arousal

However, content is only one aspect of television programming. Another, frequently overlooked aspect of programming is the form of the program. This form includes variables such as settings; frequency of change of setting; length of verbalization; frequency of change of speakers; number of characters; uncertainty of setting change; amount of camera movement; and amount of physical movement by characters. These variables are associated with arousal because they produce novelty, surprise, and uncertainty—all inducers of arousal. A program with many set and character changes, much camera movement, and an abundance of physical movement by characters (in short, a high-action program), but with a lack of violence, may also induce generalized arousal.

Recent television research has considered whether the form of programming, regardless of content, produces aggressive behavior. If high-action programming, regardless of content, produces aggression, then aggressive behavior may be due to generalized arousal rather than social learning. Research by Bryant and Zillman (1979); Huston-Stein, Fox, Greer, Watkins, and Whitaker (1981); Tannenbaum (1972); and Watt and Krull (1977) has suggested that television viewing produces generalized arousal which leads to aggressive behavior. The problem with this research, however, is in disassociating the effects of generalized arousal due to program form and the effects of emotional arousal due to program content.

Research by Greer, Potts, Wright, and Huston (1982) examined the effects of high action in neutral programming (i.e., commercials) versus low action in neutral programming on young children. They found that children exposed to high-action programs were more aggressive than children exposed to low-action programs. To some degree, therefore, the effects of television viewing may be explained as a result of generalized arousal rather than modeling. Interestingly, for young children, this generalized arousal led to aggressive behavior.

UNDIRECTED VERSUS DIRECTED AROUSAL AND SOCIAL AFFECT

In a state of generalized arousal, the individual seeks to name the condition; however, young children have difficulty naming their own emotions. They also have a limited set of experiences on which to base emotional discriminations. When adults feel irritable, they are capable of channeling that feeling into appropriate or productive behaviors. Young children, on the other hand, lack experience in channeling feelings associated with generalized arousal. Because of this lack of experience and difficulty in discrim-

inating emotions, generalized arousal in young children may result in aggression as opposed to another, socially sanctioned action.

Noting that people in a state of generalized arousal are easily manipulated, Schachter (1964) studied the effects of directed versus undirected arousal. This research indicated that aroused children who lack direction tend to be aggressive. Is it possible to arouse children and provide situational factors that direct them to engage in behaviors that are not aggressive? If the answer to this question is yes, then implications for interacting with young children are dramatic. It would suggest that prosocial affect in young children might be produced by making sure that the children are in a generalized state of arousal and that situational factors direct them to behave in a prosocial manner. Using such a technique, adults may then provide children with social cognitions that allow them to channel generalized arousal into prosocial behavior.

Video Games as a Medium for Research

In order to test the hypothesis that directed generalized arousal will effect prosocial behavior, a medium other than television must be used. When prosocial behavior is demonstrated on television, it is difficult to separate the effects of directed arousal and modeling. This confounding of arousal and modeling makes television an unsuitable medium for distinguishing between arousal and modeling theories. A more appropriate medium is the video game. Suppose two children must cooperate to play a violent game. If aggressive behavior follows game playing, then directed arousal is not a suitable hypothesis because the children did not produce the most recently elicited behavior (cooperation). In this case modeling would be the explanation of choice, since it seems that the children are influenced by the violent theme of the game. Conversely, if aggression is reduced and cooperation more prevalent after playing the game, then directed arousal would be the explanation of choice.

AROUSAL AND VIDEO GAMES

There is no evidence indicating that video games also produce undirected generalized arousal. However, video games share features with television that have been identified as arousing. These features include rapid movement of characters (objects and foreground) rapid movement of setting (background), uncertainty, surprise, and novelty. In addition, the auditory and tactile stimuli presented by video games may also have potential for arousal.

Video Game Content

In addition to the arousing aspects of video game features, concern has been expressed regarding the violent content of video games, which allow the player to gobble enemies or to blast them out of the sky. However, video game violence differs substantially from television violence. First, compared to television cartoons (e.g., Bugs Bunny) or action programs (e.g., Dukes of Hazzard), video games are highly symbolic. The characters have no explicit relationship to reality (most consist of regular geometric shapes), and their "demise" in a shoot-em-up, eat-em-up game is highly stylized. The "victims" generally pop off the screen or gradually dissolve, and this popping and dissolving is quite different from the semirealism of television cartoons—where the characters are at least recognizable—and the realism of action shows. The violence of television is carried to a conclusion. Elmer Fudd gets smashed. Boss Hogg has his suit torn to tatters in an explosion.

Video Games and Modeling

A second concern is the question of modeling. In order to be modeled, behavior must be reproducible. The behaviors and objects exhibited on television can be reproduced, while the action depicted in video games is, for the most part, irreproducible. The child who finds a gun and aims it at another may be mimicking or reproducing a behavior seen on television. Unfortunately, the gun may be loaded. The televized gun is easily recognized, and the act of shooting is easily reproduced. I have yet to hear of anyone killing another by pressing the trigger of a joystick.

Form of Violence

A third concern is the form of violence presented. Television heroes often instigate or engage willingly in violence toward persons. Shoot-em-up video games (e.g., Caterpillar, Tempest, ZAXXON™, Space Invaders) do not exhibit the personal form of violence displayed on television. Other video games such as PAC-MAN, Q*bert, FROGGER, DONKEY KONG, and Pitfall all encourage avoidance of violence. (While avoidance is not rewarded at the lower levels of PAC-MAN, it is *required* at the higher levels.) There are exceptions (for example, Tron and Berserk™) but for the most part video games do not present models of violence in the same form as television and therefore do not present the opportunity for modeling that television does. This speculation is based on selected observation, however; it is a point that merits further research.

VIDEO GAMES AND AGGRESSION: RESEARCH FINDINGS

Whether due to arousal or to modeling, video games may influence aggressive behavior. In order to test this hypothesis, Silvern, Williamson, and Countermine (1983a) exposed pairs of children to three different conditions: baseline (no stimulus), viewing a Road Runner cartoon, and playing Space Invaders. In addition, half the children actively played Space Invaders and half the children observed (the observers were to help by giving advice and warnings). After each condition the children (ages 4 to 7 years) were placed in a playroom for 10 minutes, and videotapes were made of their interactions. They were told that they could play with the toys in any way they wanted. Toys available in the playroom included blocks, an airplane, truck and people pieces, play money, Raggegy Ann and Andy dolls, plastic zoo animals, stick horses, and a child-size bobo doll (a vinyl punching bag weighted at the bottom). The videotapes were coded for verbal aggression (angry commands, teasing, derogation); physical aggression (physical attack, obstruction, threatening gestures); object aggression (physical attack on an object); solitary fantasy (solitary storytelling and/or acting out a fantasy role); collaborative fantasy (both children storytelling and/or acting out fantasy roles); and fantasy aggression (aggression as part of fantasy, e.g., playing a superhero and beating up the bad guy). These categories were taken from Greer and colleagues (1982).

Research Results and Interpretation

Play episodes were quite variable; however, some patterns emerged. Play with blocks tended to be quiet, constructive play in both solitary and collaborative settings. There were very few instances of block snatching and no instances of obstruction or block throwing. Play with trucks, airplanes, and dolls was similar to block play, with very few instances of conflict. Play with money took two themes, playing store and bank robbers. The store theme led to some arguments concerning who would handle the money. In one

case, two boys were bank robbers taking the money from the bank and riding away on their horses. When they got to the hideout they were caught by the police (played willingly by the bobo doll). The boys beat up the police/bobo doll and ended by reveling in their ill-gotten gains. The bobo doll, in nearly every play period, took some abuse. It was as if the doll gave special permission to be attacked. Usually at the beginning of the play period bobo received an attack. Several pairs of children would continue their attacks on the doll throughout the entire 10-minute period. Some attacks were particularly brutal, for example, picking the doll up and slamming it to the floor or using the stick horse as a weapon to beat the bobo doll. These attacks were seldom part of fantasy; rather, they were instances of outright aggression against the object. One pair of children attacked bobo so viciously that at one point they fell down exhausted, gasping for breath. Needless to say, the bobo doll had to be repaired and eventually replaced during the course of the study.

There were no differences in levels of fantasy play or fantasy aggression among the three conditions (baseline, cartoon viewing, and space video game play). Instances of physical and verbal aggression among the children were so few that they are not worth mentioning. Object aggression, on the other hand, nearly doubled after the television and video game play conditions. Mean object aggression at baseline was slightly more than 5 instances in a 10-minute period. Mean aggression after television and video game play was nearly 10 instances in a 10-minute period. [There were thirty 10-second time sampling observations. Thus, nearly one-third of the play period was spent in object aggression.] Object aggression differences occurred between television viewing and baseline and between video game playing and baseline. There was no significant difference in object aggression between television viewing and video game play.

These findings indicate that playing Space Invaders (and perhaps games similar to Space Invaders) has effects on aggression similar to the effects of watching violent cartoons. This video game appears to contribute to violence. Furthermore, it is not necessary to be playing the game to experience the effect. Children who watched Space Invaders being played were as aggressive as children who played the game. If video game play were cathartic, one would expect the players to be less aggressive than the watchers; this was not the case.

Explanations for Aggressive Behavior: Modeling Versus Arousal Theory

The results of this study could be explained using either modeling theory or arousal theory. In order to determine whether or not arousal theory is an appropriate explanation, a second study was conducted (Silvern, Williamson, & Countermine, 1983b). Children were exposed to a baseline (no stimulus), a cooperative video game, and a competitive video game condition. Both the cooperative and the competitive video games had violent content. In both games children played simultaneously. Arousal theory would suggest that features of the game would create generalized arousal and that the need to cooperate or the need to compete would provide the situational variables to allow children to label their feelings of arousal. Presumably the cooperative condition would induce children to be more cooperative in play and the competitive condition would induce children to be more competitive (aggressive) in play. Modeling theory would suggest that because of their content, both video game conditions would produce more aggression than that found in the baseline condition.

The cooperative game was Star Wars™. The screen has a cross-hair firing sight as the foreground. The background object is an outline of a spaceship (similar in design to the ones seen in the movie *Star Wars*). The object of the game is to manipulate the cross-hair until the spaceship is in the center of the cross-hair. When the ship is centered, it can be fired on and blown up. Firing on the spaceship at any other time will waste energy and end the game prematurely. The vertical movement of the cross-hair is controlled by one game paddle, and the horizontal movement of the cross-hair is controlled by a second game paddle. In playing the game, then, two children had to work in concert to achieve the goal of the game. The children were told that one paddle controlled up-and-down and the other controlled side-to-side movement, but they were not told which paddle controlled which movement—in truth, the experimenter did not know. Therefore, the children had to communicate with each other to identify which direction they were controlling, and they needed to control their impulse to fire.

The competitive game was called Boxing and consisted of two human-like figures in a boxing ring. The object of this game is to move the boxer you are controlling close enough to the opposing boxer to strike the opponent and knock him down. The boxers are moved using a game paddle, and blows are struck by use of the trigger on the paddle. In order to play this game each child had to control his or her own boxer. The idea was to win by knocking the opponent down more times than he or she knocked you down.

Results. In this study, as in the previous study, after each condition there was a play period that was videotaped. The observation system was also the same. There were no differences in levels of cooperative or solitary play and cooperative or solitary aggression between these conditions. However, there was a significant difference in object aggression. Mean frequency of object aggression at baseline was 3.57 incidents per 10-minute period. Mean frequency of aggression after cooperative play was 3.25 incidents per 10-minute period. Mean frequency of aggression after competitive play was .85 incident per 10-minute period. Competitive video game play significantly reduced the number of incidents of object aggression! Lang (1984), using the same paradigm, also found significant differences between baseline and competitive conditions. The means were baseline = 3.61, cooperative = 1.61, competitive = .80.

Since aggression after video game play was not higher than the baseline, it would appear that modeling is not the appropriate explanation for behavior following two-player video games. Whether or not arousal is an appropriate explanation of these findings is still open to question.

INFERENCES

Playing Space Invaders increased aggression relative to a baseline situation, playing Star Wars had no effect on aggression relative to a baseline, and playing Boxing decreased aggression relative to a baseline. Although they do not rule out the possibility, these findings indicate that modeling is not operative as an explanation of children's behavior after playing video games. However, more questions have been raised than were answered. On the surface one would guess that competitive games would give rise to more aggression than cooperative games. Why was aggression so low after the competitive condition? Why was there no effect for cooperation? Why was there such a difference in aggression among Space Invaders, Star Wars, and Boxing when the content of the games is similar?

Generalized Arousal

Space Invaders is a single-player game, while Boxing and Star Wars are two-player games. As a single-player game Space Invaders may provide generalized arousal for both the player and the observer, but there are no situational indicators to give direction to the arousal. As hypothesized earlier in the television studies, perhaps young children under conditions of undirected arousal act as if they are angry. In this case, in the absence of situational cues arousal produces aggression in young children. Boxing and Star Wars, on the other hand, do provide situational cues. The researchers assumed that the situational cues were "resident" in the objectives of the game, such that a game that required cooperation would foster cooperation, and a game that required competition would foster competition.

This assumption may be totally false. Perhaps the situational cues were resident in the interaction surrounding the game. Star Wars is a difficult game to control. The cross-hair does not always move as quickly as the target, and it is hard to isolate variables to identify which paddle controls which direction. While playing the game, children seemed to snap and fuss at each other. "Stop turning your knob; hold it still!" "Don't shoot; stop!" "Move up, move up!" "I can't!" These exclamations were frequently delivered in a whiney voice indicating frustration. Another indicator of frustration was the low level of success. Rarely did any pair succeed in destroying an alien spaceship. Boxing, on the other hand was an easy game. When a boxer fell he went straight from vertical to horizontal, simulating a comedian's pratfall. This action elicited laughter from both players regardless of which boxer was knocked down. The children did not seem to pay attention to whose boxer was whose. Both children seemed to feel they were winning in spite of the score on the monitor. Given these conditions, perhaps it isn't surprising that children were less aggressive after Boxing than after Star Wars. These observations indicate that perhaps directed arousal was operative, but not in the way the researchers expected.

Catharsis

Catharsis cannot be ruled out as an alternative explanation. Catharsis is the reduction of a drive based on an appropriate vicarious experience. In order to reduce aggression there must be the vicarious but engaging experience of aggressing against someone. Television may not provide enough personal action to be a true test of the catharsis theory. Space Invaders provides a vicarious experience of aggressing, but the aggression is not against someone. Star Wars provides opportunity for verbal aggression, but it is not vicarious. Boxing, however, provides a direct opportunity for high levels of vicarious aggression. Hence, according to catharsis theory, Boxing would be the most likely candidate to reduce subsequent aggression.

It is obvious that these are tentative inferences. Considerable research is required before either explanation can be considered satisfactory.

CONCLUSIONS

Regardless of the theoretical explanation, it seems that video games have the potential to increase or decrease aggressive behavior under varying conditions. The ability of these games to control children's aggression suggests several possibilities. The most obvious is to design games that provide environments/situations that will reduce real-life aggression. While this solution is pleasing to adult sensibilities, it does not provide opportunities for children to learn to control feelings of aggression. An alternative would be to identify games that produce aggressive game behavior. When children play these games, caregivers can provide guidance to help them understand their feelings and provide opportunities to channel their behavior

appropriately. Until situations that produce aggression are identified, it is wise for caregivers to carefully monitor children's video game play and help them realize when they are behaving inappropriately.

Finally, it must be remembered that aggression, as discussed here, is a psychological trait. It is neither good nor bad, desirable nor undesirable. There are times in Western society when aggressiveness is viewed as appropriate. For example, a person who aggressively accomplishes tasks is seen as a "go-getter" or a "self-starter." If there are appropriate situations for aggression, there may also be appropriate forms of aggression. Much of the aggression observed in the studies by Silvern and associates was against an object that was designed to accept aggression (some might say that the bobo doll invites aggression). Less than 1 incident in 60 observations was directed toward another person. In this sense the children's aggression, for the most part, was appropriate. Singer and Singer (1981) made the distinction between playful aggression and inappropriate aggression: As long as they don't interfere with or aggress against another child, children who aggress against objects in a play situation are simply playing. With these considerations in mind, perhaps video games will not turn out to be as horrible as some would have us believe.

REFERENCES

Berlyne, D. E. (1957). Uncertainty and conflicts: A point of contact between information-theory and behavior theory concepts. *Psychological Review, 64*, 329–339.

Berlyne, D. E., Craw, M. A., Salapatek, P. H., & Lewis, J. L. (1963). Novelty, complexity, incongruity, extrinsic motivation and the GSR. *Journal of Experimental Psychology, 66*, 560–567.

Bryant, J., & Zillman, D. (1979). Effect of intensification of annoyance through unrelated residual excitation on substantially delayed hostile behavior. *Journal of Experimental Social Psychology, 15,* 470–480.

Comstock, G., Chaffee, S., Katzman, N., McCombs, M., & Roberts, D. (1978). *Television and human behavior.* New York: Columbia University Press.

Greer, D., Potts, R., Wright, J. C., & Huston, A. C. (1982). The effects of television commercial form and commercial placement on children's social behavior and attention. *Child Development, 53,* 611–619.

Hanneman, G. J. (1971, October). *Message uncertainty in television violence as a predictor of arousal and aggression: Some experiments.* Paper presented to the Annual Meeting of the Speech Communication Association, San Francisco.

Huston-Stein, A., Fox, A., Greer, D., Watkins, B. A., & Whitaker, J. (1981). The effects of action and violence in television programs on the social behavior and imaginative play of preschool children. *Journal of Genetic Psychology, 138,* 183–191.

Lang, M. (1984). *The social effects of competitive and cooperative video games on six and seven year old boys.* Unpublished doctoral dissertation, Auburn University, Alabama.

Schachter, S. (1964). The interaction of cognitive and physiological determinants of emotional state. In L. Berkowitz (Ed.), *Advances in experimental social psychology,* (Vol. 1, pp. 49–80). New York: Academic Press.

Silvern, S. D., Williamson, P. A., & Countermine, T. A. (1983a, April). *Aggression in young children and video game play.* Paper presented at the biennial meeting of the Society for Research in Child Development, Detroit.

Silvern, S. B., Williamson, P. A., & Countermine, T. A. (1983b, June). *Children's play with video games.* Paper presented at the International Conference on Play and Play Environments, Austin, Texas.

Singer, J. L., & Singer, D. G. (1981). *Television, imagination and aggression: A study of preschoolers.* Hillsdale, NJ: Lawrence Erlbaum.

Stein, A. H., & Friedrich, L. K. (1975). The impact of television on children and youth. In E. M. Hetherington, J. W. Hagen, R. Kron, & A. H. Stein (Eds.), *Review of child development research.* (Vol. 5, pp. 183–256). Chicago: University of Chicago Press.

Tannenbaum, P. (1972). Studies in film and television mediated arousal and aggression: A progress report. In J. P. Murray, E. A. Rubenstein, & G. A. Comstock (Eds.), *Television and social behavior. Vol. 5. Television effects: Further explorations* (pp. 309–350). Washington, DC: U. S. Government Printing Office.

Watt, J. H., & Krull, R. (1977). An examination of three models of television viewing and aggression. *Human Communication Research, 3,* 99–112.

PART III
VISIONS

CHAPTER 7

PLAY WORLDS AND MICROWORLDS

June L. Wright
Center for Young Children
University of Maryland
College Park, Maryland 20742

Anastasia S. Samaras
Department of Curriculum and Instruction
University of Maryland
College Park, Maryland 20742

Much attention has been given to understanding the world of play. Research has focused on children's play with a variety of materials found in preschool settings, in homes, and on playgrounds. Recently, technology has produced a new and complex machine—the microcomputer—which both challenges and frightens adults. Children, however, appear to accept this wonderful machine as another kind of plaything.

BACKGROUND OF THE CYC PROJECT

The view that children perceive the microcomputer as a plaything is based on an analysis of observations conducted at the Center for Young Children (CYC), University of Maryland. At the CYC, each child is recognized as a unique and intrinsically motivated individual. Each child is encouraged to explore the environment and to invent solutions to problems. Such learning requires an atmosphere in which discovery is recognized as vital to the child's cognitive growth and skill development is seen as secondary to the more important task of concept building through experiencing and understanding.

Research Hypothesis

The introduction of the microcomputer into the CYC classroom environment was based on the hypothesis that an atmosphere that promotes free play would allow children to discover the capabilities of the machine relatively unhampered by adult definitions. The computer project at the CYC was inspired by Seymour Papert's vision that the microcomputer is an object with which to create microworlds, operated by "children who will have their own say in what they pick up and what they make of it" (Papert, 1980, p. 29). In designing the CYC project, we paired a playful atmosphere with open-ended pro-

grams in order to offer a microcomputer experience in which children would truly have "their own say."

The purpose of this chapter is to describe how 4-year-olds mastered the microcomputers and what they picked up and what they made of it. Many of the predictions made by the CYC staff were altered dramatically by what was learned from these children. This study of how children made discoveries and how they used the microcomputer to communicate thoughts and feelings offered unexpected insights into the role this new machine might play in the young child's world.

Procedure and Results

In the spring of 1983, two Astrovision® microcomputers were introduced as another play area to be used by 4-year-old children during free-choice time. The microcomputers were moved on rolling carts into the rug area after group time. Two chairs were placed at each microcomputer to permit children to work in pairs as partners. The machines were positioned so that both monitor screens could be seen by all the children. (For a more complete description of the CYC Computer Discovery Project, see Church & Wright, this volume.)

Observational logs recording the ongoing behavior of the children as they interacted with the microcomputers were maintained for a 4-month period (February–May, 1983). The observer recorded the dialogue between teacher/child and child/child, commands the children gave the microcomputer, and the affective responses of the children. These logs were analyzed to determine how the recorded behaviors related to the cognitive and socio/emotional development of children and how these responses resembled behaviors observed in other play research.

Teacher Role. The teacher acted as a facilitator who introduced the children to the basic commands needed to operate the program and then fostered their investigation. Research suggests a relationship between the degree of teacher direction and the task completed. Iverson (1982) reported that direct teaching is not significantly more efficient than free play in getting children to perform the task. "When free play is routinely discouraged and assignments are always predetermined by teachers, children's flexibility of thought and action is severely limited, and little creativity exists" (p. 694). Commenting on the crucial element of instructional style, Bruner (1972) highlighted the importance of open-ended "tool use," stating, "The crucial evolution of tool using (through play activities) helps free the organism from the immediate requirements of his task" (p. 698). He noted that a child operating in an unpressured environment has the opportunity to try combinations of behavior that might not otherwise occur.

Children's Play Sequence. Given an environment in which teachers encouraged exploration, children at the CYC were able to experiment with and attempt to comprehend their new plaything, the microcomputer. Changes in the way children played with this remarkable toy followed a sequence proposed by Smilansky (1968): functional play, constructive play, and dramatic play. The children's initial functional manipulations led to an understanding of cause and effect relationships between the control panel and the monitor display (functional play). Once aware of how to command the program, the children, sensing that they were in control, moved on to a constructive stage during which they identified and solved specific display problems. The same learnings that permitted the children to design images and create games (constructive play) eventually opened a new play world in which the power to create became the freedom to transform the symbolic meanings of those creations (dramatic play). The most exciting interactions included the sharing of pretend transformations and the realization of a micro-world in which several children expressed their thoughts and feelings through collective symbols. By following the recorded behavior of these young explorers, constructivists, and dramatists, adults may begin to grasp the rich experience and depth of mastery children achieve as they learn through play.

INITIAL EXPLORATIONS

The graphic arts programs, Scribbling and Creative Crayon, were the first programs introduced to CYC 4-year-olds. These programs were chosen because they were open-ended and because they allowed the child to be immediately in command, without requiring an ability to read. The programs were controlled by manipulating a control panel consisting of a joystick, a switch, a button, and a knob. The children were shown only the basic movements of the control panel: that the joystick directed the cursor, that pressing down the switch or the button made the cursor draw a line, and that the knob allowed the user to change the color and size of the cursor. The children were encouraged to use the controls in as many ways as possible. As the children played, they learned about new and complex microcomputer objects and events. The following illustrates an exchange between the teacher and a child discovering the invariant relationship between actions on the controls and events on the monitor.

Amin: You don't know what I get. I get it quick. [He turns the knob quickly.] When I go like this, I make an arrow [at the end of his line]. [He turns the knob in a circle.]

Teacher: Does it make a difference if you turn it fast or slow? Do you still get an arrow?

Amin: Yes, you go like this. [He tries
                 it fast and slow. He gets the
                 same result. He moves the
                 joystick in a circular motion.
                 He experiments. Some areas
                 make an arrow. He stays in
                 those positions longer.] (Sa-
                 maras, Log, 4/11/83)

As children make discoveries they apply
them in new and novel ways. In the following
example, Elaine first discovered how to de-
tach a colored area from a solid line.

Elaine: I know I did that [she has
                 turned the switch off]. . . . Look
                 at this. I had it switch "off."
                 [Her square is moving. She is
                 announcing her discovery and
                 how she did it.] (Samaras, Log,
                 3/2/83)

Some children quickly discovered that the
Scribbling menu allowed the choice of producing more cursors, thus allowing one
screen to be used by more than one child. The
menu also allowed an automatic drawing
mode called "kaleidoscope" which continually made shapes and colors. In the following example Elaine has found the automatic
draw mode.

*Elaine pushed the button on and off, slowly
at first, and then more quickly. The teacher
asked if pushing the button made it change.
Elaine nodded her head, yes. [It did not.] (Samaras, Log, 4/11/83)*

Elaine's inference of a relationship between
the button and events on the screen was incorrect but understandable. She had over-
generalized her own earlier experience in operating Scribbling. In the regular drawing
mode, the button did control whether the
cursor drew. Exposed to a new mode, Elaine
was attempting to assimilate new events to
old schemas. Her misconception made sense
from her point of view. In an inquiry proc-

ess, mistakes are an important part of learning. It required only two play sessions, however, for these 4-year-olds to gain sufficient
knowledge of the relationship between the
knobs and switches and the commands to
permit fairly accurate predictions.

PROBLEM SOLVING

In examining the children's problem solving,
it is evident that there are individual styles
in learning, usage, and mastery of a tool. The
incidents reported in the logs illustrate the
way young children define their own goals
and invent a wide variety of methods for using a creative program.

*Daek-yoo floated the square (cursor) and
changed colors; he then pushed the button intermittently leaving multicolored squares all
over the screen. Next, he put on the switch
and made a box with different colored sides.*

Soo-Young: How did he make that? I'm
                 going to follow him and see
                 how to do it. (Keenan, Log, 2/7/
                 83)

Given the desire to create the same shape,
children will use different problem-solving
techniques to obtain that end.

*After creating a large area of blue, David
made a wide horizontal line on the screen using the background color.*

Soo-Young: That line is wider than mine;
                 why?

*David then attempted to recreate the space for
Soo-Young. While he was doing so, Soo-
Young had an idea, went to the other computer, and drew a long, narrow rectangle outlined in blue, which he filled in. The two
screens looked identical, but the way that*

they were created was different. (Keenan, Log, 2/7/83)

Sometimes in solving a problem, children think out loud, with speech directed to themselves rather than to other people.

Ann had one triangle left in her picture that had not been colored in.

Ann: [to herself] Now, how do I get rid of this [the empty triangle]? [She successfully moved the cursor in the tiny triangle and selected the fill command]. Now I'm done. (Samaras, Log, 4/15/83)

Ann was operating the program Creative Crayon, which allowed her to place her cursor in an enclosed space and fill that space with a color. This program also contained a menu to which the children could turn by using the knob. Sven, operating Creative Crayon, thought out loud, asked for help, and waited for instructions from the teacher. However, once he received the information, he wanted to direct the solution by himself.

Sven: What's going on here? [He was looking for his cursor, which was at the edge of the screen. He moved his joystick as he sucked his thumb.]

How can we do that? What's going on here? . . . I don't know where it went. . . . How can we make the words? [He wanted to get to the menu.]

Sven: [After the teacher described the task] Let me push the keys. (Samaras, Log, 3/11/83)

Mastery and Self-Concept

The child's self-concept as a craftsman becomes more positive as he or she masters the machine. Problems are posed and solved more rapidly and with more internalization. The importance of a sense of mastery has been highlighted by Elkind and Weiner:

> Children's feelings of mastery begin to be shaped during infancy by the pleasure they get from being able to control their environment. . . . Children do not become capable of feeling any lasting sense of accomplishment until the preschool years, however, when their cognitive maturation allows them to recognize the difference between past and present levels of skill. The ability to apply standards of excellence to their own behavior, that is, to realize they are doing something well, or better than before results in children viewing some of their experiences as achievements. Achievement experiences in turn now begin to generate feelings of mastery that can have a lasting influence on an individual's sense of personal competence. (1978, pp. 258–259)

Many experts agree that the overwhelming attraction of the computer is "the lure of control, the pleasure of being able to think out and then make something happen, a satisfaction all too often denied children" (Golden, 1982, p. 52). The examples that follow provide observational evidence of the children's perceptions of the locus of control existing within themselves and their friends.

Amin: Hey, look what I made, look what I did. Look! Look! I'm coloring the whole thing [by knowing the correct sequence for coloring]. Hey, look, I did it all myself!

Josh: Look what I did. You have to do it like that. . . . You don't know how I did this. I did it all by myself! (Samaras, Log, 3/1/83)

The logs demonstrate that children recognized the abilities of their classmates as well as their own accomplishments and were willing to learn from one another. One 4-year-old boy who had experience at home with a nonviolent spaceship game, used the microcomputer to recreate the game he had enjoyed.

Bill: [explaining to Cindy] It's a spaceship. It goes that way. [He pointed to the nose of his ship.] That's how I build things with my tinkertoys. It's going to blast off. [He cleared the screen, then he held down the clear button and drew. He released the button and the picture disappeared. He repeated this sequence faster and it looked like it was jumping.]

Cindy: How did you do that? [Bill showed her again and they both made jumping lines.] (Keenan, Log, 2/9/83)

The children felt that they were controlling what happened on the monitor. They viewed themselves as competent, and on many occasions they demonstrated to parents and visitors how to use the microcomputer. These vignettes of autonomous 4-year-olds designing creative strategies to direct the microcomputer reveal a sense of empowerment from open-ended exploration and self-initiated processes.

PLAY TRANSFORMATIONS

The study provided numerous examples of children engaging in symbolic transformations. The movement of the cursor could produce an animated effect that may have been a factor in the creative response of the children. Lydia, who often worked at the microcomputer, humanized her lines the way a child might humanize a doll or a stuffed animal.

Lydia and Beth created lines. Their lines crossed each other back and forth.

Beth: They're sewing. [She looked at her lines.]

Lydia's line disappeared at the end of the screen.

Lydia: It's sleeping. [The line reappeared.] Now he woke up. (Samaras, Log, 3/28/83)

Language Development

The relationship between symbolic play and language was discussed by Corrigan (1982), who observed that children show increasing flexibility in both play and language when they use nonprototypical constructions. "Studies involving inanimate objects or instruments in pretending have reported that children are most likely to pretend with realistic objects, but when none are available, they may substitute less realistic objects" (p. 1344).

Bobby drew a shape that looked like a dump truck.

Bobby: [Chanting] You dump, you dump, you dump, you dump the dirt out. (Keenan, Log, 2/27/83)

Singer (1973) suggested that fantasy play is a possible mediator in linguistic and cognitive development. When playing, the children often explored and extended their language. For the significant number of CYC children for whom English was a second language, this language development was especially important. This extension occurred for Sven, a Swedish child.

Sven:	We're making a road.
Ann:	There . . . [with a sense of exhaustion].
Sven:	I have a car on the road; I'm making a road.
Teacher:	A highway?
Sven:	What's a highway? [The teacher explained a highway to Sven.]
Sven:	[Explaining to Ann] It means fast, with no home close.

Because children assimilate objects into their own world without the conventions imposed by society, they can easily incorporate different objects and images into the same fantasy.

Allen arrived at the computer first and began drawing with Scribbling. John, having finished making his bead rattlesnake (an art project), pulled it beneath his computer chair and began with Scribbling too. John listened to Allen describe his monkey house for unfriendly animals. John drew a place to house his rattlesnake. The boys were so absorbed that when a neighboring nursery class paraded into the room to display their king-sized Chinese dragon, John barely gave them a glance and Allen never looked up. (Lewis, Log, 2/18/83)

John was not concerned with how the real bead snake would actually enter the picture house. In his fantasy, anything could happen. On a later day, having mastered the use of the background color to erase, John's comment highlighted this lack of concern.

John:	You know what I'm going to do? I'm going to erase! Look at the termite eat at the wood! Yum, yum, yum! [The cursor

erased the screen.] (Lewis, Log, 2/25/83)

Fantasy, even at age 4, is affected by cultural forms. The following month the logs reported:

John:	I'm gonna pretend I'm termites [erasing] . . . no, PAC-MAN. If he can eat all the dots, the monsters turn blue and he can eat the monster. (Keenan, Log, 3/12/83)

Collective Symbolism

Make-believe during free play has been shown to lead to associative fluency (Dansky, 1980). Johnson (1976) has further claimed that there is a relationship among social fantasy play (as distinguished from nonsocial fantasy play), divergent thinking, and intelligence test performance. This distinction is "consistent with the view that collective symbolism requires greater cognitive maturity than does solitary symbolic play" (Johnson, 1976, p. 1203).

Some of the instances of collective symbolism occurred when two children drew on one monitor with separate cursors and joysticks.

Judy and Soo-Young were using two cursors of the same color and drawing random lines.

Soo-Young:	We're making a dinosaur face, right?
Judy:	Yeah!
Soo-Young:	There's a ear, there's a horn— because it's the Tryceritops— a little one. [Paused to draw lines that met the ones Judy had drawn, making a frame.] There's a box—a dinosaur box.
Judy:	There's the dinosaur; he's kicking his leg. [Pointed to the

diagonal line suggestive of motion].

Soo-Young: But it's [the box] made of iron. (Keenan, Log, 3/29/83)

Some children brought dramatic play props to the computer.

Joe and Phil were sharing one monitor. Joe brought two puppets to the computer to let each one "have a turn using it." Phil began moving his cursor to pursue Joe's.

Joe: Come on, the puppet doesn't know how to do that. This puppet wants to practice! (Keenan, Log, 2/23/83)

Collective symbolism, particularly when it is represented on a 12- by 19-inch screen, requires a high level of cooperation. One person following another person's cursor was sometimes interpreted as part of the game and other times as an intrusion. In the sewing symbolism interaction of Beth and Lydia, the separate fantasies came into conflict.

Beth: Stop, Lydia! [Lydia was following Beth's lines.] We're sewing.

[But when Beth crossed Lydia's lines,]

Lydia: Stop! Don't go the same way as I am!

Beth: I don't want to play anymore. (Samaras, Log, 4/28/83)

The interaction between the girls illustrates the difficulty of being co-creators of a "shared make-believe reality" (Giffin, 1984). The metacommunicative process of agreeing on a frame within which two or more children can share a fantasy worked for the creators of the dinosaur but not for the sewing partners. In the latter example, Lydia had not accepted the same pretend structure as Beth. When a common frame is created, an inter-

action may be sustained for as long as 15 or 20 minutes.

John and Bobby were drawing together on separate screens. Bobby made the background dark, and then light.

Bobby: I made it day; when you turn on the light, then it's morning time.

John: I want to make it night. The builders are making a building at night. You see, they got a light.

Bobby also changed his background to dark. Then he turned his red to pink with the intensity button.

John: I want to make my red pink, too. The building looks like red at night, but see, it's really pink in daytime. It's nighttime, but now they put flashlights on and it's really pink.

Bobby: I'm thinking about my building [chin in palms of hands].

John: Is his as light as mine? . . . Oh, I know, his is almost morning time. (Keenan, Log, 1/28/83)

In this example the boys are trying to maintain the same atmosphere on their two separate screens. In the next episode, what started out as a competitive event evolved into a beautiful story enactment. This episode shows how goals may change as two other children interact together on the same screen.

Rob: I'm wrecking the whole picture.

Andrea: I don't care. [Pause] I'm wrecking the whole picture.

As Rob continued to draw, the teacher asked him about his picture.

Rob:	A wolf.
Andrea:	He's speeding up the road.
Rob:	And there's the stairs. Down the stairs onto the pathway, into the jail and he steps down into a dark, dark room, a cave. I want this to be a dark, dark room, a cave. Stop, don't darken it. Leave this space; it's a window.
Andrea:	O.K., that's all; come on. [They stopped and left together.] (Samaras, Log, 3/29/83)

This fantasy took place in a matter of minutes. The ideas were a shared creation, dramatizing bits and pieces of life as the children viewed it. Working together they created an atmosphere of suspense with a window to provide a way out if needed.

PLAY AS THERAPEUTIC ENACTMENT

Children's play is not necessarily devoted to reenactment of pleasurable themes. Waelder (1983) observed that "the child, in playing with extraordinary frequency reproduces, or at least proceeds from, situations that were in actual experience devoid of pleasure" (p. 210). Peller (1954) shared Waelder's position that play is an attempt by the child to assimilate anxiety and reenact an unpleasant experience in a situation in which the child can play an active role. She explained further that a "child plunges into his play.... However, the skilled observer who knows the child and his behavior in the immediate past, his mood on the day of the observation, can with certain probability foretell the duration of the play form and the course it will take without outer disturbance" (p. 196). Consider the following episode in light of the background knowledge that Charles and his mother had had a power struggle on the playground 15 minutes earlier.

Charles:	Somebody's running from the monster.... He can fly, too. Somebody's running up and down the stairs like Dracula. The monster escaped. That's Dracula. That's a woman. ... Somebody bites the woman. Help me! I'm going up the stairs. The woman can't get me. (Wright, Log, 10/8/83)

Another instance, less intense in nature but also reflecting a child's deep desire for power and autonomy in a classroom situation where he is not one of the leaders, follows.

Amin:	I'm the police boy. I have policeman all the way to the top. I'm going 10 miles, here I go. [Made several car screeching sounds.] You'll never get me. Here I go.... Dukes of Hazzard. I'm going at fast speed. You're following me. Where's my line?
Harry:	I gotcha.
Amin:	No, you don't. (Samaras, Log, 3/1/83)

Feitelson and Ross (1973) addressed the concept of catharsis through play, describing play as an open-ended activity that is voluntary, not assigned. "Playing out his problem enables a child to gain a sense of mastery. From being controlled, he becomes the controller of events" (p. 207). The reenactment of an experience as the child attempts to direct the situation has been observed throughout the study of play interactions. These episodes of shared fantasy and emotional catharsis at the microcomputer add new questions for the educator to ponder regarding the roles this multifaceted plaything, the microcomputer, may assume in the preschool classroom.

SOCIAL INTERCHANGE

In spite of the concerns of many parents and educators that the microcomputer may foster solitary play and decrease social interaction in the classroom, observations at the CYC did not support this fear. The presence of two microcomputers made it possible for children to share the fantasies and the games they invented. An important part of the arrangement was the two extra chairs located one on each side of the microcomputer operators. This setup encouraged the observers to join the group and interact with the operators.

Ellen was working at the microcomputer and Lydia was an onlooker.

Teacher:	Turn to fill, Ellen.
Lydia:	Fill, Ellen. Press the button; turn this knob [now demonstrating with hand motions in the air]. Put it more. Can I do it with you?
Ellen:	Yea, we're painting.
Lydia:	Now, I'm going to do it. Sit here, Ellen. [They changed places.] (Samaras, Log, 3/7/83)

Some onlookers became directly involved as they began instructing the children they were watching or adding to the story they were telling.

Sven was using the computer. Amin was the onlooker.

Amin:	Cover this part, O.K.? That's a good one! Now try one more time. No, no. Wow! That's a great job! (Samaras, Log, 3/11/83)

It is evident from this log that the microcomputer provides opportunities for meaningful social interactions among peers. Through suggestion and compromise, the children developed strategies for communicating and dealing effectively with peers. Soon they began to share skills and to teach each other. Perhaps even more important, they were encouraged to consider the feelings and needs of others in order to "collaboratively sustain and experience a transformed definition of reality" (Giffin, 1984). This collaboration helped minimize risk-taking factors, and even timid children assumed control of the microcomputer. These children demonstrated and verbalized their newly acquired abilities with great competence. The pairing further generated a brainstorming of creations that might not have been realized in a structured setting.

THE FREEDOM TO PLAY

The microcomputer can provide a setting in which children may permissively explore their world. The diversity and complexity of the pretend environment created by the children themselves motivates them to think more divergently (Dansky, 1980). If the child is to explore the microcomputer as a toy and use it in his or her constructive and pretend play, what are the implications of this usage for the method of classroom implementation? Feitelson and Ross (1973) have offered the following observations: "Toys, whether store-bought or hand crafted, [are] essentially artifacts provided by adult society to be used by the child at will and without recriminations, in place of useful or precious objects whose use is denied him" (p. 206).

The use of the microcomputer as a plaything departs somewhat from this definition of the term "toy" since it is actually a useful and, if not precious, at least an expensive object. However, the experience at the CYC illustrated that children as young as 3 and 4 years of age could understand the need for care and still experience the freedom necessary to allow the microcomputer to be viewed as a plaything freely chosen and without adult-oriented goals.

It is important that adults, like children, stretch their imaginations to envision the full scope of the microcomputer.

Can you imagine a device that extends your imagination the way telescopes and microscopes extend your vision? Such a device could help you explore worlds that do not exist, bring your fantasies to virtual life, and alert you to the implications of your own creative fiats. Such a device exists today, although imagination extension is not yet its primary task. It is the computer. (Dennett, 1982, p. 33)

As children freely answer the question, "What can *I* do with the microcomputer?" they become software designers showing us alternative computer applications.

NOVEL COMBINATIONS

Research has shown repeatedly that play encourages flexibility. Play gives children experience in operations they are capable of doing, but which may seem extraneous at the time. Because the player is free of the demands imposed by having to solve a problem, he or she is capable of "combinatorial freedom," cultivating a "habit of creating novelty," which will be an asset when confronted with new problems in the future (Miller, 1973, p. 96). The ability to imagine many solutions has its roots in the child's capacity for symbolic play. The work of Piaget and Bruner and many subsequent studies based on their theories have pointed to the fact that "playful activity is an important source of flexibility and novel adaptation" (Dansky, 1980, p. 672). Divergent production

was certainly encouraged by the microcomputer software in the CYC. Using changing colored lines, the children made weather conditions like a thunderstorm, snow, and lightning. They created representational symbols such as a hammer, a machine in a box, a dinosaur, and termites. They executed car races, sewing projects, and day/night scenarios. The children autonomously designed all of these play experiences with a simple graphic arts program!

PROCEDURAL THINKING

The children discovered that ordered sequences of commands were necessary to yield special effects and combinations. In the Scribbling program, in order to separate a line, the switch that controlled the cursor had to be switched off and then on again. As observed in the anecdote of Daek-yoo and Soo-Young described earlier in this chapter, a floating cursor (turning off and on intermittently) could produce patterns other than lines. This variation of the basic drawing sequence was discovered by the children. The Creative Crayon program permitted similar extensions of the initial sequencing. In order to fill in spaces (a choice on the menu), the child had to select the word "FILL," push the button, turn the background knob until the chosen color appeared, and push the button again. Looking back at the episode describing the interaction of Ellen and Lydia, it is evident that Lydia knew the sequence to fill in the shape. Both girls shared a common goal that gave purpose to learning the initial combination of commands.

Some children tested the sequences to ascertain the effect of altering the order. If the commands were permutable, the results were the same. More often, the results were different. Choosing "FILL" before "LINE" (the draw command) in Creative Crayon resulted in a new background color. Since the teachers encouraged exploring new sequences, new combinations and effects were continuously being discovered. Because the children had been encouraged throughout to be autonomous, they eagerly discovered new ways of expressing their individual styles and concerns. There was agreement about the procedure, but the procedure was trivial compared to the richer knowledge of using it to invent and produce outcomes.

These early experiences may facilitate children's ability to use more complex software and may promote higher order thinking skills needed to design algorithms and learn programming. Among other things, the children learned, first, that the microcomputer does exactly what it is instructed to do, in exactly the same sequence as it is instructed, and second, that these sequences produce predictable effects. Whether this early experience with ordered sequences will facilitate the ability to use more complex software and whether the ability will generalize to other aspects of life are questions worthy of consideration. Conceivably, the children who most easily discover such combinations come to the microcomputer with sequencing skills already developed. More specific research can clarify such issues.

CONCLUSIONS AND IMPLICATIONS

The young child's natural tendency to relate to the microcomputer as a plaything has powerful implications for the microcomputer's potential role in early childhood education. When intrinsically motivated, children explore the machine in depth, exhibiting great intensity and involvement. While educators ponder the depth and scope of the learning that might be possible with the microcomputer, children surge ahead to show some of the possibilities. A careful study of the logs has uncovered a new perspective on

the impact of the microcomputer in the classroom and the home.

Cognitive and Affective Potential

In the CYC project, the cognitive challenge and creative potential realized through playing with the microcomputer was immediate. Children demonstrated their abilities to understand cause and effect relationships, which set the stage for designing their own problems and solutions individually and collectively. Not only could they "scribble" in their constructive play, but they could also prolifically sequence, combine, and transform those simple lines in their symbolic play. These 4-year-olds were not frightened by the computer. Their approach to the machine was zestful, uninhibited, confident, curious . . . and yet, in a special way, highly disciplined.

Accompanying this cognitive challenge was a powerful affective force. As the children determined and executed their goals, they were assured that they were indeed capable individuals. They expressed delight when they realized they were in control of their environment. This sense of efficacy, of being the controller, has implications for developing the ability to manage problems in the real world. These experiences confirmed a sense of worth and trust in themselves and in their partners.

The microcomputer also served as a vehicle for self-expression, where children represented feelings and new understandings of their world in graphic representations. This idea was further developed in the curriculum when the children were introduced to the idea of writing their own stories on the microcomputer. For some children, the microcomputer became a cathartic transport, an avenue of self-expression in a secure setting. These affective avenues gave us insights into the children's personal concerns offering a better understanding of their behaviors and learning.

Need for More Research and Careful Decisions

The potential of the microcomputer as a powerful plaything is not widely recognized. The abundance of recent commentary concerning the use of computers in the classroom suggests that computer literacy is quickly becoming as essential as reading, writing, and arithmetic. Fortunately, curriculum guidelines and implementations are still in a formative period; unfortunately, educational directions are often determined by a handful of "experts." This chapter has suggested that through careful observation of the children themselves, educators may discover how the microcomputer complements other classroom activities while contributing in a special way to personal growth and creative thinking.

As a new tool becomes available in a technological society, competition by both commercial enterprises and theoreticians soars, confusing the role and value of the tool with its power and style. It is essential that educators maintain perspective and resist reaching premature conclusions. Instructional decisions have consequences for children's learning. What role the microcomputer will take in the school and the home will largely be determined by how educators and parents choose to integrate this new tool/plaything. Its full potential is only beginning to be discovered. A crucial component in the development of this potential will be the teaching techniques employed. It is important to remember that the adult's perception of the microcomputer can easily color the child's perception. Teacher strategies that encourage autonomous exploration, problem solving, and play will sanction quite different outcomes from those that do not. The cognitive potential lies not just in what is taught, but how it is taught. Careful research must consider a variety of implementations, the immediate impact, and the long-term outcomes on children of each of those implementations.

Decisions concerning instructional setting (classroom or computer lab), appropriate software, and frequency of use as well as mode of instruction must all be governed by sound educational goals and a solid knowledge of child development. True, the microcomputer is a new tool/plaything, part of a fast-moving information age, but as in the past, children, their needs and their potential, present the same challenge to parents and educators. Young children who grow in an atmosphere that promotes a sense of worth and encourages playful exploration of their world better understand the larger world of which the microcomputer will be a part.

REFERENCES

Bruner, J. S. (1972). Nature and uses of immaturity. *American Psychologist, 27,* 687–708.

Corrigan, R. (1982). The control of animate and inanimate components in pretend play and language. *Child Development, 53,* 1343–1353.

Dansky, J. L. (1980). Make believe: A mediator of the relationship between free play and associative fluency. *Child Development, 51,* 576–579.

Dennett, D. (1982, December). The imagination extenders. *Psychology Today,* pp. 30–39.

Elkind, D., & Weiner, I. B. (1978). *Development of the child.* New York: John Wiley.

Feitelson, D., & Ross, G. S. (1973). The neglected factor—play. *Human Development, 16,* 202–223.

Giffin, H. (1984). The coordination of shared meaning in the creation of a shared make-believe reality. In I. Bretherton (Ed.), *Symbolic play: The representation of social understanding* (pp. 73–100). New York: Academic Press.

Golden, F. (1982, May 3). Here come the microkids. *Time*, pp. 50–56.

Iverson, B. (1982). Play, creativity, and schools today. *Phi Delta Kappan, 63*, 693–694.

Johnson, J. E. (1976). Relations of divergent thinking and intelligence test scores with social and non-social make believe play of preschool children. *Child Development, 47*, 1200–1203.

Keenan, K. (1983). [Computer discovery project: Log]. Unpublished raw data.

Lewis, C. (1983). [Computer discovery project: Log]. Unpublished raw data.

Miller, S. (1973). Ends, means, and galumphing: Some leitmotifs of play. *American Anthropologist, 75*, 87–98.

Papert, S. (1980). *Mindstorms: Children, computers and powerful ideas.* New York: Basic Books.

Peller, L. E. (1954). Libidinal phases, ego development, and play. *Psychoanalytic Study of the Child, 9*, 178–198.

Samaras, A. S. (1983). [Computer discovery project: Log]. Unpublished raw data.

Singer, J. L. (Ed.). (1973). *The child's world of make believe: Experimental studies of imaginative play.* New York: Academic Press.

Smilansky, S. (1968). *The effects of sociodramatic play on disadvantaged preschool children.* New York: John Wiley.

Waelder, R. (1933). The psychoanalytic theory of play. *Psychoanalytic Quarterly, 2*, 208–224.

Wright, J. L. (1983). [Computer discovery project: Log]. Unpublished raw data.

CHAPTER 8

MICROCOMPUTERS, PRODUCTIVE THINKING, AND CHILDREN

Rich Hofmann

Department of Educational Psychology
Miami University
Oxford, Ohio 45056

As a child in rural New York state, I spent countless hours by myself in the woods and swamps studying the trees and rock formations. Later I lived near an American Indian reservation located on the edge of an enormous swamp. When hunting and fishing with my Indian friends, I was always amazed at their uncanny ability to return to our entry point in the swamp, because we never returned the way we entered. This behavior was exhibited in areas that we had never before entered. When I asked them how they located the entry point so accurately, their answer was incredibly simple. They told me that they had been taught at a very young age always to be aware of where they were relative to where they had started. In other words rather than remembering their trail as they walked through the woods and swamps, they always maintained a mental map of their present location relative to their entry location. Once informed, I realized that I, too, could use this strategy.

As an adult, I have tried unsuccessfully to teach my own and other children how to use mental maps. Why was it so easy for me but so hard for others to learn this method? The answer to this question is, I believe, in my early experiences. As a child I developed an awareness and sensitivity to my natural surroundings. These perceptions often seemed to be unrelated to anything else. However, these seemingly unrelated awarenesses and sensitivities coalesced into a meaningful relationship by means of mental maps. Seldom do I get lost in the woods. Even when in a large wooded area for the first time, I have little difficulty finding my way, and I am always able to take a direct path back to my entry point. In subtle and not easily discernible ways, our experiences in certain environments give us access to elegant and efficient strategies for operating in environments never before encountered.

EXPERIENCES IN THE MICROCOMPUTER ENVIRONMENT

Within the past 4 years microcomputers have flourished, and they are now making their way into homes and schools. During the past several years my research has involved preparing software for children, providing programming instruction to children, and monitoring young children as they use microcomputers with various commercial software programs. As this research has progressed at Miami University, we have become particularly interested in identifying early experiences that the microcomputer uniquely provides. By *unique* we mean experiences that either could not or could not easily be encountered by a child outside of the microcomputer environment.

The position advanced in this chapter is that children must feel in control of their microcomputer environment while, at the same time, the experiences that children derive from microcomputer software must be under the subtle control of the software. The microcomputer environment can be designed to provide children with experiences that may have a pervasive positive influence on their future learning.

One powerful influence is the potential of the microcomputer environment to foster children's acquisition of cognitive skills and strategic attitudes that may have a long-lasting influence on their approach to new problem settings. It is hypothesized that such experiences in a microcomputer environment will facilitate the development of children's productive thinking, their problem-solving strategies. With a microcomputer available, such experiences may occur independent of adults. In this chapter, the basis for this position is briefly noted and then clarified within the context of several illustrative examples. Finally, speculations are made regarding a possible relationship between age and a child's capacity to learn from programming experiences.

A BASIS FOR PRODUCTIVE THINKING

Hebb's Theory of Learning

In Chapter 11 of *Organization of Behavior*, Hebb (1949) described brain injuries, comparing the consequences of similar types of injury in children and in adults. Specifically, he described a young child's mental functioning after a brain injury. Prior to this injury the child had been mentally active and quite intelligent; after the injury the child had a severely diminished learning capacity. The adult whose injury resembled that of the child appeared to be mentally normal in every capacity save one, arithmetic. Even here, the adult was functional in arithmetic but showed diminished capacity relative to his skill prior to the injury. In his text Hebb offered these and other anecdotes in support of his theory dealing with the acquisition of knowledge.

Hebb's theory postulates that a large amount of brain tissue is needed when new learning is taking place. However, as the newly acquired knowledge is related to previously acquired knowledge, the amount of brain tissue required to maintain the knowledge is reduced. Bits of knowledge that are in some way related are interconnected in the brain. The more interconnections there are for a bit of knowledge, the less brain tissue is required to retain that knowledge. Because of the complexities of these connections, damage to parts of the brain destroys only certain pieces of knowledge, which may be of little consequence in the adult brain because the network of connections continues to exist in a reasonably intact fashion.

Hebb theorized that destroyed knowledge may very well be reconstituted by the network of connections. It may be that the initial knowledge was only important in order to establish the connections, and once established the bit of knowledge itself is of little value, especially if it can be reconstituted when needed. Consider an analogous situation. One can think of a pile of bricks as representing pieces of unconnected knowledge or experiences. As an unorganized pile they take up a substantial amount of space. However, the amount of storage space they require can be reduced markedly if they are laid in an interlaced fashion, as in a single rectangular box or a brick wall. Not only does such an arrangement require less space than the unorganized pile, but also, once the structure has been made, it is possible to remove individual bricks without actually destroying or even weakening the structure.

Piaget's Memory Theory

Piaget (Piaget, Inhelder, & Sinclair-DeZwart, 1973) also talked of memory and intelligence. Unlike more traditional discussions of memory that allude to a deterioration of memory over time, Piaget discussed a specific aspect of memory as improving with the passage of time. In particular, he noted that in younger children memories of certain experiences become refined as the child obtains knowledge or understandings that are in some way "connected" to those experiences. For example, when posed with a question regarding the color of their home before the age of 5, many adults are able to offer an immediate response that accurately specifies the color of the house. Yet most readily admit afterwards that they did not really know colors before the age of 5. This is easily explained for individuals whose family homesteads have remained inhabited and unchanged during the individual's lifetime. It is an amazing demonstration of the refinement of memory for those individuals who have not seen these homes since childhood. This example of color recall has also been reported for cars. It is as if the brain stores away a bit of knowledge dealing with the color of the house or car, even though it doesn't yet associate the knowledge with color. Later, as the child learns about color, a connection is established between the bit of knowledge dealing with car or house color and color variation itself.

This is the same phenomenon with which Hebb was dealing: As experiences are acquired the brain becomes more efficient in utilizing and recalling the experiences. This type of memory refinement is especially prominent in children. The important implication is that the task of learning should become not only one of amassing bits of knowledge but also one of connecting bits of knowledge or even developing strategies for connecting bits of knowledge.

Tolman's Theory of Cognitive Maps

Tolman (1967) developed a theory of learning that was quite different from theories put forth by behavioral learning theorists, but quite consistent with the theoretical orientation toward knowledge advanced by both Hebb and Piaget. In particular, Tolman felt that behavior is purposive in the sense that individuals do something because they expect a specific outcome as a consequence of what they have done. Knowledge is stored in such a way that different bits of knowledge are connected with each other. He likened these connections to roads on a map, the analogy being that bits of knowledge are like cities and villages. Connections between bits of knowledge are like roads connecting the cities together. This powerful conceptual model was used by Tolman to explain how an individual creates or invents solutions to new problems. Generally, within the context

of cognitive maps the individual will frequently identify the shortest, most efficient route to a solution. One must be careful not to overgeneralize Tolman's theory to all learning and to all knowledge. He indicated that his theory dealt with "molar" behavior, that is, behavior that could be molded or modified in order to adapt to new circumstances.

Productive Thinking

In the process of reorganizing or assimilating knowledge, new and possibly unique thoughts are produced. This process may well involve putting together the pieces of an old puzzle to form a new picture. Perhaps previously obtained knowledge or information is used or recombined to solve or better understand an existing problem. This process was termed *productive thinking* by Wertheimer (1959), although most modern-day cognitive psychologists would prefer to use the term *problem solving*. It is quite likely that Wertheimer's earlier works and the work of Gestalt psychologists in general either influenced or are consistent with the referenced works of Piaget, Hebb, and Tolman. Although I will use the term *productive thought*, it is important for the reader to keep in mind that the basis for productive thinking as it is used in this chapter is from the works of Hebb, Tolman, and especially Piaget and Wertheimer.

PRODUCTIVE THINKING AND LEARNING

While it is usually possible to solve problems that others have encountered by using the same solutions, it is also possible that a better solution exists and is just waiting to be found. One of the more traditional approaches to education is the passing down of knowledge, sometimes in the form of other people's solutions to problems. However, one of the surest ways to stymie productive thinking is to teach children "blind habits" through certain types of school drill.

In order to facilitate the productive thinking process, the learner must be given an opportunity to explore and manipulate the environment in such a manner that bits of knowledge or structure can be found. The learner must be allowed to identify different parts of a problem and to recognize interrelationships within and between different parts of the problem. This effort implies that the learner will separate out those aspects of a problem that do not go together and group those aspects of the problem that do belong together. To generalize solutions to problems, a learner not only must create the necessary steps to a solution, but also must understand the necessary steps, their relationship to each other, and their relationship to the total problem. When this is accomplished the steps often lead to sensible expectations and assumptions that in turn lead to additional solution steps.

If "damage" occurs in an educational setting, it is often because the learner is not allowed to think independently. Often the learner is encouraged to rely on established textbooks or teacher answers. We then find that when encountering a new problem, one not encountered in previous settings, the learner is incapable of deriving a solution to it. The problem remains unsolvable as long as the learner tries to use old solutions.

Allowing the learner to explore and manipulate an environment is one way of facilitating the acquisition of solution structures, that is, the complex interconnections that figure so prominently in Hebb's theory. Learning connections seem to be more powerful if the learner controls the environment within which the learning takes place. A learner cannot always tell you how much has been learned because all of the pieces may

not yet be in order. However, when the learner is placed in control of the problem environment, pieces of knowledge have an opportunity to coalesce into powerful structures. These structures may be substantially more powerful than those that might have been taught by rote drill. They may be unique and "unteachable," because they provide solutions to problems whose solutions previously were not known or not understood.

ABOUT SOFTWARE

One of the common questions that I hear from children to whom I have taught programming is, "What should I do?" Perhaps what they are really saying to me is, "Hey! You taught me how to program. Now teach me what to do with it." I even hear this question from children who are programming in machine language. After listening to these types of questions for a while and after watching the children for several years, it has become clear to me that the problem may be in the software that children use. Commercial software may serve either of two purposes. First, it may be thought of as a stage for showing aspiring young programmers the vast array of things that can be done with a microcomputer. Second, and perhaps more important, microcomputer algorithms can structure experiences for a child independent of the presence of an adult. These experiences may not be replicable in a non-microcomputer environment, but they may provide knowledge and concepts that are generalizable beyond the microcomputer environment. The major thesis of this chapter is that software holds the "computer future" for children; not just any software, but rather software that allows a child to control or modify the microcomputer environment as it is created by the software.

Two Major Software Dimensions

There are at least two major dimensions of software and the generalizability of knowledge: *type of experience* and *user control*. Both of these terms are somewhat ambiguous. Experience may be thought of as the extent to which it is possible to acquire meaningful or generalizable knowledge through interaction with the microcomputer software. Control may be defined as the degree or extent to which a child has apparent control of the microcomputer environment.

Experience. There are at least two general types of experience that facilitate learning when children use microcomputer software. First, it is possible to learn through environmental interaction, which may be the most powerful of all experiences. A second type of experience is drill or sheer memorization in which learning occurs because of repeated exposure to material. It is difficult to generalize this drill learning to other experiences. However, in those situations where the drill is meaningful, learning does take place and the knowledge does generalize.

Perhaps the most powerful type of environmental experience is purposive as opposed to chance. Purposive environmental experiences are those that are under the direct control of the learner. The learner may actually manipulate the environment either in anticipation of a particular outcome or to explore a particular outcome. For want of a better term I will refer to learning associated with purposive environmental experiences as *strategy learning* (Wertheimer, 1959). Strategy learning is the type of learning that generalizes to other situations and facilitates the acquisition of additional knowledge. Such experience also refines the understanding and meaningfulness of already existing knowledge. Chance environmental experiences may be thought of as those experiences within the environment that appear to occur quite independently of the learner; that is, they do not appear to be under the learner's control. Such experiences usually do not result in meaningful learning. They neither generalize well to other situations nor facilitate the acquisition of additional knowledge.

Control. There are at least three types of control illustrated in the commercial microcomputer software currently used by children. *Strong control* occurs when the user's self-perceived role is one of developing a strategy for controlling and predicting outcomes; however, the software remains in control as it readjusts the microcomputer environment in terms of the user's strategy. In *subtle control*, the user's perception is one of almost total control of the microcomputer environment, when in reality the software is cleverly controlling and structuring the microcomputer environment to foster such a perception. *No control* is also characterized by the user's perception of no real control or adjustment of the microcomputer environment by the software. In no control, the microcomputer's total presentation is not predicated on the user's prior response; thus, the software does not exert real control over the environment, save for the simplistic sequencing of the frames on the monitor screen.

Strong-Control Software. Arcade games are an example of strong-control software. Such software requires quick motor reaction and anticipation from the user. When the desired user response either is not given or is given inaccurately, there are severe negative consequences. Alternatively, chaining together of proper responses will result in the user's obtaining control of the microcomputer, a positive reinforcer with both visually and auditorialy exciting consequences. However, such control is usually short-lived since the software will create a new environment, in microcomputer terminology a new *level*, that reestablishes control by the microcomputer and places new demands on the user. Such software is entertaining, but its potential for facilitating cognitive learning is not yet well understood.

No-Control Software. One example of no-control software is educational software that simulates a worksheet or textbook page. The user simply responds, frequently in a rote fashion, to stimuli on the screen. Either a correct or incorrect response is given by the user. The reinforcers are usually very dull, either a short tune or a short flashing phrase on the screen. There is no necessity for original decision-making with this kind of control. At best, some rote learning or memorization may occur. There is a place for rote learning in some cases, since such learning may be a necessary prerequisite for more advanced, abstract learning. However, no-control software is not very motivating, and its effectiveness with children appears to be very short-lived, especially when they realize that microcomputers are capable of offering more interesting types of experiences. Such software might also be referred to as *noninteractive*. In some instances the material presented with no-control software might be better presented outside of the microcomputer environment.

Subtle-Control Software. Subtle-control software is the software of interest in this chapter. Such software is usually quite complex from a programming point of view. The programmer must design the software in anticipation of a variety of responses from the user. When this has been done it is quite possible for the microcomputer to establish a highly structured environment in terms of microcomputer algorithms, but one that appears almost totally unstructured from the user's point of view. The user perceives the microcomputer as being under his or her control since the microcomputer seems to react to whatever response is offered by the user. In reality, the user has simply responded in one of the ways identified in advance by the programmer. The microcomputer then presents the environment

assigned to that response by the programmer. One might argue that subtle-control software is the most structured software, perhaps exerting the greatest amount of control over the user. However, the important consideration is the user's perceived control, which rests on the degree to which the user can manipulate the microcomputer environment in a purposive, exploratory fashion.

Stress and Software. Recently we have been looking at the relationship between stress and microcomputer software with preadolescents and adults. Although our efforts have been centered on arcade-type games, they should generalize to the present discussion. We have consistently found that when individuals initially use microcomputer software they show physiological signs of being stressed. As they acclimate themselves to the software and begin to exercise control over it, the physiological signs of stress diminish. Once mastery of the software is demonstrated by the user, we often find stress reduced below the basal level obtained when we initially started the stress measurement. However, if the individual who is acclimated to the software initiates a response and the outcome of the response is not the one expected, the individual rapidly shows physiological signs of being stressed.

Generally, to the extent that individuals can control the microcomputer environment to bring about anticipated results, not only may they experience no stress, but they may very well experience stress reduction. We have not yet been able to study the effects of stress and stress reduction in learning situations with children. However, we are willing to speculate that the effects of stress reduction would be quite favorable, particularly in terms of facilitating learning and productive thought. This is in contrast to stress-inducing situations that might very well militate against learning and substantially reduce the probability of productive thinking.

Strong-control software has great potential for inducing stress. We have found software to be stress-producing if it is difficult to understand, manipulate, and control. Some of the less popular "adventure" games have this problem. Interestingly, the most popular commercial adventure games, Wizardry® from Sir-tech, reduces stress and requires productive thinking from the user. Educational software that is difficult to understand and control will most likely be stress-producing.

Examples of Software that Facilitates Productive Thinking

Over the past 3 years, we have reviewed approximately 250 commercial microcomputer programs. This section presents a brief discussion of several of these commercial software packages. These packages represent some of the finest commercial software available to facilitate the growth of productive thinking in children. This section also discusses some of the experimental software we have developed in order to study productive thinking in young children and some anecdotal observations of children using the software. Each of these software packages encourages purposive experiences within the microcomputer environment. Children refer to these packages as games, and so do we in this chapter; however, they are substantial learning experiences and excellent examples of subtle-control software.

Spelling Bee Games™ by EduWare Services, Inc. This software was developed by John Conrad, a fusion physicist, for his own children. There are a series of game-type programs on a single disk; however, one program, Skyhook, is especially notable. Briefly, the user flies a helicopter that has a skyhook. The objective is to pick up some letters from a flatbed truck and fly them to the top of the skyscraper. Once the letters have been flown to the top of the skyscraper, they must be lowered to the roof. However, the letters must be lowered to specific ordinal positions on the roof. The ordinal positions spell out the name of an object whose image is being projected onto the wall of the building. If the letter is placed into the wrong ordinal position it simply drops back down to the flatbed truck. A number of different images may be projected onto the building so the software maintains high interest over a long period of time. It is important to note that the user controls the flight of the helicopter, the movement of the skyhook, the letter that is picked up, and the placement of the letter. This piece of software seems to be quite entertaining to students with spelling problems as well as to students just learning to spell.

After watching children 6 to 14 years of age play this game for long periods of time, I was amazed at their persistence in attempting to discover the relationships among the letters on the flatbed truck, the ordinal positions of the letters on the roof, and the projected image. Invariably, the relationship is one of sounding out the word associated with the projected image. For children who are either having difficulty reading or just learning to read, it is an "intellectual happening" when they discover the relationships among the letters, the images, and the ordinal positions and then try to replicate these types of relationships when a new image is projected onto the wall. The child is in total control of the operation. When using this software in a primary grade classroom where there is a waiting line, it is not uncommon to see a child prolong his or her playing time by pretending to be totally baffled on the last image of a turn.

I lent this software to the parents of an 8-year-old youngster who was having great difficulty reading. The youngster was fascinated with his ability to control the helicopter. His parents told me that this was the first time they had ever seen him attempt to sound out words. They, as well as his reading teacher, had come to believe that he was incapable of sounding out words. This boy was teaching himself to sound out words when adult instruction in this area had failed. Later, the parents told me that they were having some trouble because he was sneaking out of bed early in the morning, before anyone else was awake, to use the program.

Learning with Leeper by Sierra On-Line, Inc. This disk also contains a series of programs. Although there appear to be four different programs on the disk, each program has a variety of levels. In fact there are so many levels that I am not sure that I have actually seen all of them. What makes this software especially unique is that it was designed by Nancy Anderton, who is not a microcomputer programmer! This software, although geared for children in the 4- to 7-year age range, is also attractive to 3-year-olds and adults. This software presents no consequences for an incorrect response. One program on the disk requires the user to move a frog through a simple maze with a friendly serpent in pursuit. No matter what the user does, the serpent will never catch the frog. Therefore the user is able to investigate the consequences of taking various paths through a maze. There is also a painting program, a letter discrimination program, a shape discrimination program, and some simple one-to-one correspondence problems.

This may be the best piece of software for introducing young children to microcomputers. With it, the children are in total control of their environmental experiences. A user can mix colors or draw in any manner that is desirable. If a user miscounts the number of bones for the dogs in the one-to-one correspondence task, dogs that get "short-changed" beg for a bone. If a user doesn't match the correct shape in the discrimination problems, the shape just falls back to its original position. There is no real failure. However, there is some excitement in the form of a collection of balloons popping if the correct shape is matched. Still another task requires eye-hand coordination. With

this task the user works the left and right arms of a clown in an attempt to burst balloons moving up on either the left or right side of the clown. This piece of software provides many hours of experience for the young user with no negative reinforcement.

It is particularly interesting to watch a child attempt to figure out how to make the dogs beg! We watched some 4-, 5-, and 6-year-olds work with this one-to-one correspondence program. We were somewhat astonished by the fact that the more they used the program, the more erroneous their answers. We asked the children to tell us what they were doing while they were playing. Much to our surprise, they were attempting to maximize the error in the problem. The greater the error, the more dogs there were to beg. The children enjoyed seeing the dogs beg. These children had discovered the concept of subtraction!

The Talking Touch Pad. The talking touch pad is an experimental device that we have developed primarily to accommodate children who have difficulty in reading, letter discrimination, and motor control. It is a 12-inch by 24-inch touch pad that attaches directly to an Apple® microcomputer. The pad has a collection of numbers, letters, and colors on its face. It consists of numbers from 0 to 15, lower- and upper-case letters arranged in alphabetical order, and some 10 to 13 colors. When a child touches a key on the pad the corresponding symbol is displayed on the screen and pronounced, including colors. A pair of red lips have been drawn in the middle of the touch pad. When the lips are touched, the letter or number collection currently on the screen is pronounced. This pronunciation is accomplished with text-to-speech and number-to-speech algorithms in conjunction with a synthetic voice. Thus, children may experiment with the sounds associated with certain letters or various letter combinations, an experience that is not readily available elsewhere. They may experiment with arithmetic operators and numbers. They may even experiment by having the microcomputer pronounce large numbers.

When they use this software, the children are able to generate their own experiences with letters and numbers. It is an exemplar of true purposive environmental experience. There are a variety of methods for teaching reading, but the touch pad requires no method. Through their own controlled experience the children begin to learn letter sounds, diagraph sounds, and so on. We have watched children—even 3-year-old children—come to recognize the sounds that certain letters and letter combinations make when they are entered into the touch pad. We have not yet had an opportunity to watch the children with numbers because they seem to prefer the letters.

Shortly after the touch pad was completed we placed it in a kindergarten room to see if the children could "crash" the exploratory software that we had written. When we placed the pad in the kindergarten room we were especially interested in observing the children's reactions to the pad's pronunciation of letters and numbers. The teacher did not provide any instruction to the children; rather, they were allowed to interact with the pad in any way that they wished.

When I came back to talk with the children a week later they were excited about a discovery that they had made with the pad. They informed me that they had discovered magic letters on the pad. Because I could make no sense of their excited discussion, they showed me what they meant. At first they entered the letters BCD and touched the lips. The microcomputer voice synthesizer pronounced the names of the letters B, C, and D. Then they entered the letters BAD and pressed the lips. The microcomputer voice synthesizer then pronounced the word that is spelled "BAD"! Eventually I was able to figure out what they were saying to me. If they entered a collection of letters and pressed the lips, the microcomputer would usually pronounce the letters. However, if they entered a magic letter or magic letters with the other letters, the microcomputer would make a sound or word that was not a letter name. These children had discovered the difference between vowels and consonants. They had discovered that you need vowels to have words. If you do not have vowels then you only have a collection of letter sounds. The teacher assured me that this discovery had been made by the children independently of any adult interaction. What is most interesting about this is that the children did not know all of the letter names, yet they had learned certain phonological characteristics of the letters. One must wonder what wonderful benefits this will have for these children when they receive their initial reading instruction.

On another occasion some first grade children in a rural school who were not yet capable of reading many words were using the talking touch pad. These children were given 3- by 5-inch cards with their names printed on them. The children would enter their names letter by letter on the touch pad. As they entered the letters the touch pad would pronounce the letters. When they had completed the task of entering the letters of their name they knew that all they had to do was touch the set of smiling red lips in the center of the touch pad and the letters appearing on the screen would be pronounced in word form. The children quickly tired of entering their names and were looking for other words to enter when they discovered the word *PAC-MAN* on a lunch box. They entered the letters "P" and "O." As the child entering the letter pressed the "O" rather than an "A," another child yelled, "No!" This caused the child entering the letters to hold his finger on the touch pad. As a result another "O" was entered. All of the children standing around the microcomputer and the touch pad knew that "P-O-O" was not going to say *PAC-MAN*. But before they could figure out what to do, the boy entering the letters entered a "P" to start spelling PAC-MAN again. Unfortunately he had not cleared the letters from the screen by pressing the lips, so now the screen showed the letters "P-O-O-P." When the children pressed the lips to clear the screen, it seems that every child within earshot heard the pronunciation. Suddenly the children decided that the bathroom walls were a good source of words. One can only speculate as to why the children didn't think of using their school books! It is important to realize that these children were using the touch pad during a play period and that the preceding events and those that followed occurred out of earshot of the teacher. I was a very inconspicuous observer.

The children began "drawing" or copying four-letter words from the bathroom wall. They came back with one forbidden word that was written in upper-case letters. They entered the letters and were delighted at their ability to make the microcomputer pronounce the naughty word. Of course, they reentered these letters several times. Meanwhile a second child came back with a "new" word, which was actually the previous four-letter word in lower-case letters. The children entered this word and were astonished that the touch pad pronounced the same previously entered word. Suspecting that they had done something wrong, they entered the lower-case word again and again. Finally they concluded that the two spellings were indeed the same word. They fiddled around with the letters on the touch pad and discovered a relationship between capital letters and lower-case letters. They discovered that capital letters make the same sound and are indeed the same letters as lower-case letters. What a terrific insight these seven or eight children had, and the whole experience occurred within 20 minutes!

General Dolch Spelling Program. Several years ago we developed a generalized spelling program for use in a rural first grade classroom. Over the previous 4-year period, a progressively larger and larger proportion of second grade children had been qualifying for remedial reading instruction. The spell-

ing program dealt with the Dolch sight words, which the teacher was also using for reading instruction. Each week the teacher selected five to nine Dolch words. The words then became part of the spelling program. This spelling program is unique because a child does not have to read in order to use it. The spelling algorithm involves synthetic speech. When a child sits down at the microcomputer and "initiates" the program, the microcomputer asks the child to enter his or her name. The weekly words are then displayed in an animated fashion so that the child can have some initial familiarity with the words. The actual spelling task is presented in two phases. First, a word is displayed at the bottom of the screen and the child is asked to spell it. The displayed word serves as a crutch. Once the child works through all the words with the crutch, the second spelling phase begins. The child is once again asked to spell the words, but now the words are not spelled out on the bottom of the screen.

A powerful feature in this spelling program is that the program will not allow the child to enter a letter immediately after an incorrect letter has been entered. The child must correct the incorrect letter before continuing with the spelling. Effectively, the algorithm never allows a child to spell a word incorrectly. To the extent that a child can read the words, he or she is able to use the provided crutch. The motivating factor for the children is a second spelling exercise, a hangman game with a talking hangman.

This "backward" approach to reading may be a totally different method of establishing the early learning and "understanding" of the Dolch words. How effective is this approach to reading? It appeared to be so effective with these first grade children that only one child needed remedial reading work at the beginning of second grade. This was a statistically significant reduction over previous years, which averaged around 12 remedial readers. The first grade teacher in the school was the same individual who had taught first grade in the school for 2 years prior to the study. While we are quite willing to admit that the teacher was very good, we, as well as the teacher, feel that the special experiences provided by the spelling algorithm made her even more effective. The teacher felt that the fact that a word could never be spelled incorrectly using the spelling program, coupled with the fact that the spelling words were also reading words, yielded an experience that neither she nor any other teacher could provide without the aid of a microcomputer.

ABOUT PROGRAMMING

Programming and Problem Solving

One commonly misunderstood aspect of microcomputers is the relationship between programming and problem solving. Some argue that learning how to program develops critical thinking and perhaps even problem-solving skills. In the earlier years of American education a similar argument appeared in the "mental discipline" theory of learning. For example, studying Latin was assumed to be a mental exercise that made the brain stronger. This hypothesis was refuted with such regularity that it was finally abandoned. At the present time research results regarding the relationship between programming and critical thinking are just beginning to trickle in. A majority of the early results deal with Logo, a language specifically developed to facilitate the acquisition of problem-solving skills and critical thinking. So far, the results are virtually unanimous: Children studying Logo show no greater problem-solving skills or critical-thinking skills than children who are not studying Logo. Indeed the results are especially disappointing because those children considered most proficient with Logo seemed not to understand fundamental pro-

gramming instructions (Pea, 1983). That is, neither specific nor generalizable knowledge was associated with the children's experiences.

Programming and Formal Thinking

I am convinced that programming has redeeming features. I am convinced that there is an interaction between programming, thinking, and age. Perhaps this relationship is similar to the relationship between mathematics and age. Children aged 10 or younger are taught mathematics in the same way that they think, concretely. Older children and adults, who are formal thinkers, are able to think about abstract concepts. The term *formal thinker* is borrowed from Piaget and refers to a sophisticated level of thinking involving multidimensional thinking, multiple solutions to a single problem, or hypothesis thinking. Children under 10 years of age are seldom formal thinkers, while many individuals over the age of 10 are concrete thinkers in many subject areas. Concrete thinkers generally approach problems in a fixed manner, often learning by rote rather than by understanding.

Many students of algebra and calculus who are unable to think in a formal manner impose concrete thought models on mathematical structures. They never develop a conceptual understanding of the subject matter. Unfortunately, mathematics teachers often cater to the concrete thinker by stressing a specific rather than a conceptual approach to the solution of a particular problem. For example, there is frequently more than one way to solve a calculus problem. Typically, however, a particular solution approach to a particular type of problem is taught. Yet a student who masters the given solution may generate additional solutions to the same problem. This student, the one who develops additional solution approaches, is not only a formal thinker, but a thinker who understands the problem conceptually. Such students might also be called productive thinkers. When generating these additional solutions, the problem solvers develop an information "background" that generalizes to other problems.

What I am suggesting is that age may be a critical variable when it comes to teaching programming. Furthermore, there may be many individuals who are simply incapable of acquiring much more than a rudimentary knowledge of programming. Finally, I am suggesting that when we teach programming we should focus on the student's experience of generating and studying solutions to problems that are understood.

Developing Problem-Solving Skills Through Programming

Programming in its purest form is the creation of a solution or set of solutions to a given problem. It is much more general than mathematics and requires a more generalized form of study than does mathematics. I am making a distinction between matching a known solution to a particular class of problems as opposed to understanding a problem and then generating diverse solutions. It is the latter that involves productive thinking. In order to understand a problem, the problem solver must have the freedom or control to manipulate the problem parameters. Once the parameters are manipulated, it becomes clear to the problem solver that some solutions fail, often for different reasons. Thus, the problem solver becomes a learner, learning not only *that* some solutions fail but also *why* some solutions fail. Computer programming provides the ideal environment within which such problem-solving skills may be developed and studied by children.

Several years ago I observed an 11-year-old boy as he wrote an algorithm to determine the square root of a number. He knew that there was a square root function in the microcomputer, but he preferred to see if he could compute a square root using his own algorithm. His solution was fundamentally a Newton iteration, a numerical methods procedure typically taught to university-level students. The iteration serves as the basis for computing approximate solutions to complex matrix algebra problems. Yet, this 11-year-old boy had developed the iterative solution independently of adult interaction. He developed it with the aid of a microcomputer.

More recently, I have had occasion to interact with a 14-year-old who was attempting to understand a four-by-four magic square problem. Squares are sectioned into rows and columns. Numbers are entered into the cells defined by the intersections of the rows and columns. In a magic square the numbers in the cells of the rows, columns, and diagonals of the square all sum to the same number. This youngster developed a conceptual model based upon matrices and then began writing a microcomputer algorithm to aid him in studying the effects of various cell manipulations on the magic square. This fundamental work with matrices, cells, and subscripts will give this youngster invaluable insight into matrix operations. Most likely the solution approach would have never been conceptualized without microcomputer programming experience.

A number of years ago while I was attending a professional conference, I had occasion to discuss a complex statistical topic with a stranger. Aside from his brilliant conversation regarding this particular statistical topic, he seemed to know little about statistics. Somewhat amazed at this apparent paradox, I asked him how he had amassed so much knowledge about such a complex topic, especially when there were no books yet written on it and most articles were incredibly complex. His answer stunned me. He said that he was initially unable to read the published articles, so he studied circulating microcomputer algorithms that dealt with the topic. A similar experience occurred several years ago when I had the good fortune to listen to a lecture on Logo given by Harold Abelson (see Abelson, 1982). This lecture, given to a group of scientists, was one of the most intellectually stimulating lectures I have ever attended. Using the Logo language, Abelson not only demonstrated the migratory behavior of birds, he demonstrated how birds keep from getting lost when they migrate. All of this information was communicated using Logo algorithms as illustrative examples. It is possible to use well documented algorithms to communicate information that is either too burdensome or inappropriate for communication in typical prose or equation form.

CLOSING COMMENTS

Most people are speaking of a microcomputer revolution. It is my belief that while adults are experiencing a microcomputer revolution our younger generation is experiencing an intellectual evolution. Until recently many biologists adhered to the Darwinian notion that evolution is a slow process that occurs over many generations primarily as a function of chance and survival of the fittest. An alternative theory of evolution is Lamarck's theory, which originally formed the basis for Darwin's theory and a variation of which is enjoying renewed respectability today. Lamarck viewed evolution as rapid change that occurs within a single generation as a function of adaptation.

For years psychologists have unsuccessfully attempted to accelerate the acquisition of certain cognitive skills in children. In attempting to accelerate these cognitive skills, psychologists typically have manipulated the experiential environment of the children. However, these researchers may not have truly altered the environment of the children; they may have just rearranged it! With the advent of microcomputers we may be creating a more dynamic environmental modification in the form of a highly efficient medium for communicating complex information. A dynamic environmental modification such as this will most likely yield changes in intellectual development. In particular, the microcomputer environment can simulate experiences from other environments as well as create unique experiences. These environments may facilitate the acquisition of knowledge at ages earlier than educators and psychologists thought possible. One result of such early knowledge acquisition may be that children will reach adulthood with not only more knowledge but a greater variety of knowledge, stored more efficiently than ever believed possible. Such experience-rich adults should be better productive thinkers than the adults in today's world.

In this essay I have provided illustrative examples that suggest that certain types of microcomputer software that provide a subtle structure and appear to give total freedom to the user can provide extensive experiences in relatively short periods of time. These experiences are not easily replicated outside the microcomputer environment even though they clearly will generalize beyond the microcomputer environment. Such experiences appear to hasten the acquisition of certain types of problem-solving strategies for children. The end result may be that our younger generation will evolve into adults who are capable of formulating solutions to very complex problems—problems that are beyond the conception of most present-day adults. Such generation differences will occur because of the dramatic early experiential differences in the two generations provided by the microcomputer environment. Finally, it is possible that we may have created a new and highly efficient medium for communicating complex information. This medium, which is a combination of mathematical equation and written prose, is called a *computer algorithm*.

REFERENCES

Abelson, H. (1982). *Logo for the Apple II.* Peterborough, NH: BYTE/McGraw-Hill.

Hebb, D. O. (1949). *Organization of behavior: A neuro-psychological theory.* New York: John Wiley.

Pea, R. D. (1983). *Logo programming and problem solving* (Technical Report No. 12).

New York: Bank Street College of Education, Center for Children and Technology.

Piaget, J., Inhelder, B., & Sinclair-DeZwart, H. (1973). *Memory and intelligence* (A. J. Pomerans, Trans.). New York: Basic Books.

Tolman, E. C. (1967). *Purposive behavior in animals and men.* New York: Appleton-Century Crofts.

Wertheimer, M. (Ed.). (1959). *Productive thinking* (2nd ed.). New York: Harper & Row.

CHAPTER 9

LEARNING AND LOGO

Judith A. Kull

Department of Education
University of New Hampshire
Durham, New Hampshire 03824

James, seated beside the computer, is the 6-year-old "Logo expert" in his class. He took private lessons last summer and is now teaching Jason, a novice, how to use the commands RT 90 and PENUP (PU). As the eager pupil tries to make the "turtle" go forward (FD) on the screen, James peers over his shoulder and assumes a nondirective teaching posture.

James:	[Knowing that his pupil has made a typing error] Is that FT 9?
Jason:	Oh, yea. [He uses the ESC key to erase, and then makes the correction to FD 9.]
James:	[Referring to the turtle trail on the screen] That's pretty tiny.
Jason:	Yea.
James:	Wanna do more?
Jason:	Yea. [Jason types FD 99.]
James:	[Apparently satisfied with his pupil's progress] Wanna turn?
Jason:	Yea. [Jason has not looked up from the keyboard except to check the turtle trail on the screen. He types RT 90.]
James:	Try FD 1.
Jason:	Okay. [Jason types FD 1.]
Jason:	[Both boys laugh.] It didn't go anywhere.
James:	Let's try PU. Hold your nose!
Jason:	[Giggling] PP?
James:	[Assertively] No, PU.
Jason:	[Jason types in PU.] There.
James:	Let's go far. [Jason obligingly types in FD 9999999.]
James:	Too far. [Jason types FD 99.] Yea, that's a smaller number, but we need PENDOWN (PD) to draw a line.
Jason:	This is going to be fun.

The two children depicted in the preceding scenario were learning Logo, a computer programming language developed by Seymour Papert and others, primarily at the Artificial Intelligence Laboratory at the Massachusetts Institute of Technology in the 1970s. The language is well-suited for children in style, vocabulary, and problem-solving capabilities (Papert, 1980).

As educators, however, we must ask ourselves, "What are the children learning when they work with Logo?" James and Jason did not seem to have a particular plan in mind as they practiced using commands in this new language, but they were gaining control over the microcomputer environment. They also were acquiring or reinforcing a concept of number. They were beginning to recognize the fact that there is a direct correspondence between what they typed and what appeared on the screen. They were becoming aware of the precision required in communicating with the "turtle" (drawing cursor). They were also, perhaps, developing a style of communicating with each other. The interchange was natural and playful, but on-task.

BACKGROUND

The purpose of this chapter is to acquaint the reader with young children who are learning Logo in the classroom. Examples are drawn primarily from two typical first grade classrooms. Logo is taught within the discovery learning cultural context described by Seymour Papert in *Mindstorms* (1980). Although Logo is a computer language, and can be used for solving problems on the computer in much the same way as with other, higher level computer languages, Papert (1980) has attached a much larger significance to the learning of Logo:

> The child programs the computer. And in teaching the computer how to think,

children embark on an exploration about how they themselves think. The experience can be heady: Thinking about thinking turns the child into an epistemologist, an experience not even shared by most adults. (p. 19)

The behaviors exhibited by James and Jason are typical of those observed in two first grade classrooms as children began to learn Logo. The research team consisted of the two first grade teachers, Bert Cohen and Joyce Shea, two graduate students, one of whom was a teaching intern in Joyce's classroom, and myself.[1] The classrooms are housed in two different schools. Joyce's school serves about 330 pupils and is located in a rural academic community. Bert's school serves 450 pupils and is one of several elementary schools in an urban coastal town. Both are fairly typical public schools with two possible exceptions: A number of parents have taken an interest in the educational process in both classrooms, particularly as it relates to microcomputers; and, historically, there has been good administrative support for sound educational innovation.

Most of the descriptions of children and how they learn found in this chapter are taken directly from observations made by one or more members of the research team. Vignettes are illustrative of behaviors and behavioral patterns seen over and over again in many children. For the most part, these children were at the beginning stages of their Logo experience. Observations confirm those made previously in other classrooms and during a summer Logo project for young children.[2] We have found this experience usually stimulating, sometimes frustrating, often surprising, and always rewarding for both ourselves and our pupils.

There are several general ways in which learning Logo or learning with Logo might be viewed.

1. *Learning the language itself.* This refers to the mastery of the structural and syntactical tools of the computer language and, by logical extension, the use of those tools to solve problems.

2. *Learning mathematical concepts or concepts basic to other disciplines.* It has been postulated by Papert (1980) and others that Logo provides a forum for the acquisition of certain concepts. Children may, for example, acquire an intuitive understanding of angle, radius, or circle as they work with Logo.

3. *Learning about learning.* Logo provides a forum whereby children can pose problems, take stock of the tools they have mastered, and develop strategies for solving the problems posed. In this case the *process* of the child's problem solving is emphasized over the product.

In addition to these aspects of learning, a number of factors integral to the learning process were noted by observers as they watched children and teachers. There was continuous discussion about how to solve the problem at hand. This took place at the microcomputer among children working there or between teacher and child. The tone was always positive and collegial. Other children in the vicinity of the microcomputer often joined in for a time. Completed graphics projects were displayed for others in the school to see.

It is helpful to keep in mind the three aspects of learning Logo and the interactive patterns just described while reading the descriptions of the various learning stages and strategies that follow.

GETTING STARTED

Based on earlier difficulties in introducing young children to Logo on the microcomputer and the teachers' concern that children have an introduction to Logo that was rooted in concrete experience, a series of gross motor "turtle activities" was devised. Both in the summer class and in Joyce's class, these activities and the Logo microcomputer experience were introduced simultaneously. Bert did not have a microcomputer during the first few weeks of the school year, so such activities served as pre-Logo exercises for his pupils.

These Logo activities were not simply a series of games, but a carefully planned sequence taking into account the needs of the children relative to their subsequent or concurrent mastery of Logo commands. In Logo, a triangular cursor or "turtle" on the screen is manipulated through commands typed in at the keyboard. The turtle can be commanded to turn on its own axis and to move a specified number of "turtle steps" forward or backward.[3] "Playing turtle" was helpful in gaining an understanding of the commands and how they work. A number of 5- and 6-year-olds had difficulty distinguishing right from left and became confused about how to turn the turtle right or left as they looked at it. Many adults show the same confusion when first learning Logo. Mastering these concepts, recognizing letters on the keyboard, and typing, in some cases for the first time, were all a bit overwhelming for some youngsters.

The activities were designed to assist children in orienting themselves and in taking the perspective of the turtle. One of these activities was a board game using a portable 4-by 4-foot grid and a velcro turtle that could be moved around the grid.[4] Problems were posed concerning movement of the turtle from one place on the grid to another, and the children took turns playing two roles, that of "turtle mover," and that of "commander." Commands were chosen by the commander from a pile of cards, for example,

RT 90 (degrees) LT 90, etc.
FD 1 (turtle step) FD 2, etc.
BK 1 BK 2, etc.

HOME
STOPPED!

In this manner, the children learned the relationship between commands and the turtle's orientation. We eventually transferred the board game to the wall, putting the microcomputer and monitor screen beside it. Two children were then invited to solve some simple problems at the gameboard and microcomputer simultaneously, for instance, "How can we move the turtle from the middle of the screen to the upper righthand corner?" The children who watched observed the effect of typing the commands. They also noted proportional differences in the size of turtle steps on the gameboard versus those on the screen. Other games such as turtle aerobics (set to music) helped to reinforce the difference between right and left and the relationships of turtle commands to the orientation of the turtle on the screen.[5] Invariably, the child who turned left in response to a "RIGHT 90" dance command was the same one who had difficulty deciding which command should be used to turn the turtle in the desired direction on the screen.

These games facilitated the children's development of what Papert called "body syntonicity." That is, maneuvering the turtle on the screen became "related to children's sense and knowledge about their own bodies" through physical actions involved in "playing turtle" (Papert, 1980, p. 63). In their thoughtful article concerning potential dangers of introducing children who might be at a preoperational level to the microcomputer, Barnes and Hill (1983) warned that, "When using microcomputers, children may be actively engaged but their physical participation is limited to eye-hand coordination" (p. 11). Incorporation of three-dimensional games into the microcomputer curriculum addresses this concern. It is also likely that some physical expression of body syntonic turtle moves would be demonstrated spontaneously by children even without the games. But the games offered planned facilitation and modeling, which are crucial to "getting started."

GAINING CONTROL

The next phase consisted of the children's struggle to gain control over the microcomputer. Initially this meant learning how to use the keyboard relative to symbols and signs used in Logo. There were several levels of abstraction and interaction involved. First, the children learned the symbolic representations for moving forward and back: FD, BK. Next, or simultaneously, they learned the direction symbols for pivoting on an axis: RT, LT. They learned to use numbers as inputs signaling "amounts" (in turtle steps or degrees) following each command and began to get a sense that entering different amounts would quantitatively vary the graphic result. But at the same time, they had to contend with the psychomotor coordination required to find and type in the letters. After all, these first graders were just beginning to read! Many of them used the phonetic rules that they were learning in reading to recall the commands. We encouraged this happy integration of computer skills and language arts. The children also learned quickly how to erase a typing error. They displayed an amazing degree of patience! In some ways, it was the hardest time for us. We viewed ourselves as facilitators, not directors, of the learning process and found it difficult to keep quiet while a child doggedly typed in a misspelled command.

Brian sat beside Matt, who was at the keyboard.

Brian:	How do we turn right, TR?
Matt:	No, r-r-right-t-t, RT.
Brian:	What now? [Brian typed in FDD9. An error message flashed on the screen.]
Matt:	What's wrong? You put two D's.

The children cleared the error message and all previous commands by hitting the spacebar until the text area at the bottom of the screen was completely clear. Brian and Matt made many mistakes while trying to learn the FD command, but they began to recognize the specific nature of each mistake, describing it aloud each time, clearing the text portion of the screen, and attempting to type an accurate FD command.

Enhancing Self-Esteem

The contrast in keyboarding skills was striking when a new child arrived in class a few weeks after the start of the semester and the children assisted him in gaining proficiency. As skills improved, children displayed a sense of power over the micro environment, and it became a source of self-esteem for some. One developmentally delayed child told his parents proudly, "My best subject is computers with turtles." Another little girl, who during art time had drawn the same picture featuring a house, a tree, and a rainbow 10 times in a row, drew a picture one day of the gray computer screen featuring a straight vertical line with the turtle at the top. She proudly displayed it to the class and, when asked to comment, pointed to the barely visible "FD 60" in the lower lefthand corner and explained the relationship between the command and the line.

The role of Logo in enhancing children's self-esteem should not be underestimated. The speed with which some degree of success can be achieved, the impermanence of and ease in correcting "mistakes," and the public graphical display of a completed task all add to this feeling of self-esteem.

Children gained control over the system at different rates. For instance, Scott had demonstrated some comprehension of certain commands in an isolated fashion but was unable to integrate them as useful tools.

Scott typed CS (CLEARSCREEN) explaining that this would erase the unwanted line in his drawing of a face.

Author:	Tell me what CS means.
Scott:	CLEARSCREEN.
Author:	What would happen if you used CS?
Scott:	[After thinking about this a minute] It would clear the screen.
Author:	Is that what you want to happen?
Scott:	No, I just want to erase the line I don't want.
Author:	Do you know how to erase a line?
Scott:	No.

Retracing the unwanted line using PC 0 (pen color same as background) would have erased it. He had done this before, but it did not seem relevant to him now.[6]

Learning to Use Color

A good example of the children's struggle to master the system is the acquisition of new knowledge in Logo such as how to make the turtle draw in color (PENCOLOR or PC). Color was introduced by posting a chart on the wall noting the name of each color (printed in that color) and its pen color code, for example, PC 0 = black or PC 1 = white. Earlier, as the children entered the classroom, they may have glimpsed some colored drawings on the monitor screen. The teacher mentioned the new commands and suggested that children try them if they had a chance, but he did not demonstrate their use.

A second chart with the commands HT (HIDETURTLE), ST (SHOWTURTLE), PU (PENUP), PD (PENDOWN), SPLITSCREEN, FULLSCREEN, and TEXTSCREEN was also placed on the wall and mentioned to the children. (The two observers thought this was too much at one time. We were wrong.) No actual teaching about these commands took place because the teacher did not want to model a possible learning style. The children worked individually in 20-minute time blocks. They exhibited a number of different styles in learning the new information.

Kathy moved the turtle RT 90 and FD 10. Satisfied that the turtle was controllable in the usual way, she read through the color chart. Staring at it for a full 2 minutes, she finally typed PC7, reciting the commands aloud. She got the usual THERE IS NO PROCEDURE NAMED PC7 error message and turned to me.

Kathy:	Won't it [the command] turn the turtle yellow?

We discussed the probable error; she typed PC 7.

Kathy:	That was fun, turning the turtle yellow. [In this version of Logo, the turtle cursor turns color.]

She then typed FD 90.

Kathy:	I made a yellow line.

Kathy repeated this sequence a number of times, integrating her new knowledge with what she already knew. First she turned the turtle a chosen color, using the chart as a reference, then she drew a line.

James used a similar strategy for assimilating this new knowledge, initially, and then began wrapping the lines to form a design of bright colors.[7]

James: Oh, neat. [He began to delib-
                  erately add to the pattern
                  changing the pen color and us-
                  ing FD 9999.]

Jason also quickly assimilated the use of
color, making wrapped designs in various
pen colors as James had.

*At one point the turtle disappeared and Jason
hypothesized that when he typed PC 0 (black),*

Jason: It made the turtle the same
                  color as the screen so you can't
                  see it.

His hypothesis was correct. Jason exhibited
a fairly sophisticated understanding of the
system at an early point. Other children had
more difficulty.

*Brian changed the pen color a number of
times. Finally,*

Brian: How do I make him move
                  around in a color?

*Even after this was explained, he had diffi-
culty. He did not comprehend the fact that the
turtle could have two attributes at once.*

Timmy struggled for awhile and finally,

Timmy: Oh, yeah, you get him to go
                  purple first, then get him to go
                  forward.

Timmy had reasoned through the process,
then verified this new knowledge by drawing
a simple figure in several colors. His words
also suggested that he felt in control of the
turtle but had to be precise in communication. He reinforced this observation by reciting a series of commands aloud, including
his errors and corrections. In the end, he
taught Brain how to draw in color.

Different Learning Styles

In analyzing the learning styles of these children, we noted that Kathy began by verifying
her current knowledge about turtle commands, then turned her attention to the new
information. She studied the new commands
intently until she thought she knew how they
worked, then she used one. It did not work.
Kathy mistook a typing error for a conceptual error and looked to the teacher for help.
Once she was sure that her conceptual understanding was correct, she integrated new
information with old, first changing the pen
color, then drawing a line. She repeated the
pattern again and again. James displayed the
same knowledge acquisition strategy but
went a step further. He had a "powerful
idea." Colored lines would be especially useful in making a wrapped design. Thus, he
tried a second, more creative application of
the new information, integrating it with the
old in order to accomplish a new effect.

Jason skipped over the early single-line
drawing steps, going directly to wrapping
various pen colors. Thus, he immediately
tested his initial assumption about how to
use this new information to serve a particular purpose. In doing so, he made a discovery (the turtle disappeared), hypothesized
correctly about why it happened, and subsequently used this new information in other
ways. Later, when changing the pen color to
the background color was introduced as a
means of erasing lines, Jason had already
been using it for several weeks.

For Brian, this new information about pen
color did not relate in any way to what he
already knew. Changing pen color and drawing were separate, disconnected turtle attributes. It took a great deal of modeling by a
peer (Timmy) who had had a similar problem, before Brian could use pen color effectively. Timmy's struggle to assimilate new
information took a form similar to that of
Kathy and James except that he initially just
tried out commands at random, never study-

ing the chart as intently as Kathy. He finally articulated the "rule" for integrating pen color and drawing. He then applied the rule to the drawing of a figure, finding it unnecessary to try out the rule on a simpler problem first as Kathy had.

Levels of Competence

These struggles to acquire new information exemplify struggles for mastery of Logo in general. Logo seems to unfold in overlapping levels. The children gain a competence at one level, making a discovery somewhere along the way that suggests pursuit of a higher level. But in pursuing the higher level, they reinforce tools and concepts within the mastered level to ensure accurate connections between what they already know and what they are trying to master. The process is repeated, sometimes through all levels attained thus far, each time new information is acquired. A conceptual misunderstanding at a lower level surfaces when a new piece of information cannot be comfortably assimilated. Usually, an intellectual struggle ensues until some accommodation can be made within the child's existing notion of how things work. Are these "existing notions" analogous to Piaget's "schema"? This may be a metaphor for learning in general in young children. Logo has, perhaps, provided us with a view of the dynamics of learning—at least given the conditions described.

MATHEMATICS AND LOGICAL REASONING

Once the children understood a reasonable number of commands and knew how to operate the mechanical system at an elementary level, they began to define and solve graphics problems. This was the point at which we observed discovery and use of mathematical concepts and operations. These were not chance discoveries but products of what might be called in Piagetian terms, "logical-mathematical reasoning" (Papert, 1980; Wadsworth, 1978). Some of the observations in this area are very powerful, particularly from the standpoint of a first grade teacher. A great debate arose concerning ways of facilitating such discoveries and reasoning skills without destroying the discovery-oriented cultural context in which Logo was being taught. The debate is yet to be resolved, and I am not sure that it can be or even should be resolved.

Emily gave us an unexpected insight into how some of the children were conceptualizing numbers in Logo. She began by typing a pen color:

Emily: (Types in commands) PC 2

                  FD 99
                  BK 88

                  I put 8 and then 8 again.

                  RT 66
                  FD 67
                  PC [Nothing happened.]

                  Oh, I forgot to put *how many*.

                  PC 99 [There is no PC 99. The numbers following PC go from 0 through 11.]

To Emily, numbers in Logo answered the question, "How many?" (turtle steps). She did not have a concept of number as symbol or "sign." The number was an accumulation of turtle steps that she visualized in fairly concrete terms. Numbers, in this sense, did not mean anything when coupled with the command PC. Another question we had was whether or not Emily thought that FD 88 meant the same as FD 8 plus FD 8. Upon careful questioning, we finally discerned that

Emily knew that 88 meant 88 steps. She, as many others, typed in double numbers—88, 66, 99—when first working in Logo. Most of the children said that they did so because they "wanted a big number and it was easiest to hit the same key twice." Later as the children became more precise in planning turtle moves and better at typing, this practice disappeared. Emily eventually accepted the notion of numbers as signs in the case of pen color, but we think that her concept of number when used with FD and BK is a different one. In the case of a number that represents an accumulation of turtle steps, the "sign" was a more concrete meaning.

Logical-mathematical reasoning was apparent, but the building of mathematical operations was not always accurate.

Linda was making a square, the "frame" for her house. She had progressed this far (see Figure 1).

Linda: [Typed FD 50. She saw that the line was too long.] I forgot it was 40.

              PC 0 [Pen color changed to background color.]
              BK 9

              [When asked why she chose to go back 9] Because I pushed 50 and I knew it should be 40, so it needed 9 less.

FIGURE 1.

Using a Favorite Number

The product of Ryan's mathematical reasoning was more accurate. He received important assistance from his partner. Many of the children used a favorite number time and time again. When watching Ryan, we were able to consider why this may be the case. From an adult perspective the task of drawing a rectangle seemed simple enough, a four-sided figure with the lengths of equal measurement and widths of equal measurement, and four 90-degree angles. Ryan, a first grader, did not know this.

He began his rectangle by constructing it. His turtle began at home.

Ryan: [Enters commands.]
             FD 33
             FD 22
             FD 1
             FD 11

After Ryan's RT 90 turn, he moved FD 33 again. In fact, Ryan consistently moved FD 33 after every right angle command.

For Ryan, 33 is a number that he knows in Logo and is comfortable with. Rather than beginning the corresponding sides of his rectangle by using equal numbers as an adult would, he experimented with numbers after the initial FD 33. The distance of 33 was a point of reference, his standard of measure.

When Ryan's rectangle was complete, he decided that he would add a mouth, nose, and eyes to make a face. Again, when working on the inside of his rectangle he consistently moved FD 12 before moving in smaller steps.
While constructing the second side of the rectangle, Ryan had been talking aloud as he went along.

Ryan: It went 33. [Then he typed FD 55.]
             What's 33 plus 55?

Author: [Jotting down the two numbers in her notebook]
First we add the ones . . .

Ryan: Eight.

Author: And then the tens. . . .

Ryan: [Pleased with his achievement] Eighty-eight. That's the furthest I've ever gone in Logo. Before I only went up to 81. [A "Piagetian purist" would probably not have formally operationalized addition of the numbers!]

Ryan, apparently, had already added 33 and 22 to get 55—his method for ensuring that the second side was longer than the first. This conversation indicated that Ryan remembered other numbers that he had used previous to this drawing. This confirmed my suspicion that number choices were not random guesses. Ryan was experiencing a number through a unit of measure, a turtle step. The turtle step is quite small, so Ryan had devised larger units of measure, 33 for the outside of the rectangle and 12 for the inside.

John was experiencing these numbers by observing Ryan's strategy. After Ryan's second FD 33–FD 22 sequence,

John: I knew it! . . . I just knew he would go 22!

The number strategies that Ryan used to create his rectangle were reinforcing his understanding of what a 33 is, as well as giving subsequent numbers a point of reference. He was assimilating this understanding of 33 through repetition.

Estimating Distances

Does this repetition and experimentation with numbers help a child to become better at estimating distance?

Ryan had just about finished closing his rectangle with the exception of a very small space that was left (see Figure 2).

This seemed like a perfect time for me to introduce how to hide the turtle in order to better see exactly how much space was left. Both boys scrutinized the screen.

Ryan: About 9?

John: Yup.

And 9 it was. I was so amazed at this estimation that I looked back into my notes of the boys' previous Logo activity together. Nine was a number that they had tried on their first drawing.

Upon completing the rectangle, Ryan decided to put the pen up and move diagonally into the area of the figure from the lower left corner so that he could start the mouth. He knew that RT 180 would reverse the turtle's direction, in this case from left to right, so he typed that in with this result (see Figure 3).

Ryan: [Turning to the teacher] What's half of 90?

Teacher: [Not knowing what he had in mind] 45.

Ryan: [Typed RT 45.] Oh, I went the wrong way.

FIGURE 2.

FIGURE 3.

FIGURE 5.

John had said nothing, eyes glued to the screen. He continued staring and finally,

John: Try LEFT 90.

This command produced the desired effect. The turtle was now facing what would become the left corner of the mouth (see Figures 4 and 5).[8]

Constructing Mathematical Structures with Logo

There were a number of behaviors here to suggest that the boys in this scenario were constructing mathematical structures, at least within this microworld.

- They developed and used a standard unit of measure.

- They estimated distance using that standard unit.
- They combined units to construct a symmetrical figure.
- They constructed an inverse operation using a part-part-whole concept in order to start a mouth.

This is most likely an example of what Piaget meant when he talked about the "spontaneous mathematical intelligence of the young child" (Piaget, 1973, p. 97). The children constructed structures and operations in order to solve problems that were important to them. This was the crux of Piaget's concern that problems be posed in a manner that has meaning to the child.

We thought Laurel might have developed an accurate concept of "radius" while mak-

FIGURE 4.

ing DESIGN6, but the following excerpt indicates that she did not quite have the right idea.[9]

Laurel had recently learned to draw circles. With her partner, Melissa, reading the letters aloud from the wall chart, Laurel typed RCIRCLE 54. The turtle drew a circle to the right with a radius of 54 turtle steps. "Radius" had never been discussed in class, but Laurel seemed to have some notion of the connection between 54 and the circle size. She gave a knowing nod when a 90-degree right turn plus FD 54 produced a horizontal line ending at the center of the circle (Figure 6). She then went on to construct a rectangle with a width of 28 (Figure 7).

At this point, Laurel typed FD 54 and was very surprised when the final 54 steps did not end within the circle (Figure 8). She doggedly moved BK small numbers of steps in order to put the turtle back within the circle. This seemed like a good time to introduce her to HIDETURTLE. It was difficult to see exactly where the line ended with the turtle in the way. She tried this and agreed that estimation was easier with the turtle hidden. She decided to save this as a picture which would replace her previous "design." She left the

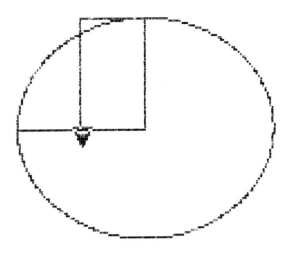

FIGURE 7.

computer still puzzled about why "54" moved the turtle outside the circle.

Was this an instance of disequilibrium? Would she try more circles and work at discovering "radius"? Teacher facilitation of this concept, at an appropriate level, is probably a good idea. But when? Laurel did con-

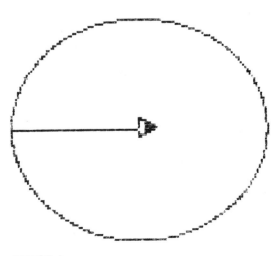

FIGURE 6.

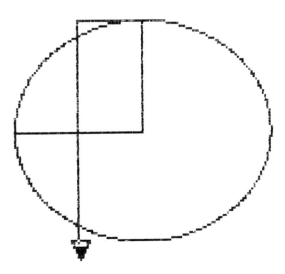

FIGURE 8.

tinue to draw and wonder about circles but has not yet grasped the concept of "radius."

PLANNING

Planning is a problem-solving step that has recently gained much attention in the Logo literature. Watt (1979) addressed planning as he compared the problem-solving styles of two sixth grade children:

> Donald was a "planner." He made an overall plan for his project, and created separate plans for each subpart of his project. Deborah had an overall idea of what she was trying to accomplish, but her actual project was carried out in an exploratory manner, one step at a time. (p. 90)

We saw similar behavior in the first graders. Some children were very deliberate, carrying out a preconceived plan and requesting additional tools as they went. Others developed a plan as they worked, allowing discoveries to move them in a new direction if the results of such discoveries were interesting enough.

Reasons for Abandoning Plans

Rampy and Swensson (1983) talked about planners who stick to a plan in order to produce a product and those who give up or stray from their original plan, seemingly more interested in process. Our observations suggest that there may be several reasons for "giving up" on a plan:

1. The child may not feel "ownership" of the problem to be solved and so does not perceive it as important enough for continuation if difficulties are encountered. Or the child may redefine the problem in his or her own terms and solve it. This is particularly true if someone other than the child poses the initial problem. A casual observer might record this as giving up on a problem even though the child may never have perceived the original "problem" in the same way as the person who devised it. For example, early in his Logo training, someone suggested to Tommy that he draw an E. After drawing the vertical line, all he could manage was to make a right angle at the bottom of the E. It was very hard for him, but he persevered right through recess. Tommy never perceived the problem to be "drawing an E." To him, it was lining up the turtle to draw two lines juxtaposed in a certain way. He verbalized his whole plan, citing the necessary corrections as he made them along the way.

2. The children do not have the tools to finish solving the problem in accordance with the solution they have envisioned, or the tools at their disposal are not acceptable. We saw this a great deal and, happily, were sometimes available at the "teachable moment" to assist the child in acquiring the necessary tools. Jonathon, for example, had given up on drawing a series of orange bullets coming out of his gun. (He owned this problem. We did not suggest it!) It was just too much trouble to repeat PC 4 FD 5 PC 0 FD 5 enough times to make the gun fire (- - - -). He gave up and worked on the stock. The next day we taught him the repeat command, and the gun shot bullets in a matter of seconds. He was ready for this tool. He had recognized the necessary pattern, knew he had to repeat it a number of times, but did not know *how*.

3. Something along the way suggests a more interesting problem, and the plan

is changed along with the problem. This may be particularly likely when two or more children are working together. The benefit may be a sharing of strategies. Andrew, for example, wrote a procedure for drawing an angle. He then ran his procedure five times and produced a star. He had not anticipated this result, but upon looking at it closely decided to reproduce the star 25 more times, overlaying the original each time to make a multipointed star. He then decided that the graphic result resembled a flower and posed the problem of drawing a stem without altering the "petals." This proved to be a difficult task, but he accomplished it with the help of his peer assistant, who agreed with Andrew's interpretations along the way.

Preplanning Activities

In light of these considerations and the ensuing examples, our findings relative to planning were different from those reported by Pea (1983) in a study of 8- to 12-year-old children who were learning to program in Logo. These investigators observed "very little pre-planning activity" (p. 30). We saw quite a bit, but it developed very slowly. At first, the children planned only two or three moves ahead, tracing some lines on the screen with their fingers and reciting the commands they would use when typing in the procedure. Others used PENUP or PC 0 to try out several moves ahead without making a line. To us, this was strong evidence of preplanning even before procedures were introduced. We *did*, however, note that some children had difficulty understanding the conceptual difference between "drawing mode" and "procedure mode." Certainly a misunderstanding here could frustrate even the most determined procedure planner.

Melissa's story suggests this. The story also illustrates her problem-solving strategy.

Like many of the children, Melissa sometimes exhibited a profound understanding of the power of Logo and then forgot "where she was" and seemed confused about devising the next step. We think, in particular, that there is a distinct difference between the children's understanding of how to use Logo tools to solve problems and their understanding of how the mechanics of the system work.

Melissa had become quite sophisticated in her problem-solving techniques. She had been drawing letters for several weeks, her goal being to spell "LISSA," her nickname. She was now working on the "S." During her last exposure to Logo, Melissa had drawn and saved the bottom curve of the "S" (Figure 9).

The final position of the turtle was actually the original starting position, HOME. Melissa, who had already drawn the L and I of her name, had originally planned to make an S using right angles ("straights," she called them), but she learned about circles and arcs when making the "I" and agreed to employ arcs to make the curved "S." She planned out her strategy for the drawing shown in Figure 9 on the bus one day on her way to school. At the time of this particular observation, we no longer had her written plan (Melissa now "plans" in a notebook), but Melissa remembered the lengths of the first three arcs, which together formed the bottom curve of the "S," and she retraced them with the pen up to be

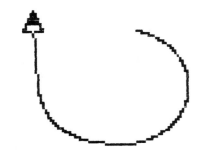

FIGURE 9.

sure. The next part of the plan was to correctly position the turtle and repeat the series of different-length arcs, but in the reverse order, to make the top curve of the "S" symmetrical to the bottom.

Having completed the bottom curve, Melissa typed a command that put the turtle in the wrong position for drawing the next arc. Upon seeing the error in her drawing, Melissa patiently brought the turtle back to the starting point at the bottom curve and began again. Whenever Melissa made a mistake, she went back to the beginning and retraced the desired pathway on the screen with her finger, then recited aloud why her previous strategy had failed. After four well-thought-out attempts, she achieved the symmetrical "S" (Figure 10).

We had witnessed preplanned use of symmetry and a careful process of revision and refinement. The teacher suggested that Melissa write in a notebook the steps used to make her "S." Then she could type them into a procedure and save it. Her response illustrates confusion about the mechanics of the system. Melissa asked, "Do I have to write down the bottom part, too?" meaning the commands for the bottom curve that had been typed during the previous session. She had difficulty comprehending the difference between drawing mode and procedure mode as they related to the "S" on the screen. Practice in "drawing" and "writing and saving procedures" resulted in a successful grasp for most children.

FIGURE 10.

Like Melissa, many of the children envisioned the graphical solution to problems before beginning to solve them. They actually "drew out" the desired picture on the screen with their fingers before typing in the turtle commands to execute the drawing. When prompted, many declared their general overall strategy aloud: "I have to make him go up to here, turn this way, then go over to here and down." The solution was then refined as the problem-solver actually began the command moves.

Often if the exact or most efficient tools were missing, the children employed the tools that they had already mastered (and were comfortable with) even though they were aware that a more efficient solution might be possible. For example, Mary Ann wanted to make a right-angle turn. She turned the turtle to the right by 10-degree increments until it "looked right." She knew there was a specific number she could use, but she had forgotten it. Her RT 10 typed in nine times worked, and she was pleased. She had used RT 10 previously and was comfortable with that tool. There seems to be a pedagogical payoff in this. The children had become quite adept at estimating distances in turtle geometry. As discussed earlier, some had devised standard units of measure similar to Mary Ann's RT 10 which they employed quite consistently in constructing their drawings. Amy, for example, had used a series of "FD 9s" to reach a certain point and needed just a little more to close the gap. Checking the size of the gap with her finger to determine "how much of a 9" was needed, she typed in FD 7 with the other hand to complete the drawing. She was gaining a sense of proportion.

The children were very young, and this was their first set of experiences with Logo. There is no point in discussing how efficient or sophisticated their programming skills were relative to problem-solving. We agree with Watt (1979) that the alert teacher should try to recognize different problem-solving styles and use this information to assist the child in his or her learning. But, as we have mentioned before in this chapter, such skilled observation and its translation into practice are not always easy.

BUGS AND DEBUGGING

Papert interpreted children's need to clear away errors and later resistance to debugging as an internalization of the concept of error as "bad." He and others have argued that children are taught in school that "missteps" are wrong, bad, to be devalued or not dwelled upon (Papert, 1980, p. 114). We have seen this type of error-erasing behavior, but our interpretation differs. To us, this need to wipe out missteps seems a happy opportunity to get rid of what is "gumming up the works." The children can physically eliminate the troublesome missteps and start over. The painstaking care with which some of them then go through the beginning steps again seems to be their way of gaining a firmer hold on the solution to the problem. Perseveration is common in young children as a method of acquiring new information. How often does the small child point to the stove and declare "hot" in the struggle to gain control over the concept and make it his or her own? I think that, for some children at least, debugging at a particular point without starting the problem over again would be an isolated, out-of-control exercise.

For example, while running her "S" procedure, Melissa noticed a bug. The bottom half of the "S" was white, and the top half was orange. Diagnosing the problem in the text of the procedure and correcting it seemed to be two separate tasks to Melissa. She noted that PC 4 (orange) appeared just prior to the instructions for the upper half of the "S." She thought for a moment and said, "That's okay, I like it in two colors." When asked how she might make the corrections, she thought for about 30 seconds,

traced through the whole procedure again with her finger, and finally said with assurance, "The pen color has to go at the beginning." It was time for the next class activity, so Melissa decided to leave the picture as it was and declared that next time she would check the L and the I to see what color they were and then amend the current procedure accordingly. She was originally reluctant to edit the "S" procedure because she was unsure of the process. Assurance that such editing did not require retyping and redrawing the whole procedure prompted her willingness to edit the next time. For Melissa, conceptual debugging required retracing the problem, physical elimination of the bug did not!

Many children used Melissa's strategy of working through a problem from the beginning after a bug had been encountered. Papert, Watt, diSessa, and Weir (1979) described this behavior in some of the children in the Brookline Logo Project. Perhaps it was necessary in order to put the "bug" back in context. Many of the children did eventually develop superprocedures containing subprocedures, but they consistently reaffirmed all the connections when a bug was encountered. Given the way we saw children work, I suspect that most of them would have failed a first grade version of the "debugging test" as reported by Pea (1983). He reported that although "many children were able to locate and eliminate surface errors of syntax or missing variable values (in written programs shown to them), very few found procedural errors in which the order of lines in a program was mixed" (p. 28).

I think that the children in our classes who had experienced only a problem-solving approach to learning Logo would not even have recognized a sequence of written code as being the same thing that they were doing in Logo. They, of course, saw programs being written and wrote them themselves, but even if a child in passing wished to help another, the first question, before even looking at the code, was, "What are you trying to do?" The next could be translated as, "What have you done so far?" Perhaps we must look more closely at how a child goes about debugging and how this is related to his or her problem-solving style. This may even be similar to the difference between decoding and encoding as children learn to read and write.

GAINING POWER

The notion that modular programming was possible came once the children realized that they could save their drawings and add to them at will. Some developed an early notion of modular programming. Scott, for example, wrote a procedure for a basic house (HOUSE1); HOUSE2 was developed by adding a chimney to HOUSE1; HOUSE3 featured an attached garage but no chimney; and so forth. This may have been the teachable moment for introducing the concept of a superprocedure called NEIGHBORHOOD!

Jason discovered modularity one day by accident. He wanted to add several colors to the screen at once, so he wrote the following procedure:

```
TO COLOR
PC 0
PC 1
PC 2
PC 3
PC 4
PC 5
PC 6
PC 7
PC 8
PC 9
PC 10
PC 11
END
```

To his surprise the colors flashed on the screen one at a time. He changed the name to POW, and we assisted him in writing a superprocedure containing POW

```
TO BOOM
POW
POW
POW
POW
END
```

Jason taught Sherrie the POW procedure, and she used it in another procedure that she called JASON in honor of its creator! Another child saw the JASON procedure and asked Sherrie to teach it to her—an instance of peer tutoring. In addition to the power gained via modular programming, the incident suggests that there may be some power in naming procedures. Watt (1982) alluded to this:

> While classmates often gave pictures and procedures single letter names to avoid laborious typing, Jamie (age 8) was content to take the time to type "Door Through Time," "Sparkle in the Night," "Experience in the Fifth Dimension," delighting classmates with his naming as much as with his pictures. (p. 119)

Syntonicity and Play

Consider now syntonicity and its relation to play. Papert distinguished between learning that is body syntonic and learning that is ego syntonic in the child who has traced out a circle by *walking* through it as the turtle might.

> . . . the Turtle circle is body syntonic in that the circle is firmly related to children's sense and knowledge about their own bodies. Or it is ego syntonic in that it is coherent with children's sense of themselves as people with intentions, goals, desires, likes, and dis-

likes. A child who draws a Turtle circle wants to draw a circle; doing it produces pride and excitement. (Papert, 1980, p. 63)

Again, "ownership" of the problem becomes important, and feeling good is important. In the sequence of events reported in the following example, body syntonicity, ego syntonicity, peer tutoring, and a sense of play are apparent as several children work together to solve a problem.

Gregory and Mike sat down at the computer. Mike announced that he would "go first," and FACE4 was read from his diskette so that he could continue working on it. FACE4 appeared on the screen. It consisted of a square for the head and a line going across the bottom for the mouth, in need of a nose and eyes (see Figure 11). The boys had been working in Logo for only a few weeks.

As Mike and Gregory were discussing a good number with which to begin, Ryan slid into a chair behind the boys, put one foot up on the back of each chair in front of him, and leaned back to comfortably observe what was about to take place. Mike began with small numbers, retracing the right side of his square to find a satisfactory place to turn in for the nose.

FIGURE 11.

Mike:	[Pointing to the screen] His nose is gonna be right there . . . PENUP!
Gregory:	Which way do you turn?
Ryan:	[Hopping up from his observing position and facing Mike] Face the way the turtle is facing.

Mike complied.

| Ryan: | [Taking Mike's hand] You want to turn this way. What hand is it? |
| Mike: | Left! [He typed in LT 90.] |

I was pleased to see Ryan help Mike with the strategy that he had seen his teachers model. But I was more surprised when I witnessed the collaboration to follow.

Mike moved the turtle forward, with the pen up.

| Mike: | PENDOWN
FD 3
HIDETURTLE . . . H . . . T |

Mike typed in another forward command.

| Mike: | Oh! The line moved! [Jumping up from his chair in complete surprise] |
| Gregory: | Yeah, that's because you hid turtle. |

Mike called over to Ryan, who, by then had moved a few feet away.

| Mike: | Hey, Ryan, want to see some magic? |

Mike was obviously impressed with his discovery that the turtle would move when hidden.

Ryan: Mike, your nose is gonna be like this? [Ryan pulled his nose to one side with his fingers to demonstrate the kind of crooked nose he saw on the screen.]

Peals of laughter emerged as Mike and Gregory imitated Ryan. Mike, not fully recovered from this humor, hit the return key to get started again.

Gregory: B . . . K . . . NEEDS MORE INPUTS.

Ryan: That means you forgot the space and the number. [He explained on his way over to the drinking fountain.]

Mike: [Typing as he spoke] Turn left . . . L . . . T . . .

As Mike was directing the turtle I noticed that Ryan had returned and was standing in the middle of the rug, turning left.

Ryan: O.K. I went LEFT 90. Mike, what do I do now?

Mike: FORWARD 10.

Ryan took five steps forward, "wrapped" to the other side of the rug, and counted five more steps forwards.

Mike: H . . . T . . . RETURN . . . HIDETURTLE.

Ryan ran off, and ducked behind some desks.

Gregory: Hey, Mike, Ryan hid.

Mike: S . . . T . . . SHOWTURTLE. Hey Ryan! [enjoying the new twist to his commands.] You have to show, show turtle!

Ryan ran back to the middle of the rug, jumped up, and called out:

Ryan: I'm home!

Mike was just about finished with his last eye.

Mike: I just want to hide this to see how it looks. [Obviously satisfied with his drawing] It looks good.

Gregory: It looks good to me.

Ryan: It looks good to me.[10]

Mike's fifth face was complete (see Figure 12). He, Ryan, and Gregory had spent 20 minutes "playing" at the computer. It has taken educators many years to understand that children in the primary grades need an experiential approach to learning in the classroom. Many life skills and academic skills are developed through play. It is a natural medium of self-expression for a young child. Logo fit in with the developmental learning needs of Mike, Ryan, and Gregory, who had initiated and orchestrated the body syntonic and ego syntonic Logo "play."

Social Interaction Effect

Another powerful aspect of Logo and learning is the social interaction that arises among children as they work together on a task.

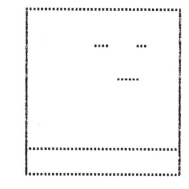

FIGURE 12.

Most of us who have worked with children at the microcomputer dismiss an early concern on the part of educators that the technology would be intrusive, stifling social interaction. On the contrary, there was constant dialogue among the children we studied. These were not just trivial interchanges. The children were focused on solving problems in a collegial fashion. The teacher's role was one of colleague/facilitator. Many of the children exhibited excellent questioning and helping strategies similar to those of Mike, Ryan, and Gregory in the episode just recounted or Jason and James in the opening scenario.

TRANSFER AND INTEGRATION

Although we were concerned about the Logo learning process during our observations, we were not concerned about the transfer of Logo skills to other areas, mainly because we *did* see the learning as a process, not as the producer of a specific product. Logo is really a series of tools in a special environment for problem solving. Taking one piece of the process out of context to see if it "transferred" to another area did not seem a worthwhile pursuit. But the nagging question remained. If Ryan had developed an understanding of inverse operations in Logo, would he apply it in areas other than Logo? Our experiences suggest that transfer of skills learned in one area to another area does not necessarily occur spontaneously.

In their discussion of this topic, Cole and Means (1981) noted that despite the practical importance of being able to generalize such tasks as counting, addition, finding geometric areas, and reading comprehension, "transfer of different problem sets to other settings might still prove elusive" (p. 159). They went on to say that even when training for transfer takes place, it does not always work. Our observations have corroborated the first point, and we have not tested the

second. As teachers, we are more comfortable watching children as they work with Logo and documenting their mastery level and skill development relative to system control, attainment of mathematical concepts, reasoning skills, and problem-solving strategies. Until we have a clearer picture of what children are learning with Logo, it is premature to deal with the transfer issue.

We did, however, see spontaneous integration of Logo into other parts of the curriculum and vice versa by children. A number of the learning experiences already described reflected this integration. For example, depiction of the Logo turtle in one child's artwork seemed to be a creative breakthough. During Jonathan's work with the bullet-making sequence, he observed a pattern:

```
PC 4  FD 5  PC 0  FD 5  PC 4  FD 5
PC 0  FD 5
```

He had learned to recognize patterns while using manipulative materials during "math time," and now he recognized an entirely different kind of pattern in Logo. Patterns were also noted during a lesson in origami taught by a visitor from Japan. Several types of folds were made more than once. "Just like REPEAT," observed James.

The writing process as described by Graves (1983) has been an important focus of the two first grade classrooms. Children have had much practice in communicating their thoughts via pictures and words. Choosing a topic is not always easy, but one day, after working feverishly during "writing time," Stephen discussed the rough draft of his story, called "The Cnputr."

The children later developed some "publishing" criteria for producing hard copies of procedures or drawings much in the same manner as they had for their stories.

- It should look good.
- It should be a real picture. (Not "just" wrapping)

- It should be finished.
- It should have a name.

They became quite critical of their own procedures and rarely chose to publish new versions of previously published procedures that showed only minor alterations. (Figures 13 through 16 are illustrative of the children's art work.) There continue to be many instances of integration between Logo and other curriculum areas as the children hone their skills. The teachers have deliberately encouraged this.

A NOTE TO TEACHERS

Throughout this chapter, I have been describing the discovery-oriented learning context in which Logo has been taught. Yet there is much controversy concerning the effectiveness of the indirect manner of instruction inherent in the "Logo culture." In his discussion of academic work, Walter Doyle (1983) defined "indirect instruction:"

Such instruction emphasizes the central role of self-discovery in fostering a sense of meaning and purpose for learning academic content. From this perspective, students must be given ample opportunities for direct experience with content in order to derive generalizations and invent algorithms on their own. (p. 176)

He went on to describe some of the problems inherent in this approach:

The propensity to invent can have both advantages and disadvantages . . . invention enables students to learn routines and concepts that are difficult to teach directly. At the same time, invention can lead to "buggy" algorithms and misconceptions of content. This

possibility underscores the central role of corrective feedback in learning and the need to base that feedback on an understanding of the processes that lead students to make mistakes. (p. 178)

Suggested here is the role of the teacher as a keen observer who can use what he or she has observed as children work in classrooms to effectively improve instruction. I think that the manner in which we worked with children as they learned Logo blurred the line between direct and indirect teaching. Children did explore the microworld environment, but we assisted them in avoiding or correcting "buggy" algorithms and pushing on to another level of Logo learning. Avoidance was not always a good idea. Children learned from their conceptual errors with and without us.

We do not yet have a clear picture of the outcomes, however, so teacher facilitation of learning thus far has been spontaneous, unrehearsed. We never knew exactly what would happen next, so we observed more carefully, recorded what we thought were signs of cognitive growth in children, and did our best to help. At least we now have a picture of what happened in the classroom described here as children began to learn (with) Logo. There are some stages emerging, but they are not necessarily sequential, partially because Logo seems to have so many conceptual levels. Just when one seems to have gained some control over the system and is happily moving along in the development of some logical-mathematical reasoning skills, a knowledge gap regarding the system emerges that precludes further reasoning. Help! If the reacher recognizes this point, he or she *can* help.

Hopefully, communication of our observations will assist other teachers. But only the beginning stages are addressed here and by people who had little in the way of roadmaps for guidance. The reader is referred to other Logo and learning discussions, although mostly of older children (e.g., Papert

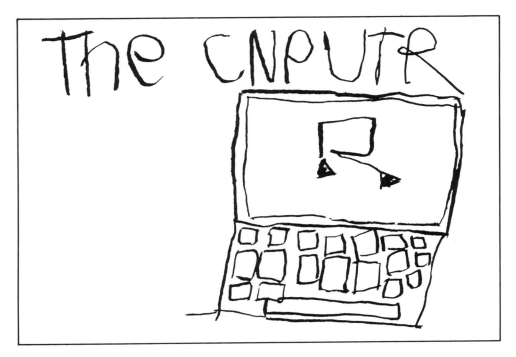

FIGURE 13.

FIGURE 14.

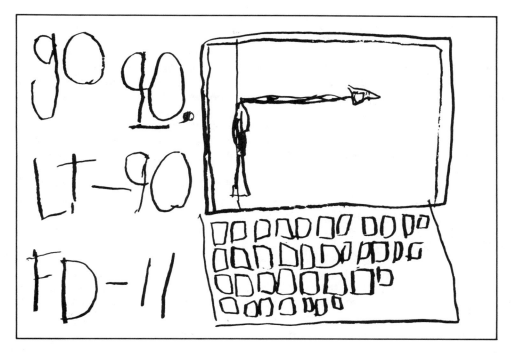

FIGURE 15.

FIGURE 16.

et al., 1979; Rampy & Swensson, 1983; So-loman, 1982; Watt, 1979; Watt, 1982; Weir, 1982). Our next step is to continue along in the mode, but to focus on translating what we have observed and continue to observe into effective instruction.

We have learned a few things about Logo, learning, the children, and ourselves.

Logo

The language does seem to provide an environment in which children and adults can construct and practice powerful ideas. It is a very complex language, but it can be mastered at a number of different intellectually satisfying levels. Although welcomed by the children, Logo did not become all-encompassing.

Learning

The children were able to comfortably pose and solve graphics problems in Logo. They developed and assisted each other in creating various strategies. Sometimes several strategies were developed to solve the same problem, prompting articulation of criteria for choosing one plan over another. Perhaps discussions about "what to do next" or "why this is a better plan than that" fall under the heading of epistemology.

A number of mathematical concepts were constructed and used many times such as standard unit of measure, estimation, inverse operation, angle, proportion. In addition, Logo seemed to facilitate children's understanding of their own orientation in space and spatial relationship to other objects. We also found that there is some integration between Logo and other areas of the curriculum.

Children

The children continuously surprised us. The "aha's" from both learners and teachers were abundant, yet flashes of brilliance did not always lead to new plateaus.

The children worked well with one another. They served as peer tutors, often emulating our nondirective teaching style. One outside observer suggested that older children might serve as tutors for the younger ones, bypassing the teacher completely! Certainly such an arrangement would be helpful when starting Logo in a busy classroom.

TEACHERS/RESEARCHERS

The role of teacher as researcher is an important one. The commitment stimulated us to do a number of things that will make us better teachers:

- We divulged our underlying assumptions about teaching, learning, and children.
- We developed a positive attitude toward classroom management, stubbornly refusing to perceive the computer as an "intruder."
- We were very deliberate and analytical in our observations of children's behavior.
- We constantly debated the relationship between teaching and learning.
- We supported each other in what was for us, initially, a risky venture, despite our enthusiasm.
- The project had a positive effect on our approaches to teaching in general.

Despite the overwhelmingly positive response to Logo in the classroom by all concerned, we still do not see Logo as a panacea. It is a powerful vehicle for learning, but it is not unique in exhibiting that capacity. The teacher who introduces Logo into the classroom requires support from peers, just as he or she would for any initially unfamiliar innovation. The enthusiasm is usually contagious. Logo becomes a luncheon topic. Teachers sneak in to catch a glimpse of children at the microcomputer. But if Logo is to become a cultural context for learning, it must merge with the existing classroom culture, comfortably in tune with other parts of the curriculum and not relegated to or exalted as "Logo time."

END NOTES

1. The research was supported by a grant from the Central University Research Fund of the University of New Hampshire. See Kull, Cohen, Shea, Ferraro, and Bonnano (1984). The model is based on the collaborative model described by Oja (1983) and a descriptive research model employed by Graves, Hansen, Stebbins, and Hubbard (1983).

2. A course in Logo for teachers was taught by Judith Kull, Kathleen Kelsey, and Wallace Reed at Plymouth State College, New Hampshire. During the second half of the course, participants taught Logo to gifted and talented children enrolled in Ventures in Learning, which was coordinated by Gail Glidden Flickenger.

3. Simple commands include: RT (RIGHT), LT (LEFT), FD (FORWARD), BK (BACK).

4. Devised by Jean Cornell, a second grade teacher in Colorado and a participant in Project Venture.

5. Devised by Kathleen Kelsey.

6. Submitted by Lorraine Ferraro.

7. "Wrapping" occurs when commands send the turtle trail off the screen and it reappears on the opposite side of the screen. For example, if the turtle were positioned in the center of the screen facing north and commanded to go FD 300, it would draw a trail which led off the screen at the top and "wrapped" around, coming up again from the bottom of the screen. Initially, most of the children spent a great deal of time making wrapped designs. "Wrapping," when the turtle is faced in a nonvertical or nonhorizontal direction, produces an interesting effect.

8. Submitted by Joyce Shea.

9. DESIGN6 is so named because it is the sixth version of an original design created by Laurel. Children often saved each newly refined version of an original drawing using a single name followed by a number (in sequence).

10. Submitted by Joyce Shea.

REFERENCES

Barnes, B. J., & Hill, S. (1983). Should young children work with microcomputers: Logo before Lego? *The Computer Teacher, 10*(9), 11–14.

Cole, M., & Means, B. (1981). *Comparative studies of how people think.* Cambridge, MA: Harvard University Press.

Doyle, W. (1983). Academic work. *Review of Educational Research, 53,* 159–199.

Graves, D. H. (1983). *Writing: Teachers and children at work.* Exeter, NH: Heinemann Education Books.

Graves, D., Hansen, J., Stebbins, A., & Hubbard, R. (1983). *The writing process research project.* Durham: University of New Hampshire, Department of Education.

Kull, J. A., Cohen, B., Shea, J., Ferraro, L., & Bonanno, A. (1984). Unpublished memos, University of New Hampshire, Department of Education, Durham, New Hampshire.

Oja, S. N. (1983). *A two-year study of teachers' stages of development in relation to collaborative action research in schools.* Final Report. Durham: University of New Hampshire.

Papert, S. (1980). *Mindstorms: Computers, children and powerful ideas.* New York: Basic Books.

Papert, S., Watt, D., diSessa, A., & Weir, S. (1979). *Final report of the Brookline Logo Project. Part II: Project summary and data analysis* (LOGO Memo No. 53). Cambridge, MA: Massachusetts Institute of Technology, Artificial Intelligence Laboratory. (ERIC Document Reproduction Service No. ED 196 423)

Pea, R. D. (1983). *Logo programming and problem solving* (Technical Report No. 12). New York: Bank Street College of Education, Center for Children and Technology.

Piaget, J. (1973). *To understand is to invent.* New York: The Viking Press.

Rampy, L., & Swensson, R. G. (1983, June). *The programming styles of fifth graders us-ing Logo.* Paper presented at the Fifth National Educational Computing Conference, Baltimore, MD.

Solomon, C. (1982). Introducing Logo to children. *BYTE, 7*(8), 196-208.

Wadsworth, B. J. (1978). *Piaget for the classroom teacher.* New York: Longman.

Watt, D. H. (1979). A comparison of the problem solving styles of two students learning LOGO: A computer language for children. *Creative Computing, 5*(12), 86–90.

Watt, M. (1982). What is Logo? *Creative Computing, 8*(10), 112–129.

Weir, S. (1982). Logo: A learning environment for the severely handicapped. *Journal of Special Education Technology, 5,* 20–22.

PART IV

APPLICATIONS FOR YOUNG AND HANDICAPPED CHILDREN

CHAPTER 10

CREATIVE THINKING WITH THE MICROCOMPUTER

Marilyn J. Church
Department of Curriculum and Instruction
Center for Young Children
University of Maryland
College Park, Maryland 20742

June L. Wright
Director, Computer Discovery Project
Center for Young Children
University of Maryland
College Park, Maryland 20742

Some educators believe that a developmental approach to early childhood education would dictate that young children be given only sensory experience, saving abstractions for a later time. If this view has merit, does the introduction of the microcomputer to 3-, 4-, and 5-year-old children represent good educational practice? The Center for Young Children (CYC) at the University of Maryland subscribes to a child-centered philosophy in its approach to developing a curriculum for young children. The Center also recognizes that the microcomputer has quickly become a learning tool that children will encounter in their education just as they encounter books, rulers, and pencils. Therefore, rather than summarily dismissing the microcomputer as being too abstract for young children, the staff decided to see whether or not there were creative, child-directed ways the microcomputer could be used.

BACKGROUND

In the spring of 1982, the CYC began to explore positive uses of the microcomputer in the education of young children. The CYC fosters the development of knowledge as a network of ideas, not as a collection of specific facts or isolated sensory experiences. Because the Center staff believes that children learn by interacting with their environment, it offers children a physical setting they can explore with a wide variety of materials to shape and change. Child- and teacher-initiated activities encourage the children to ask questions, seek answers to those questions, and develop problem-solving skills. The intellectual, emotional, social, and physical development of the child are interrelated. The CYC places equal emphasis on all four areas of development and seeks to understand each child as a unique person with his or her own developmental pattern.

Microcomputer activities were initiated against this background of an experiential approach to learning. One of the authors (Wright) directed the Computer Discovery Project and provided the technical skill and expertise needed to translate CYC philosophy into an ongoing microcomputer curriculum.

THREE MAJOR CONCERNS

Not having other preschool computer curricula to emulate, the Center staff decided to examine the use of microcomputers in a preschool setting from the perspective of three questions. The first question was *could* young children remain engaged in front of a monitor screen long enough to interact with the microcomputer? In addition to the problem of attention span, there was the question of manual dexterity. Could young children successfully manipulate a small lever in relation to images on the screen? Could children this age manipulate a keyboard?

A second question was *would* children wish to work at the microcomputer? What types of programs might interest children, and would these programs be selected by the children when other activities were available?

Perhaps the most important question, which concerned the adults who were planning and implementing the program, was *should* young children be exposed to microcomputers during their preschool years? Is this experience consistent with a child-centered curriculum? All three questions were ultimately answered in the affirmative. The last one, "Should young children be exposed to microcomputers during their preschool years?" was answered, "Yes, but. . . . " The qualification concerned the kind of software chosen and the way in which the microcomputer activities are implemented in the classroom.

INITIAL OBSERVATIONS

It is not surprising that the microcomputer was initially introduced into classrooms in the "tutor" (Taylor, 1980) mode as a directive teaching tool to reinforce an ongoing curriculum. Computer programs written for preschool children typically capitalized on the traditional idea that young children need to learn their letters and numbers. The most widely recommended first programs included Hodge Podge, Nine Games for Preschool Children, and Caterpillar (Lathrop & Goodson, 1983). Variations of these themes reappeared a year or two later in ABC's, Early Games, and Sticky Bear's ABC's. Now, a second level of programs is offering to teach concepts such as above/below and right/left (Juggle's Rainbow™), and to involve children in instructional games that call upon skills such as attribute recognition (Gertrude's Secrets™) and one-to-one correspondence (Moptown™).

Standing in sharp contrast to these A-B-C and 1-2-3 tutorial programs are the powerful ideas of Seymour Papert, who believes that Logo, a computer language designed to be understandable to the beginner as well as the expert, offers a "new kind of learning environment" (Papert, 1980a, p. 16). The teaching strategy employed in introducing Logo is commonly referred to as the "tutee" mode (Taylor, 1980). As more programs become available, distinctions between "tutor, tool, and tutee" are increasingly apparent. At last, teachers might find a "match" (Hunt, 1966) between their philosophy of education, their teaching style, and the use they make of the microcomputer.

> People often ask whether in the future children will program computers or become absorbed in pre-programmed activities. The answer must be that some children will do the one, some the other, some both and some neither. But which children, and most importantly, which social classes of children, will fall into each category will be influenced by the kind of computer activities and the kind of environments created around them. (Papert, 1980a, pp. 29–30)

The challenge for early childhood educators is both bewildering and exciting. The bewilderment arises because no one has done it before, available programs are in flux, and the microcomputers with their accompanying array of peripherals are still under development and constantly changing (or being discontinued). The excitement arises because there are no rules, no precedents, and this new machine offers immense possibilities.

This challenge is tempered by warnings from noted educators who caution that

> Young children sitting at microcomputers are being short-changed in terms of fulfilling those needs which are fundamental to learning and to their optimal development. . . . They are being limited to dealing with two-dimensional abstractions of real objects that are represented on a screen. (Barnes & Hill, 1983, p. 13)

Juxtaposed to these warnings are positive reports from teachers at the Lamplighter School in Texas and the Capital Children's Museum in Washington, D.C., and observational data from researchers at Stanford University's Bing Nursery School (Piestrup, 1981), the University of Wisconsin Lab School (Borgh & Dickson, this volume), and our own program (Campbell & Schwartz, this volume; Wright & Samaras, this volume). These educators and researchers agree that children appear to be learning from interacting with the computer, that they are highly motivated, and that they are having fun! At the same time comparison of these reports indicates that teaching style and the software program influence children's experience with the microcomputer.

THE PILOT PROJECT

At the Center for Young Children, the microcomputer was first introduced to 3-, 4-, and 5-year-olds as one of many activity centers available during a free-choice period each day. The microcomputer was located in a Computer Discovery Room near but separate from the children's classrooms. This placement permitted careful observation of the children's responses to the new machine without distraction and disruption of the existing CYC curriculum. In the style of Jersild (1946), who defined the child development approach to the curriculum as "an effort to apply to the education of children the lessons learned from the study of children themselves," the CYC approached the use of the microcomputer with "a spirit of inquiry and a desire to learn about the ways of children" (p. 1). Consistent with the philosophy of the Center, children were encouraged to explore the potential of the microcomputer. The teacher served as a facilitator to that exploration.

After a careful review of the very limited supply of software available for preschool children in the autumn of 1982, two programs were chosen, Scribbling and Creative Crayon. Both of these graphic arts programs were produced by Astrovision and used on Astrovision Computers. They were selected because they offered an environment in which children could exercise control over what happened on the monitor screen through a series of simple commands given from a control panel. The control panel executed the functions of a typical joystick, but it was built to the specifications of the CYC staff by Tom Meeks, a representative of Astrovision. Its uniqueness lay in the positioning of the joystick (at an angle) so that mov-

ing the joystick up corresponded to an upward motion on the screen. In addition to the joystick, the control panel had an easily turned knob, an enlarged button, and a switch, all of which were simple to manipulate. Because the control panel was heavy, it did not move around as the children used it; thus it met the needs of early learners still developing their small muscle control.

EXPLORING THE GRAPHIC ARTS POTENTIAL

For children who had passively watched many hours of television, the programs on the computer were a real surprise. At first, the children expected the monitor to give them a show. However, they soon discovered that Scribbling and Creative Crayon reversed the locus of control, putting them in control of what occurred on the screen. This active role is essential because knowledge is not given to a passive observer. Knowledge of reality must be discovered and constructed by the activity of the child (Piaget, 1970). In the spirit of Piaget and Papert, children who were using Scribbling and Creative Crayon became "the active builders of their own intellectual structures" (Papert, 1980a, p. 19). There were no adult expectations of what should be created; instead the child was free to use a new medium that encouraged fluency and originality by its rapid responses and its multiple possibilities for original productivity.

When using Scribbling, the child can choose the color and size of the drawing cursor. The child can also choose one of eight directions with the joystick and one of four colors and widths with the knob on the control panel. A switch allows the child to choose whether to draw or to move the cursor without leaving any line. Because of the novelty of the operation, it was necessary to teach the children how to use the control panel before they could operate the program. Once these operations were understood, the teacher facilitated the child's independent use of the program fostering looking, touching, and intuitive hypothesizing about what would happen. Each session was audiotaped by the teacher so that the children's verbal responses could be analyzed. This analysis provided insights into the children's abilities and interests.

Discoveries with Scribbling and Creative Crayon

Given the natural curiosity of children, many discoveries involving color choice, switch options, and keypad selections were made. For example, one of the drawing colors the children could choose using the control panel was the color of the monitor screen. By choosing this background color and reversing direction, the children could erase what they had drawn. The children were delighted with this ability. One child filled the whole screen with green and then proceeded to "cut the grass" as he methodically moved the cursor back and forth across the screen leaving behind a "path" of background color.

The switch could serve to create dots of color rather than lines. Two boys (twins) developed a game that involved placing dots on the screen and then playing "connect the dots." With the switch off, the cursor would move freely. Based on this principle, several children drew mazes and then went through them with a cursor of a different color. One child explained, "I made a game and you try to get through all that little place" (i.e., the spaces between the lines).

The Astrovision computer also had a keypad that resembled a hand-held calculator. This keypad had a CLEAR button. One girl combined that function with the control panel. An animated effect could be achieved by drawing and clearing in rapid succession. "See, the water is pouring out of the bottle— now it's gone—here it comes again," she ex-

claimed. In addition to the CLEAR button, the keypad had a variety of other buttons that the teachers had assumed the children would ignore because of the smallness of the pad and the buttons. However, the children were fascinated with the buttons and soon realized through experimentation that they had the capacity to increase and decrease the intensity of the various colors. This discovery led to activities such as "day and night" and "Halloween." In the "day and night" sequence, two boys drew pictures of their homes, then told stories about what was happening as they changed the background from white to dark gray and back to white. The inventor of the technique was happy to teach it to his friend. "Halloween" involved changing the white background to black and the red drawing cursor to orange, after which one 5-year-old girl delighted in drawing ghost and pumpkin pictures.

These novel uses of the commands could not have occurred without an environment that fostered spontaneous exploration. One component of creative thinking is the promotion of "nonevaluative ideational productivity" (Dansky, 1980, p. 577). The microcomputer may well offer a new avenue for fostering such divergent thinking.

Kamii and DeVries (1978) defined four levels of children's acting upon an object. These are:

1. Acting upon an object to see how it reacts.
2. Acting upon an object to produce a desired effect.
3. Becoming aware of how one produced the desired effect.
4. Explaining causes.

As noted by Kamii and DeVries, the first two levels frequently occur with young children while the most advanced level, explaining causes, is in fact often impossible for them. With the microcomputer, it was noted that after the children had obtained sufficient mastery of the program (level 1), they began to move from experimenting with the machine's responses to carefully planned symbolic representations (level 2). The planning that occurred was followed by explanations to friends of how to do something (stage 3). This sequence indicates that if computer programs are changed too rapidly, they may not be used to their maximum potential.

After the children mastered Scribbling, they were introduced to Creative Crayon, a somewhat more complex program involving the use of a menu. The menu offered a "fill" option that allowed the children to color enclosed areas of the screen. Interestingly, after the children used Creative Crayon, many preferred to return to Scribbling, which utilized commands they had mastered. In some cases the children expressed a preference for the wider line available in Scribbling. In other cases children were not at ease with the additional sequence of commands necessary to use the menu in Creative Crayon.

The types of representations that occurred using these two programs varied widely, from "That's a superrabbit. See his blue ear!" to "See, this is a map of where I live. You take Riggs Road and South East and you can see lots of houses down there." Some children chose to practice drawing letters and numbers on the screen. Each child was encouraged to use these programs in his or her own unique way. A comparison of children's uses of a graphic arts program on the microcomputer and their art activities in other centers would be valuable in evaluating the impact of the new medium of expression.

Using the Electronic Easel Program

After 12 weeks, a third graphics/simulation program, Electronic Easel, was introduced using the Apple II Plus microcomputer. This program was selected because it was easily integrated into the CYC curriculum unit on color. The program offered the child two options, either to draw with the primary colors using the joystick or to mix primary colors and create secondary colors. Having mixed the secondary colors, the child could draw with all six colors. This simulation of mixing colors was offered after the children had mixed real paints and colored waters in the classroom. Thus each child was able to approach this program with his or her own knowledge base and operate it accordingly. Very few 4-year-olds can initially predict which secondary color will emerge when they select two primary colors. For some, this skill increases with repetition. After repeated experiences it is not uncommon to hear 4- and 5-year-olds remark, "Oh, I like purple, so I'll put in red." One 4-year-old girl was not interested in the draw option of Electronic Easel until she had committed to memory the primary color combinations needed to produce all three secondary colors. She then faultlessly filled her paint cans, each with a different secondary color.

In discussing the challenge of forming all possible combinations (colors and types) of beads into subsets, Papert (1980a) suggested that our culture has traditionally been lacking in models of systematic procedures. It will be interesting to study whether children's problem-solving skills will be enhanced by working with the procedural functions of the computer. A delightful aspect of the example just cited is that this child defined the problem for herself; the program does not demand that each paint can contain a different color. Having found the solution to her own problem, the child proceeded to paint a picture, as pleased with her growing knowledge of colors as she was with her purple mountain framed in orange. In an atmosphere that accepts each child's level of expertise, advanced programs create their own challenges.

Summary of Findings

Our experiences at CYC indicate that the specific graphic arts program chosen is not crucial to the success of this initial exploratory stage, as long as the program is age-appropriate. Because of mechanical difficulties with the Astrovision computer, several comparable programs were used on the Apple II Plus in the second year of the Computer Discovery Project (e.g., Finger Paint and Magic Blackboard). What is crucial is that the child be able to master the commands easily, thus experiencing a sense of power and self-confidence. Initial success determines how the child will view himself or herself in relation to the microcomputer. Two important criteria for choosing software for preschool children are that the software be simple to operate, freeing the child to create imaginatively, and that the software foster exploration of this unique machine.

DEVELOPING COMPUTER LITERACY

In planning the children's first interaction with the microcomputer, we questioned what kinds of perceptions of the microcomputer would be encouraged by our approach. Unless planned experiences show children otherwise, they may readily conclude that what appears on the monitor screen is "magic." Program names such as *Magic Paintbrush* and *Magic Spells*™ foster this sense of the mysterious. The name *Electronic Easel* on the other hand, is an accurate description of the process that occurs as the child interacts with the machine. Further understanding of the process can be achieved by the availability of a programmer to interact with the children. If a programmer comes to class and demonstrates commands that result in the large red square or the small green square appearing on the screen, children may begin to grasp the real essence of this new technology, i.e., that microcomputers are programmed by people who understand how electronic equipment works. Coburn, et al. (1982) observed that adults as well as children are naturally suspicious of the unseen processes.

A major difference between the computer and the calculator examples is the degree of visibility of the process to you, the user. In using the calculator, you are involved with each generation and see each intermediate result as it is generated. Once you have accepted the minor marvel that the calculator does indeed perform its operations correctly, the whole thing becomes routine and trivial. In the case of the computer example, all of the calculation is concealed from you: you enter the numbers, it gargles them and regurgitates the answer. The process by which the result is achieved is hidden.... This often has the effect of making the computer seem more distant, forbidding, and magical than it really is. The user is potentially isolated from the process, and this isolation can be alienating. (p. 62)

The staff at the CYC was fascinated by the rapidity with which 4- and 5-year-old children seemed to grasp the concept that programmers decide what each program does. The children readily accepted the notion that "Computers, for all their power, are entirely stupid, useless, and helpless without instructions" (Coburn et al., 1982, p. 60). Sally, at age 4, showed an understanding of this concept when she attempted to correct a discrepancy in the operation of Hodge Podge. Convinced that if the picture of a farm said "farm" under it, then the picture of an apple should say "apple" under it, Sara tried to add the word "apple" to the screen. Since the program was not written to accept this type of input, it went on to show Sara more pictures. Some of these pictures had words under them, others did not. "Oh, well," said Sally, "I guess Betty will have to fix it." Betty was one of the programmers Sally knew. Sally had correctly identified the fact that the computer could not fix itself; it needed a programmer to change it.

Certainly not all preschool children will comprehend cause and effect to the same degree. A broken microcomputer was described by one 5-year-old girl as "sick," an age-appropriate response reflecting an animistic understanding often found in the "precausal period" (Piaget, 1930). These "false theories" are a necessary part of the process of learning to think.

In sharp contrast was the response of another 5-year-old girl, who set out to discover whether the monitor attached to one microcomputer would work with other microcomputers. Her investigation was facilitated by a teacher who believed that an introduction to computer science begins with such simple experiments as connecting different peripherals to different microcomputers and observing the effects. This 5-year-old demonstrated that she could go beyond the "egocentric" assumption that elements go together because they occur together and could look for causal relationships (Flavell, 1963). Designed by the child, this activity added much to a growing awareness of the interactive functioning of computer components. This type of productive thinking can occur in an atmosphere that encourages investigation. The Computer Discovery Curriculum allows children to generate and test their hypotheses within the limitations necessitated by safety, that is, not connecting equipment that is turned on.

As children learned to operate more programs, they soon discovered that some programs use both buttons on the joystick while other programs use one or neither. They also encountered a variety of uses for the same keys on the keyboard. The ease with which children moved from one program to another depended upon the individual child's ability to group individual commands and to discriminate one grouping from another. In general the children at the CYC have been consistently more capable than their teachers would have predicted. Just as children exhibit unique learning patterns when beginning to read, so too with computer literacy. Children differ in their readiness to operate more complex and varied programs.

PROCESSING SYMBOLS AND WORDS

Because it is a nonspecialized tool (Coburn, et al., 1982), the microcomputer is difficult to define, even for adults. Its many applications make it bewildering. Is it a word processor? A data processor? A game machine? In designing the curriculum at the CYC, an effort was made to introduce several facets of the microcomputer's capabilities. Following the lead of children who expressed strong interest in the keyboard (wanting to "type my name" or "type letters"), the graphic arts unit was followed by a language arts unit that includes keyboard exploration and word processing.

The transition from graphic arts to language arts was a natural one. In several drawing programs, children entered their names and gave names to their pictures. Keyboard Fun allowed the children to explore all of the keys and to choose to write in any of the high-resolution colors. Some children typed their names and names of friends. They all had name tags and soon realized that they could borrow these to copy the letters. One group of children chose to create the alphabet and sing the alphabet song. A pair of 4-year-olds counted from 1 to 9, then paused and studied how to type "10." A third original approach to the keyboard involved learning to use the shift key to make an asterisk and then creating a design with that image.

Self-initiated projects are more meaningful to the child than are drill and practice alphabet games. If a printer is available, the activity can be enhanced by a printout of the child's work. A study of the wide variety of responses young children originate using very simple, open-ended programs indicates that an important criterion for software evaluation is flexibility in the program's acceptance of diverse responses.

There are many motivating factors at work as the young child interacts with the microcomputer, some of which result in serendipitous learning. While introducing 4-year-olds to several programs she designed as part of a Logo environment, Coletta Lewis (personal communication, June 10, 1984) unintentionally inspired her students to want to call up these games independently.

Very soon the children were pecking their way about the whole keyboard spelling out the Logo commands that would interrupt one game and set up the next! They were on their way towards two new worlds of intellectual endeavor: writing and programming.

A similar sequence of events is reported in the logs of the Discovery Project. While working with Picture Book Fun, the children quickly discovered that along with the ability to choose a set of shapes, create a picture, write a story (assisted by a teacher's aide or parent), name, and save that picture story, there came an additional bonus. They recognized their friends' names on the catalog and learned to call up their picture stories. Designed as a computer adaptation of a language experience story, Picture Book Fun can be related to class field trips (at the pond, on the farm), class projects (hatching chicks, planting a garden), or unit topics (autumn, winter, firefighter). For each topic a unique set of images is drawn and placed in the memory of the computer as a shape table. The child may then call up these images from a picture and word index of shapes and use

them to create a picture. Having created the picture, the child adds a word story to accompany it.

Following a trip to the farm, Bobby wrote, "The pig is lonely. The pig needs more pigs so he will have friends." His picture showed one pig alone and then four others coming to play. John's story read, "The ducks are mine and the sheep. In the summer I give the sheep a haircut." Lydia said, "Ellen and Lydia had a picnic together. Ellen had a dress and Lydia has shorts and a T-shirt. After they had a picnic they fed the cows." Printed and bound together, these picture stories formed a special class book about "Our trip to the farm." The stories are often playful in nature and display a delightful sense of humor. Ellen captioned her bound picture, "Frog, you stay here. I'm going to the store!" The capacity to create beginning reading books that grow from the children's experiences opens the door to exciting educational possibilities limited only by the ingenuity of teacher and students.

The language arts component of the curriculum has been expanded to include writing stories about "Me," "My School," and "My Home." These programs were designed by a parent who is both a reading educator and a computer specialist. Her presence in the classrooms helped to develop in the children a sense that computers are for everyone—including parents. Consistent planning between the classroom teacher and the parent/programmer fostered curriculum integration and generated new implementations of the microcomputer. Children delighted in simple name banners, gift tags, and valentines.

It is also possible to use a combination of computer programs to provide a creative writing experience for the children. Using a simulation, Star Gazer, in connection with a study of the sky, 5-year-olds chose their favorite constellations. They then renamed the constellations and wrote stories about them with BANK STREET WRITER™. Many of the children chose to type in a number of the words themselves. They were able to copy the letters from word cards placed above the keyboard. They were also able to read a number of those words when their stories were printed for the class book. Excerpts from one such story read: "The crab is digging a hole. It's trying to find fish underground. That part looks like a fish. It lost one fin. He's swimming away from a shark."

Within the pre-Logo environment described thus far, children as young as 3 years of age can perceive the microcomputer in its role as an electronic easel (graphic arts) and a word processor (language arts). Concurrently, they give evidence of an awareness of the microcomputer as a machine that can be programmed by people to do a variety of functions. When shown a series of photographs of the microcomputer and its peripherals, a group of kindergartners could readily identify the parts and list their functions. The same class, when writing a story entitled, "A Teacher Can:", included the phrase "read, write, and use a computer" (computer literacy).

DISCOVERING A COMPUTER LANGUAGE

The full power of the microcomputer is available to the child when he or she is able to use words to create commands, that is, to program the computer. Increasing numbers of educators are using the world of the "turtle" to introduce programming to beginners. Seeking to encourage a natural exploration of the microworld inhabited by the turtle, Logo teachers are encouraging each child to think through the solution to the problems she or he poses.

> This environment of exploration demands a non-authoritative role for the teachers. When a learner asks, "Can I accomplish this?," the answer may be,

"How do you think that might be done?" or "Show what you want the turtle to do." These replies are invitations for learners to extend their skills. Some people discover new applications for known skills as they describe their intended goal. Others seem to refuse the challenge of thinking about their own questions. They are discouraged because Logo is not automatic . . . like a video game. (Bull & Tipps, 1983, p. 4)

Perspective Taking

The children at the CYC were introduced to Logo first through the three-dimensional Tasman Turtle, a computer-controlled robot. The robot has a clear plastic dome that allows full view of its motor, wheels, circuit board, two-tone horn, pen, and bright green eyes, which light on command. Some children are readily able to identify the direction the robot is heading and type in commands that send it across the floor to a chosen location. The commands used are all single-key commands designed to give rapid response so that the focus of the learning can be on commanding the robot rather than locating keys (i.e,. F = forward 6 inches, R = right 30 degrees, B = blink eyes, S = sound horn).

The challenge for the young child is to be able to take the perspective of the turtle. The observations of Piaget and others have led to the conclusion that taking the perspective of someone or something else is difficult for the preoperational child (Flavell, 1963). Papert (1980a) has suggested that the reason children have not developed certain intellectual abilities at a younger age is that they have not had access to microworlds in which to develop these capabilities. The world of the screen turtle and the novelty of the robot appeal to young children. Some kindergartners in our program enjoyed directing the robot; others enjoyed engaging in symbolic play—creating a pretend pond by drawing fish, plants, and snakes to live with the turtle or a town with houses, stores, and a playground. Each child entered into the play at his or her own level of understanding and interest.

As the children drew, first with the robot and then with a representation of the turtle on the monitor, they were estimating distances and angles with intuitive hunches. Their discoveries using Advanced Instant Logo (developed by Soergel & Soergel, 1982), were small but significant in the overall scheme of learning perspective-taking and geometric concepts:

- The turtle's right turn may not be the same as my right turn.
- To return to a location the turtle can go backward or turn halfway around and go forward.
- There are two ways to face in a particular direction, for example, turn left three times (90 degrees left) or turn right nine times (270 degrees right).

Because each command entered on the keyboard was immediately executed on the screen, the child could see the sequence of the procedure step by step and comprehend the cause/effect relationship.

Problem Solving and Programming

The implications of these insights are endless. Papert (1980b) observed that "perhaps learning to make small discoveries puts one more surely on a path to making big ones than does faultlessly learning any number of sound algebraic concepts" (p. 190). It is too soon to say how much knowledge and problem-solving ability a child can gain from any given Logo experience. It is apparent from studying CYC videotapes of kindergartners using Logo that children have very different learning styles and that the problem-solving nature of Logo allows for valuable assessment of these strategies. Being able to assess

a child's thinking processes in an open, playful environment enables the observer to estimate the capacity for divergent thinking as well as convergent thinking. Perlman (1976) noted, "the most important thing the child learns from an imaginary computer environment is a fearless, joyful attitude toward learning" (p.8).

Delta Drawing™ is a derivative of Logo that offers a simplified introduction to the world of the turtle. Its most unique feature is the ability to fill the spaces created by the child. However, in the Apple version it presents a basic problem. Once a child has created a procedure, or list of commands, the only way to edit the procedure is to erase back to the command to be changed. This action may involve erasure of a major part of the program. We used Delta Drawing in the kindergarten, assuming that 5-year-olds would not reach this level of programming sophistication. Of the 20 children in the class, 2 requested editing capability within the first 2 months. These incidents led the children to write a letter to Spinnaker Software asking that the program be revised. Because a significant number of educators (and some children, who are truly the best critics) highlighted this problem, new versions of Delta Drawing on the IBM® PC and the Commodore 64 allow such editing to occur.

The ability to change a procedure is of crucial significance to the development of the child's thinking processes. The capacity to alter a creation, debug a problem, or find a new solution is an essential part of learning. One delightful experience intrinsic to the Logo language is that often a "bug" surprises the programmer and turns out to be a beautiful creation. Then the challenge is to figure out how it happened. Logo provides the teacher with a window into the thinking processes of young children. Looking through that window, the teacher can discover how children perceive things and match his or her responses to this discovery.

Educators who are experimenting with versions of Instant Logo and Delta Drawing are unsure of the advisability of providing ready-made shapes (square, circle, and triangle) called by single-key commands (S, C, T). Records of the procedures created by 4- and 5-year-olds at the CYC indicate that children can accurately draw squares and triangles within the first two sessions using either Instant Logo or Delta Drawing. Circles begin to emerge in the fourth and fifth sessions. The more perceptive 5-year-olds are able to observe a design (such as a pinwheel) created by a classmate and decide that one four-sided shape is the basic unit that was drawn again and again by turning the turtle. It should be noted that the Instant Logo used at the CYC was designed to allow children to automatically save a procedure under a name and recall it (Soergel & Soergel, 1982).

Perhaps the key to the question of why Logo and programs similar in philosophical approach elicit meaningful responses from children is that the challenges are not being taught and there is no expectation of a "right" answer. A refreshing phrasing of a cognitive objective was made by Eleanor Duckworth, who suggested that a first cognitive objective be "the having of wonderful ideas" (cited in Kamii & DeVries, 1978).

> Children work long and hard at the problems and questions that they invent. And teachers who use these principles of teaching are frequently astonished at the difficult problems children set for themselves, problems they would never think of suggesting. (p. 45)

DEFINING THE CHALLENGE

Torrance (1965) has observed that educational programs should be based on (1) an analysis of the learning task, (2) the stage of development and preferred way of learning of the child, and (3) the settings that facilitate or impede achievement. Two and a half

years of observation at the CYC suggest that the young child can perform many creative activities with the microcomputer, which is a multifaceted tool. Graphic arts, language arts, mathematics, and preprogramming concepts all appear to be viable learning areas to explore. A guided discovery approach coupled with open-ended interactive programs has allowed CYC children to experience mastery and invent and solve their own problems.

Teachers and parents are key variables in the meaningful utilization of the microcomputer by young children. Children at the CYC have taught the staff that interaction with the microcomputer provides a unique opportunity for children and adults to discover together. Creating a microworld can result in a charming array of teacher/learner encounters in which neither the adult nor the child can predict who will be teaching and who will be learning. In one sense, the microcomputer is a value-neutral device. Its impact on children who fearlessly accept the microcomputer as a part of their culture will depend on the aims and insights of their teachers and parents.

REFERENCES

Barnes, B. J., & Hill, S. (1983). Should young children work with microcomputers—Logo before Lego? *The Computer Teacher, 10*(9), 11–14.

Borgh, K., & Dickson, W. P. (1986). Two preschoolers sharing one microcomputer: Creating prosocial behavior with hardware. In P. F. Campbell & G. G. Fein (Eds.), *Young children and microcomputers* (pp. 37–44). A Reston Book. Englewood Cliffs, NJ: Prentice-Hall, Inc.

Bull, G., & Tipps, St. (1983, December). Problem spaces in a project-oriented Logo environment. *The National Logo Exchange, 2*(4), 3–5.

Campbell, P. F., & Schwartz, S. S. (1986). Microcomputers in the preschool: Children, parents, and teachers. In P. F. Campbell & G. G. Fein (Eds.), *Young children and microcomputers* (pp. 45–59). A Reston Book. Englewood Cliffs, NJ: Prentice-Hall, Inc.

Coburn, P., Kelman, P., Roberts, N., Snyder, T., Watt, D., & Weiner, C. (1982). *Practical guide to computers in education.* Reading, MA: Addison-Wesley.

Dansky, J. L. (1980). Make-believe: A mediator of the relationship between play and associative fluency. *Child Development, 51,* 576–579.

Flavell, J. H. (1963). *The developmental psychology of Jean Piaget.* Princeton, NJ: Van Nostrand Reinhold.

Hunt, J. McV. (1966). The psychological basis for using pre-school enrichment as an antidote for cultural deprivation. In F. M. Hechinger (Ed.), *Pre-school education today* (pp. 25–27). Garden City, NY: Doubleday.

Jersild, A. T. (1946). *Child development and the curriculum.* New York: Teachers College Press.

Kamii, C., & DeVries, R. (1978). *Physical knowledge in pre-school education: Implications of Piaget's theory.* Englewood Cliffs, NJ: Prentice-Hall.

Lathrop, A., & Goodson, B. (1983). *Courseware in the classroom.* Reading, MA: Addison-Wesley.

Papert, S. (1980a). *Mindstorms: Children, computers, and powerful ideas.* New York: Basic Books.

Papert, S. (1980b). Teaching children to be mathematicians vs. teaching about mathematics. In R. P. Taylor (Ed.), *The computer in the school: Tutor, tool, tutee* (pp. 177–196). New York: Teachers College Press.

Perlman, R. (1976, May). *Using computer technology to provide a creative learning environment for preschool children.* (Logo Memo No. 24, Artificial Intelligence Memo No. 360). Cambridge, MA: Massachusetts Institute of Technology, Artificial Intelligence Lab.

Piaget, J. (1930). *The child's conception of physical causality.* New York: Harcourt.

Piaget, J. (1970). *Science of education and the psychology of the child.* New York: Orion Press.

Piestrup, A. M. (1981, January). *Preschool children use Apple II to test reading skills programs.* Portola Valley, CA: Advanced Learning Technology. (ERIC Document Reproduction Service No. ED 202 476)

Soergel, D., & Soergel, E. (1982). *Advanced INSTANT Logo* [Computer program]. College Park, MD: University of Maryland, College of Library Science.

Taylor, R. P. (Ed.). (1980). *The computer in the school: Tutor, tool, tutee.* New York: Teachers College Press.

Torrance, E. P. (1965). *Gifted children in the classroom.* New York: Macmillan.

Wright, J. L., & Samaras, A. S. (1986). Play worlds and microworlds. In P. F. Campbell & G. G. Fein (Eds.), *Young children and microcomputers* (pp. 73–86). A Reston Book. Englewood Cliffs, NJ: Prentice-Hall, Inc.

CHAPTER 11

EDUCATIONAL MATCHING: MICROCOMPUTER APPLICATIONS IN THE EDUCATION OF HANDICAPPED CHILDREN

Linda McConville
Gail McGregor
Marion Panyan
Dianne Tobin
Education Division
School of Continuing Studies
The Johns Hopkins University
Baltimore, Maryland 21218

While microcomputers are being integrated into the regular curriculum in many subject areas from the elementary school through the college level, their application in the domain of special education has been less widespread. However, according to a report from Education Turnkey Systems, this situation will soon change ("Report Sees," 1983). This report suggested that by 1985 the number of microcomputers used for instruction in special education would increase nearly ninefold, compared with a projected fourfold increase in the number of microcomputers in general education. This increase should not be surprising since the very features that make microcomputers attractive to regular teachers are just as, if not more, critical when instruction involves a handicapped student. This chapter will explore some of the uses and benefits of the microcomputer with handicapped infants and children. Because the needs of mildly retarded and learning disabled children differ from the needs of more severely handicapped children, microcomputer applications will be discussed separately for these groups.

MILDLY RETARDED AND LEARNING DISABLED CHILDREN

Characteristics

A salient characteristic of mildly retarded children is their reduced ability to learn associated with deficiencies in attention and short-term memory. Children who have problems in attending require a longer amount of time to learn material (Zeaman & House, 1963). Likewise, students who have problems remembering often need more practice, which means that they also need a longer time to learn something. Although retarded children go through the same stages of learning as do normal children, they do so at a slower rate and need more practice.

A different set of characteristics is often associated with learning disabled children. These children may exhibit attention and memory deficits, but they also may exhibit hyperactivity, perceptual-motor impairments, emotional lability (frequent shifts in emotional mood), general coordination deficits, distractibility, perseveration, impulsivity, and specific academic problems (reading, arithmetic, writing, spelling) (Hallahan & Kaufman, 1978). Not every child classified as learning disabled will necessarily manifest all of these characteristics, but each manifested characteristic will require a different set of instructional strategies for the child.

In addition to the special learning characteristics of learning disabled and mildly retarded children, it is important to address their personality characteristics. These children often have emotional problems, due at least partially to the frustrations produced by their learning difficulties. Many of these children begin to question their self-worth. In fact, some specialists believe that school difficulties can lead children to become passive learners and develop a high expectancy for failure (Hallahan & Kaufman, 1978).

Instructional Needs

Because of both their learning and emotional characteristics, mildly retarded and learning disabled youngsters often need some combination of the following instructional strategies adapted to their specific individual needs:

1. Adjustment to the child's rate of learning.
2. A variety of immediate and appropriate reinforcements to the child's responses.
3. Multisensory approaches with emphasis on the child as an active rather than a passive learner.

4. Provision for meaningful repetition and/or drill and practice activities.

5. A nonthreatening environment in which there is continuous encouragement that learning is possible and the task can be mastered.

In addition, teachers of these children need relief from clerical activities related to diagnostic testing and individualized education plans, and recordkeeping chores related to grading daily activities and providing specific follow-up assignments. If the learning needs of the students and the management needs of the teachers are compared to some of the following suggestions for using microcomputers in the schools, it becomes clear that there are areas where needs and microcomputer capabilities match well:

1. The child may use the microcomputer in an individualized setting, regardless of the concurrent activities of the other children in the classroom.

2. Feedback on correct and incorrect answers in microcomputer programs is immediate. The child does not have to wait until a teacher can grade the work. This ability of microcomputer instruction to provide continuous feedback and positive reinforcement or praise when deserved contributes to a higher sense of self-esteem.

3. The speed of a child's work is not a factor in his or her learning. Because the microcomputer is inanimate, it cannot lose patience when the child takes longer to complete assignments. In addition, this important feature of microcomputer instruction rarely requires adaptation of existing software.

4. Drill and practice can be made exciting through the use of animation, sound effects, and game-playing situations. Additional meaningful practice can be built in to programs where needed. Programs can be adjusted so that once

the student understands the materials, as evidenced by the ability to do several exercises correctly, practice can be discontinued.

5. The microcomputer creates a non-threatening environment in which students can learn. It can call the student by name when giving lessons, and it can eliminate the stress associated with giving the wrong answer by privately suggesting that the student try again.

6. The microcomputer is uniquely suited to the discovery method of learning. This is particularly useful for learning disabled children. The amount of time required to set up a discovery learning situation in a regular classroom dooms those activities to infrequent occurrences. Working within a regular curriculum, microcomputer software can model characteristics of real situations so that they can be better studied by the students. Software that simulates real life experiences allows students to make decisions and see the consequences as if they were actually reliving an historical situation or doing an experiment. The ability of the microcomputer to hide the answers from the student until the student has actually made a decision prevents second-guessing the system, which a child might attempt if the answers were fixed or retrievable from a fixed location such as a textbook.

7. Problem solving is a skill that learning disabled and mentally retarded children need and rarely acquire because emphasis is traditionally placed on drill and practice activities. Strategies related to problem solving can be adapted easily for the microcomputer through both simulations and learning to program, which is itself an exercise in problem solving because the student goes through all the steps of the prob-

lem-solving method. Simulation activities, especially adventure game programs that require the children to make decisions, are problem-solving vehicles as well. When they are rewritten to match specific curriculum and content objectives, they can become extremely powerful learning tools.

Although ordinary learners could benefit from many of these advantages of microcomputer instruction, learning disabled and retarded students have an even greater need for the individualized learning that microcomputer technology can supply. In addition, advances in technology will soon make possible multisensory approaches to learning through microcomputer instruction. For children with learning disabilities, approaches that combine visual, auditory, and kinesthetic stimuli are often more effective than single-stimuli approaches. Graphics tablets are already available that allow students to write rather than type into the microcomputer. Voice synthesizers are available that allow computers to speak, and giant strides are being made in voice recognition devices so that it is expected that these, too, will be commonly available shortly. Interfacing computers with videotape and videodisk machines will allow the interactive capabilities of the microcomputer to be combined with clear audio and visual reproductions. With educators and microcomputer technologists teaming up to produce innovative approaches, the possibilities for improving the education of learning disabled and mentally retarded children are limitless.

SEVERELY HANDICAPPED INFANTS AND YOUNG CHILDREN

As might be expected, children who are identified as handicapped during the preschool years tend to exhibit more severe handicaps than children who are identified as delayed later in life (Beck, 1977; Hayden, 1979). They are also apt to exhibit a deficit or delay in more than one sensory or skill area. Although the term *multihandicapped* does little to describe the heterogeneity of children subsumed under this label, it is generally used to refer to individuals who have two or more physical, social, mental, and/or emotional problems, the combination of which impedes development in any or all of these areas (Ficociello, 1979).

While it is perhaps easiest to recognize the health and medical needs of multihandicapped youngsters, these children and their families are also in need of early educational intervention. According to Hayden (1979):

> While nonhandicapped young children may make acceptable progress without early educational intervention, handicapped or at risk children do not. To deny them the attention that might increase their chances for improved functioning is not only wasteful, it is ethically indefensible. (p. 510)

Personnel teaching multihandicapped children under 5 years of age are challenged with the task of providing high quality, innovative intervention for a difficult-to-serve population. Whereas expectations for success among severely handicapped learners were previously quite limited (Brown, Nietupski, & Hamre-Nietupski, 1976), the development of systematic forms of instruction has enhanced the rate of learning for these individuals (Gold, 1976; Schworm & Abelseth, 1978; Snell, 1983; Williams, Brown, & Certo, 1975).

In spite of advances in the area of instructional technology, improvement is still needed to create learning environments that will enhance skill acquisition among individuals unresponsive to existing approaches (Sailor, Wilcox, & Brown, 1980). The microcomputer represents a major advance in the nature and structure of special education services for such students (Hagen, 1984; Taber, 1983), with its potential for improving communication, environmental control, and instruction (Jordan, 1984; Myers, 1982; Thomas, 1982).

Facilitating Learning with Microcomputers

By providing content tailored to a specific child's skill level and by differentially responding to each child's input, the microcomputer can provide the flexibility to fit individual student needs. Moreover, the microcomputer has the capability to instantly process and analyze responses to redirect the course of instruction (Brinker & Lewis, 1982). In addition to these capabilities for improving instruction for handicapped students, microcomputers can also provide numerous trials in a consistent manner for the many handicapped students who require repeated exposure to a problem before mastering a concept. Finally, the microcomptuer is nonjudgmental, predictable, and "patient."

Because of these characteristics, microcomputers are increasingly being used with handicapped preschoolers (Hagen, 1984). For example, Lutz and Taylor (1983) described the use of a computerized home-based curriculum with 80 high-risk preschoolers ranging in age from 3 to 5 years. The microcomputer-based behavioral curriculum was effective not only in teaching concepts but also in providing continuous records of progress.

The educational progress of handicapped children is clearly dependent on the availability of instructionally sound software that is introduced and followed up in appropriate ways. Taber (1981) specified educational standards by which to evaluate software for use in the home or classroom, and Chin (1984) offered guidelines on selecting software for preschoolers. Raleigh (1983) highlighted the most recent programs to teach basic concepts; discrimination skills; and letter, number, and object recognition. Horn and Finn (1983) provided an update of software producers in special education. Journals such as *The Computing Teacher, Digest of Software Reviews, Education, Electronic Learning, School Microware Directory,* and *School Microware Review* regularly publish critical reviews of new software to enable teachers to make judicious selections.

Facilitating Communication with Microcomputers

Deficits in language comprehension and production are common among students with severe handicaps. Microcomputer applications have been explored in relation to a variety of communicative skills with this population. Computers have been used:

- as a communication prosthesis for those who are physically unable to produce speech (Cohn, Curtis, & Purvis, 1982).

- as an augmentative communication device and language development tool for young children with delayed speech (Trachtman, 1984).

- as a tool to teach nonspeech symbol systems to handicapped children (Romski, White, Millen, & Rumbaugh, 1984).

- as a tool to improve the reading and language skills of children with communication handicaps (Geoffrion & Goldenberg, 1981).

- in combination with a printer to facilitate the expressive skills of students unable to use pencil and paper (Meyers, 1984).

The work of Laura Meyers at the University of California (Meyers, 1984) exemplifies innovative microcomputer-based language approaches with young handicapped children. In her work, the computer is used to enable a child to exercise control within developmentally meaningful routines that parallel the type of dialogues normally occurring between a child and a primary caretaker. In one situation, a 26-month-old blind child with cerebral palsy was taught to communicate with his primary caretakers through a microcomputer equipped with a speech synthesizer. The child's parents were asked to identify routines or games their child enjoyed. Since they reported that the child enjoyed having songs sung to him, a computer program was developed so that whenever a membrane keyboard was touched by the child, a speech synthesizer produced the word "sing," which signaled to the parents the child's desire for that activity. The strategy was subsequently expanded so that a number of diverse messages could be created by touching different locations of the membrane keyboard. Thus, through a highly individualized approach, young handicapped children can participate in language experiences that enable them to understand the nature of communicative exchanges.

Among the contributions of Joe Cohn (1982) to the field of technology for handicapped individuals is a microcomputer augmentative communication device. An automated, elevated system provides data-based decisions regarding the most appropriate content and access modes. The programs include pictures, symbols, or words on successive screens. Thus, children with a wide variety of neuromotor handicaps have access to an extended vocabulary for communicating messages.

It is sometimes difficult to separate the functions the microcomputer serves with young children. A single microcomputer can serve multiple functions. For example, it can be used as a communication board, an environmental control unit, a word processor, and an instructional aid, as well as for recreational and leisure time purposes.

Facilitating Environmental Control with Microcomputers

Behrmann and Lahm (1983) described the uses of technology to effect environmental control by multiply handicapped infants. Their project used an Apple II Plus microcomputer, a Votrex Type 'N' Talk voice synthesizer, a color monitor, various custom-made switches as input devices, and, more recently, the HERO-1 robot. Their findings suggest that infants understand the cause/effect relationship between the pictures on a monitor and their switch and that the infants' response times become consistent within a very short period of time. Furthermore, Behrmann and Lahm showed that the infants could use the microcomputer system to functionally control their environments by turning a television or battery-operated toy on and off. These preliminary results highlight the capabilities of microcomputer systems to extend environmental interactions to infants of limited motor ability and thus to affect their cognitive growth.

Brinker and Lewis (1982, 1983) also studied ways to give infants control over their environment. These investigators worked with 21 moderately to severely handicapped infants in a contingency intervention project based on an Apple II microcomputer. The twofold objective of this project was to (1) foster a generalized expectancy that the infant can control his or her world, and (2) lead the infant to use specific responses to explore the available contingencies. Brinker and Lewis (1983) provided one of the first and few examples of the use of the microcomputer to modify contingencies based on the ongoing analysis of the infant's movements. If the movements did not accelerate with a given consequence, the computer automatically switched to a second sequence. Through these contingencies children aged 3 months to 4 years have acquired in Piagetian terms both primary and secondary circular reactions. For example, the movements of a 4-

month-old Down syndrome infant illustrated that the infant learned the contingency between specific movements and the consequences, or spectacles, that the movements produced.

Providing Access for Severely Handicapped Students

As noted earlier, the unique capabilities of the microcomputer provide special educators with a teaching tool that holds great promise in providing responsive, individualized programming for handicapped students. A large segment of this population, however, is hampered by an inability to use a standard keyboard to access the microcomputer. Young children may simply not have yet developed the fine motor skills to adequately control a keyboard. Many other children are limited by physical and/or sensory handicaps that make using the keyboard an impossibility at any time.

Fortunately, technological applications in special education have a history that predates the proliferation of microcomputers by many years (Joiner, Sedlak, Silverstein, & Vensel, 1980). Personnel working with nonvocal individuals have developed a variety of electronic devices to provide alternative communication systems (Cohn, Curtis, & Purvis, 1982; Jefcoate, 1977; Vanderheiden & Grilley, 1976). Special educators working with physically handicapped children who are unable to use toys and other materials commonly adapt materials so that they may be manipulated by these children via some type of single-switch device (Burkhardt, 1980; Hewson, McConkey, & Jeffree, 1980).

With minor modifications, interfaces used in these other educational and therapeutic pursuits are available for use with microcomputers. Coupled with new developments that have emerged specifically for microcomputer applications, it is now possible for even the most minimally controlled physical

response to be a child's key to the world of microcomputer-assisted instruction. An overview of student input options is contained in Table 11–1. While specialized input devices will be described briefly, our discussion will highlight single-switch devices since they are the most inexpensive input alternative for a majority of individuals who are unable to use the standard keyboard.

Single-Switch Devices

It is evident from Table 11–1 that there is tremendous variety in the types of single-switch devices available to handicapped users of computers. Therefore, the first step in preparing a system for use by an individual is to identify the most reliable input mechanism. In applications with multihandicapped children, consultation with a physical and occupational therapist may be necessary to select an optimal interface arrangement. One investigation, however, provided evidence that consideration of a child's motor skills alone may be insufficient to identify a viable interface for the child. Working with a group of 14 multihandicapped preschool students, McGregor (1983) asked both the students' physical therapist and the classroom teacher to identify one switch from a set of six that, in their opinion, would be the best interface for each of the 14 children. An assessment procedure was then conducted in which the response latency for each of the switches was determined. This evaluation was supplemented by behavioral observations recorded during each assessment trial to determine the percentage of the child's time on- and off-task while using each switch. When this process was completed for each switch with each child, the switch that produced the best combination of response latency and on-task behavior was identified. The switch selected on the basis of this empirical information was in agreement with the professional judgment

TABLE 11–1.
Computer Input Modalities and Assistive Devices*

Input Source	Student Response Requirements	Variations	Adaptations
1. Conventional keyboard • space bar • key press	Child depresses designated location on keyboard	Responses made by hitting key in given area of keyboard, e.g., keyboard divided into quadrants or halves Responses made by hitting any key	Color code keys used for responses in a program Add keyguard to maximize chances of depressing correct key
2. Game paddle	Typically, child is required to press button or move joystick		Paddles can be mounted or positioned to accommodate child's motor patterns
3. Single switch • Activated by extremities (fingers, hands, feet, elbows)	Child depresses switch with given body part	Push-button switch Paddles & levers Pillow switch	All switches can be mounted or positioned to accommodate individual needs Multiple switches can be used
	Child pushes stick off center in any direction to activate	Wobblestick Joystick	
	Child pushes/pulls switch to slide along track	Sliding or trolley switch	
	Child pokes pointer into hole or indentation on switch	Poke switches	
	Child tilts switch in one direction for "on" and the other for "off"	Tilt or tip switches	
• Switches a specific body part	Child uses lateral head rotation	Head switch	
	Child squeezes switch between chin and chest	Chin switch	
	Child raises eyebrows	Eyebrow switch	
	Child moves knee	Knee switch	

152

TABLE 11–1. Continued.

Input Source	Student Response Requirements	Variations	Adaptations
	Child presses tongue against switch molded to fit in the palate	Palate switch	
	Child uses tongue movement	Tongue switch	
	Child depresses thumb	Thumb switch	
	Child rotates wrist	Wrist switch	
• Pneumatic switch	Air movement is created by the child's blowing		
4. Voice input	Child activates through sound production		Systems can be "trained" to understand sound/verbal repertoire of any person
5. Touch screen	Child has physical contact with screen, but no physical pressure		
6. Light pen	Child holds pen; directs it to designated location on screen		
7. Membrane keyboard	Child directs body part or device to designated location on keyboard	Response locations on keyboard vary in size from small squares to quadrants of the keyboard	

*Information adapted from Vandeheiden & Grilley, 1976.

of therapists and teachers familiar with the child only 14% of the time. The importance of an empirically based performance evaluation was highlighted in this study.

Once an effective switch match is found, it is necessary to train the child to use the device to make responses. The game selection in the program First Words (Wilson & Fox, 1982) and the Random Tones/Random Colors program on the Motor Training Games disk (Schwejda & McDonald, 1983) are good beginning programs for this pur-

pose, particularly for children who have cognitive impairments. Beyond a half dozen or so disks that have been programmed to accept single-switch input, however, there is very little software available for students who must use this type of input. Fortunately, one device has recently been marketed to overcome this barrier. The Adaptive Firmware Card (Schwejda & Vanderheiden, 1983), developed for the Apple microcomputer, works in such a way that programs not originally written to accept single-switch input are transparently intercepted by this card as they are run and manipulated so that responses can be made through a single switch as opposed to the keyboard. A horizontal display of characters on the bottom of the screen enables the user to select, through a variety of scanning or stepping modes, characters to answer questions or construct messages. Thus, rather than being restricted to a small number of software packages designed for single-switch users, the entire range of software becomes accessible to those unable to use the standard keyboard.

Specialized Input Devices

Other, more sophisticated adaptations are being developed to enable handicapped users to independently operate a microcomputer. While the cost of these systems, in most cases, greatly exceeds that of a single-switch device, each one broadens the potential range of computer users and applications.

Speech recognition systems, for example, enable standard software packages to be activated through the production of speech sounds. These systems must be trained to recognize the unique voice patterns of the user, and they may be extremely sensitive to variations in the user's voice patterns or background noise in the environment. The size of their vocabulary may also be limiting to some users. Nevertheless, these systems provide an input option that may prove to be the most efficient input modality for a number of handicapped users (Haas, 1984).

Touchpad technology is another vehicle for bypassing keyboard entry (Schrage, 1984). Touchpads are flat tablets that link to the computer. Because they are programmable, specific functions can be designated via a series of Mylar overlays. For example, a typewriter could be emulated and the location of the keys rearranged, or pictures of animals could be placed on the touchpad and questions or information about those animals could appear on the screen. Because it is a relatively new technology, its implica-

tions for handicapped children have only begun to be explored.

Finally, light pens and touch screens permit individuals to point to a certain area on the monitor itself (Sandberg-Diment, 1984). While this input is much more concrete than the keyboard, it is not applicable for children with certain types of physical disabilities because well-developed fine motor skills and eye-hand coordination are required.

In summary, microcomputers and related technology appear to offer many advantages to young handicapped children. Progress has been made to enable these children to access microcomputers more readily and benefit from them more substantially in the areas of instruction, communication, and environmental control.

CONCLUSION

Special education and computer technology have come a long way in the last 8 years. Handicapped children have unprecedented opportunities and support to reach their goals and fulfill their destinies. The potential for the microcomputer's use in special education is mindboggling, but its true potential can only be achieved when special educators who know what they want to teach team up and communicate with hardware developers, computer scientists, programmers, and handicapped persons. Professionals must work together to aid the disabled population, if not for their professional souls, then for the souls of the handicapped children they profess to love.

REFERENCES

Beck, R. (1977). The need for adjunctive services in the management of severely and profoundly handicapped individuals: A view from primary care. In N. Haring & L. Brown (Eds.), *Teaching the severely handicapped*

(Vol. 2, pp. 287–301). New York: Grune & Stratton.

Behrmann, M., & Lahm, L. (1983, April/May). Critical learning: Multiply handicapped babies using computers. *Closing the Gap*, pp. 1, 6–8, 14.

Brinker, R. P., & Lewis, M. (1982). Discovering the competent handicapped infant: A process approach to assessment and intervention. *Topics in Early Childhood Special Education*, 2(2), 1–16.

Brinker, R. P., & Lewis, M. (1983). Making the world work with microcomputers: A learning prosthesis for handicapped infants. *Exceptional Children*, 49, 163–170.

Brown, L., Nietupski, J., & Hamre-Nietupski, S. (1976). The criterion of ultimate functioning and public school services for the severely handicapped student. In M. A. Thomas (Ed.), *Hey, don't forget me: Education's investment in the severely, profoundly, and multiply handicapped* (pp. 2–15). Reston, VA: The Council for Exceptional Children.

Burkhardt, L. (1980). *Homemade battery powered toys and educational devices for severely handicapped children*. Millville, PA: Author.

Chin, K. (1984, February 20). Preschool computing: Too much, too soon? *Infoworld*, 6(8), 24–27.

Cohn, J. T. (1982). Microcomputer augmentative communication devices. *Technical Digest*, 3, 240–243.

Cohn, J. T., Curtis, P., & Purvis, A. W. (1982). CD: A microcomputer based communication prosthesis for the profoundly handicapped. *Family Medicine Review*, 1(3), 67–76.

Ficociello, C. (1979). Early intervention with multihandicapped children. In E. Shroyer & D. Tweedie (Eds.), *Perspective on the multihandicapped hearing impaired child* (pp. 11–22). Washington, DC: Gallaudet Press.

Geoffrion, L. D., & Goldenberg, E. P. (1981). Computer based learning systems for communication-handicapped children. *Journal of Special Education*, 15, 325–332.

Gold, M. (1976). Task analysis of a complex assembly task by the retarded blind. *Exceptional Children*, 43, 78–84.

Haas, M. (1984, June). The Texas Instruments Speech Command System. *Byte*, 9(6), 341–346.

Hagen, D. (1984). *Microcomputer resource book for special education*. Reston, VA: Reston Publishing.

Hallahan, D., & Kaufman, J. (1978). *Exceptional children: Introduction to special education*. Englewood Cliffs, NJ: Prentice-Hall.

Hayden, A. H. (1979). Handicapped children birth to age 3. *Exceptional Children*, 46, 510–516.

Hewson, S., McConkey, R., & Jeffree, D. (1980). The relationship between structured and free play in the development of a mentally handicapped child: A case study. *Child Care, Health and Development*, 6, 73–82.

Horn, C. J., & Finn, D. M. (1983). Sources of computing. *Focus on Exceptional Children*, 16,(2), 1–16.

Jefcoate, R. (1977). Electronic technology for disabled people. *Rehabilitation Literature*, 38, 110–115.

Joiner, L. M., Sedlak, R. A., Silverstein, B. J., & Vensel, G. (1980). Microcomputers: An available technology for special education. *Journal of Special Education Technology*, 3(3), 37–42.

Jordan, J. B. (Ed.). (1984). Technology in special education [Special issue]. *TEACHING Exceptional Children*, 16(4).

Lutz, J., & Taylor, P. (1983). A computerized home based curriculum for high risk preschoolers. *AEDS Journal*, 15, 1–9.

McGregor, G. (1983, April). *Microcomputer applications with multihandicapped preschoolers*. Paper presented at the Conference of The Association for Behavior Analysis, Milwaukee, Wisconsin.

Meyers, L. S. (1984). Unique contribution of microcomputers to language intervention with handicapped children. *Seminars in Speech and Language*, 5(1), 23–34.

Myers, W. (1982, February). Personal computers aid the handicapped. *IEEE Microcomputer*, pp. 26–40.

Raleigh, C. P. (1983, November). Give your child a head start. *Personal Software*, pp. 36–54, 185–186.

Report sees use of micros in special education rising dramatically. (1983, October). *Electronic Learning, 3*(2), 18.

Romski, M. A., White, R. A., Millen, C. E., & Rumbaugh, D. M. (1984). Effects of computer-keyboard teaching the symbolic communication of severely retarded persons: Five case studies. *Psychological Record, 34,* 39–54.

Sailor, W., Wilcox, B., & Brown, L. (Eds.). (1980). *Methods of instruction for severely handicapped students.* Baltimore, MD: Paul H. Brookes.

Sandberg-Diment, E. (1984, June 20). Light pen: Clever but clumsy—And is it needed? *The Baltimore Sun*, p. C-8.

Schrage, M. (1984, January 16). Programmable touchpads open versatile link with computers. [Business Section]. *Washington Post*, p. 19.

Schwejda, P., & McDonald, J. (1983). *Motor training games.* Seattle, WA: University of Washington.

Schwejda, P., & Vanderheiden, G. (1983, February/March). Adaptive firmware card for Apple II. *Closing the Gap*, pp. 1, 10, 13, 14, 19.

Schworm, R. W., & Abelseth, J. L. (1978). Teaching the individual with severe learning problems: Strategies which point to success. *Education and Training of the Mentally Retarded, 13,* 146–153.

Snell, M. E. (1983). *Systematic instruction of the moderately and severely handicapped.* Columbus, OH: Bell & Howell.

Taber, F. M. (1981). The microcomputer—Its applicability to special education. *Focus on Exceptional Children, 14*(2), 1–14.

Taber, F. M. (1983). *Microcomputers in special education.* Reston, VA: The Council for Exceptional Children.

Thomas, M. A. (Ed.). (1982). Microcomputers' place in special education. [Special issue]. *Exceptional Children, 49*(2).

Trachtman, P. (1984, November). Putting computers into the hands of children without language. *Smithsonian, 14*(11), 42–51.

Vanderheiden, G., & Grilley, K. (Eds.). (1976). *Nonvocal communication techniques and aids for the severely physically handicapped.* Baltimore, MD: University Park Press.

Williams, W., Brown, L., & Certo, N. (1975). Basic components of instructional programs for severely handicapped students. *American Association for the Education of the Severely and Profoundly Handicapped Review, 1,* 1–39.

Wilson, M. S., & Fox, B. J. (1982). *First words.* Burlington, VT: Laureate Learning Systems.

Zeaman, D., & House, B. J. (1963). The role of retention in retardate discrimination learning. In N. E. Ellis (Ed.), *Handbook of mental deficiency* (pp. 159–223). New York: McGraw-Hill.

PART V

SOCIAL REALITIES: EVALUATION, MEDIA, AND PUBLIC POLICY

CHAPTER 12

EVALUATING THE EFFECTS OF TEACHING WITH COMPUTERS

James A. Kulik
Center for Research on Learning and Teaching
The University of Michigan
Ann Arbor, Michigan 48109

During the past 20 years, computer technology has changed the way researchers carry out their research. During the past 10 years, it has changed the way writers compose their articles. During the next 10 years, it will change the way teachers teach. Microcomputers, computer communications, computer-controlled videodiscs, and other electronic marvels will enter the classroom and alter forever the methods teachers use to pass on knowledge and skills to future generations.

What impact will all this have on learners? Will children learn more easily with computer help? Will they enjoy school when more of their learning is computer-mediated? Will computers help teachers achieve a variety of educational goals, or will they be useful for only certain goals in certain subject areas? Will computer technology be worth its cost?

For more than two decades now, educational evaluators have been examining the effects of computers on learners. They have carried out hundreds of studies comparing results from classes taught with and without computer aid. And for the past 10 years, reviewers have attempted to synthesize findings from the various studies into a coherent picture. The purpose of this chapter is to describe the product of all these efforts and to indicate what work still remains to be done to fill in the missing parts of the picture.

THE MAKING OF A REVOLUTION

The Carnegie Commission on Higher Education in 1972 forecast a computer revolution in education and predicted that it would sweep over all levels of education before the end of this century. The Commission labeled it "the fourth revolution" because it was to rival in importance three earlier transformations of education. The first of these occurred when societies first shifted the task of educating the young from the home to the school and from parents to teachers. The second came with the adoption of the written word as a tool of education. And the third occurred after the invention of printing made books widely available for use in teaching. The Carnegie Commission thus considered the computer to be as significant an invention for education as were schools, teachers, writing, and books.

Programmed Instruction

The fourth revolution in teaching began modestly enough three decades ago. The event that marks its beginning was the publication of B. F. Skinner's 1954 article, "The Science of Learning and the Art of Teaching." Skinner argued that the application of technology to education would make teaching more scientific and thus more effective. He reported that he had already developed machines that could present material in controlled sequences, keep learners responding actively, reinforce correct responses immediately, and give learners freedom to move through material at their own learning rates. The machines seemed capable of doing nearly everything that good teachers did.

Instructional programs were soon available for every subject and grade level, and Skinner's programmed machines seemed destined to transform education. Within a few years, however, critics began to find flaws in Skinner's machines. Their fill-in-the-blank format atomized lessons and sometimes left the structure of course material unclear. The sequence of instructional frames in the programs was the same for all learners, no matter what their backgrounds, and the frames were often lifeless and dull. Research and evaluation findings did not reassure the critics. Experimental studies sometimes supported premises of programmed instruction, and sometimes did not (Gage & Berliner, 1979). Field evaluations raised as many questions about programmed instruction as they answered (C. Kulik, Shwalb, & Kulik, 1982; Kulik, Cohen, & Ebeling, 1980; Schramm, 1964).

Individualized Instruction

Although Skinner's teaching machines began to lose some of their appeal, the dream of an instructional revolution did not die. The revolution's prophets simply hitched their hopes to a new approach: individualized instruction. Like programmed instruction, individualized instruction is a "low," paper-and-pencil technology that allows students to work independently on school tasks. It differs from programmed instruction, however, in requiring students to work on longer units—often called learning activity packages or modules—and in giving them freedom to choose among different means of achieving unit objectives. In the middle 1960s, individualized instruction seemed to incorporate the best features of programmed instruction while eliminating the main drawbacks.

Individualized systems, however, fared no better in experimental evaluations than did programmed instruction (Bangert, Kulik, & Kulik, 1983; Miller, 1976; Schoen, 1976). Evaluators carried out numerous studies of the effectiveness of individualized instruction at the precollege level, for example, and few of the studies reported dramatic results. In study after study, use of individualized systems of teaching improved neither student learning nor student attitudes toward school. Reviewers finally had to conclude that the effects of individualized instruction were either trivial or slightly negative on elementary and secondary students.

Development of Computers

Although instructional technologists were discouraged by the poor showing of this second-generation technology, they did not abandon hope for an instructional revolution. Two events encouraged them in their work. The first was the development of high-speed computers. By the early 1960s these machines were already doing a variety of research and administrative tasks at educational institutions, and their potential for use in instruction was becoming evident. Carter (1962), for example, considered the computer's relevance to major goals of educational systems. His list of school goals included imparting subject matter, training in thinking and creativity, developing skills and techniques, developing attitudes, socializing, physical development, and "child care." He concluded that computers could help schools achieve each of these goals.

The second thing that changed the prospects of a fourth revolution in education was the invention of the microcomputer chip. The cost of computing has declined dramatically in the years since the chip was developed, and cost is no longer an obstacle to the widespread use of computers in education. A teacher who only a few years ago had to persuade a state or city school board to make a commitment of $10,000 or $20,000 for a minicomputer or access to a time-sharing system now needs only to persuade a parent-teachers' association to purchase a $1000 microcomputer. The microcomputer has put computing power into the hands of teachers.

Together, these two developments are making these watershed years in the history of education. Signs of change are everywhere. Computer stores carry full lines of educational software. Advertisements for computers and instructional programs fill the pages of magazines for teachers. Parents send their kids off to computer camps and agitate at parent-teachers' meetings for more computer instruction in the schools. Meanwhile, school personnel are facing hard decisions about which machines and programs to buy, and they are wondering about the effects that the computer revolution will have on children.

EVALUATION STUDIES

Evaluation studies do not give answers to all the questions that teachers ask about computer-based instruction (CBI), but they do provide a concrete starting point for thinking about the effects of instructional technology on learners. In a typical evaluation study, a researcher divides a class of students into an experimental and a control group. Members of the experimental group receive part of their instruction at computer terminals, whereas students in the control group receive their instruction by conventional teaching methods. At the end of the experiment, the researcher compares responses of the two groups on a common examination or on a course evaluation form. Researchers carried out more than 150 such studies during the 1960s and 1970s.

Three of the largest-scale evaluations were carried out by the Educational Testing Service (ETS). The first two focused on major CBI systems developed with National Science Foundation support (Alderman, 1978; Murphy & Appel, 1977). The systems were PLATO (Programmed Logic for Automatic Teaching Operators) and TICCIT (Time-shared, Interactive, Computer-Controlled Information Television). PLATO, which was developed at the University of Illinois under the direction of Donald Bitzer for a large-scale computing network, has been extensively used for providing supplemental CBI. TICCIT, which was developed under the direction of Victor Bunderson at the University of Texas and Brigham Young University, uses minicomputers and modified television sets to provide full courses of instruction.

The evaluation of PLATO was based on field tests in five community colleges in Illinois. The evaluators of PLATO reported that both students and teachers reacted favorably to this computer-based system, but that PLATO had little impact on student achievement. The evaluation of TICCIT was based on field tests in two community colleges in Arizona and Virginia, where TICCIT minicomputers provided the total instruction in courses in English and mathematics. Evaluators of TICCIT reported that this system resulted in improved achievement of students who completed the courses, but students in TICCIT classes were less likely to complete course work in a semester's time. Neither evaluation provided evidence that CBI had reached the potential that developers had been claiming for it.

The third ETS evaluation gave a very different picture of the effectiveness of CBI (Ragosta, 1983). The study was a 4-year project carried out in four elementary schools in the Los Angeles School District. In each of the schools half of the first through sixth graders were given access to 10 to 20 minutes of computer-assisted drill and practice in mathematics and language arts each day; the other half of the students did not receive this computer assistance. Significant gains occurred in both areas, but the pattern of increases was clearer in mathematics. At the end of the first year, the CBI mathematics students were at the 64th percentile compared to the 50th percentile for non-CBI students. At the end of the second year, the CBI students were at the 71st percentile; at the end of the third year, they were at the 76th percentile.

Although these were large-scale evaluations, they do not provide the last word on CBI effectiveness. These evaluations have too many special characteristics to be truly representative. They used specific research designs with specific populations; they investigated specific computer systems; and they were produced at specific times in the development of CBI. How do the results from these evaluations compare to the results of a hundred other evaluations, carried out at other times in different settings and in different populations?

NARRATIVES AND BOX SCORES

Review articles on CBI effectiveness provide an overview of results from the evaluation studies. The early reviews can be classified into two basic types: narratives and box scores. Narrative reviews usually provide verbal descriptions, arranged thematically or chronologically, of relevant studies and then draw general conclusions about the topic of the review. Box-score reviews report the proportion of studies favorable and unfavorable toward an experimental treatment or hypothesis.

Narrative Reviews

Feldhusen and Szabo (1969) wrote one of the first narrative reviews on CBI research. Their review verbally summarized procedures and results of 14 comparative studies. They cautioned that some of the studies were of poor quality and poorly reported, but nevertheless they felt justified in concluding that CBI teaches at least as well as live teachers or other media, that it results in a saving of instructional time, and that students respond favorably to it. Feldhusen and Szabo's final words on CBI were optimistic. The classroom, they stated, "has a new viable heart, the computer, which will bring new levels of instructional vitality to the classroom and enable education to survive the challenge of the decades ahead" (p. 271).

Chambers and Sprecher's (1980) article provides a more recent example of a narrative review. These authors also reviewed 14 outcome studies, and like Feldhusen and Szabo, they reached favorable conclusions about CBI's potential. They found that students learned as much or more from CBI as from traditional classroom instruction. They also concluded that students learned the course material in less time with computer help and that students developed positive attitudes toward the use of computers in teaching as a result of their exposure to computers.

Narrative reviews have come in for heavy criticism in recent years. Reviewers who use the approach usually report so little about their methodology that readers cannot judge the validity of their conclusions. Readers cannot tell whether the studies selected for a review are truly representative, whether the results of the studies are reported impartially and precisely, or whether conclusions follow directly from study results. Evidence from narrative reviews cannot stand alone. It needs to be supplemented with other evidence.

Box-score Reviews

Box-score reviews of CBI effectiveness have also concluded that the computer can be used to enhance student achievement. Vinsonhaler and Bass's (1972) review, for example, reported on results from 10 independent studies of computer-based drill and practice in elementary schools. Three of the studies covered instruction in language arts, and seven covered mathematics teaching. Together, the 10 studies described results from a total of 34 separate comparisons of computer-based and conventional teaching. Results of most of the comparisons were statistically significant and favored CBI; only 2 of 34 differences favored conventional instruction.

Edwards, Norton, Taylor, Weiss, and Dusseldorp's (1975) box-score review also reached positive conclusions about the effectiveness of CBI. Their review, however, covered a broader range of educational levels and content areas, and examined use of the computer not only in drill and practice but also in tutorial instruction, problem solving, and simulations. Findings were especially clear when CBI was used to supplement conventional teaching. Of the nine relevant studies reviewed, all showed that normal instruction supplemented by CBI was more effective than was normal instruction alone. Findings were less clear when CBI substituted, in whole or in part, for traditional instruction: nine studies showed that CBI students achieved more than non-CBI students, whereas eight studies found little or no difference and three studies showed mixed results. Finally, all studies of instructional time showed that it took less time for students to learn through CBI than through other methods.

These box-score reviews overcome some of the limitations of narrative reviews, but they have shortcomings of their own. First, the validity of the box scores depends to a large extent on the reliability with which studies can be sorted into the two categories of "favorable" and "unfavorable." Different reviewers sort studies differently, and their tallies often turn out to be unreliable. Second, box-score reviewers do not say *how much* better one method is than another; they simply report *how often* one of the methods comes out on top. Readers need to know whether a given method wins by a nose or in a walkaway. Finally, box-score reviewers do not use statistical methods to find the characteristics that distinguish studies with positive results from those with negative findings. Trying to distinguish between the two types of studies without using statistics is like trying to grasp the sense of hundreds of test scores without using statistical methods to organize the data.

QUANTITATIVE SYNTHESES

To overcome the limitations of narrative and box-score reviews, Glass (1976) introduced a set of objective procedures that he dubbed "meta-analysis" in his presidential address

to the American Educational Research Association. By meta-analysis, Glass simply meant the statistical analysis of a large collection of results from individual studies for the purpose of integrating the findings. Researchers who carry out a meta-analysis first locate studies of an issue by clearly specified procedures. They then characterize the outcomes of all studies on a common scale of effect size. The effect size for a given study describes in standard deviation units the difference in performance of the experimental and control groups. Meta-analysts next describe study features in categorical or quasi-quantitative terms. Finally, they use multivariate techniques to describe findings and relate characteristics of studies to study outcomes.

Achievement Effects

Hartley, who was the first to apply meta-analysis to findings on CBI, focused on mathematics education in elementary and secondary schools (Hartley, 1978). She reported that the average effect of CBI in 35 separate studies was to raise student achievement by .41 standard deviations, or from the 50th percentile to the 66th percentile. Hartley also reported that the effects produced by computer-based teaching were not quite so large as those produced by programs of peer and cross-age tutoring, but they were far larger than effects produced by programmed instruction or the use of individual learning packets.

Burns and Bozeman (1981), like Hartley, used meta-analysis to integrate findings on computer-assisted mathematics instruction in elementary and secondary schools. These reviewers located 40 studies in which CBI drill and practice or tutorials supplemented traditional classroom instruction. They found an overall increase in achievement scores of .45 standard deviations with computer-based tutorial instruction and an improvement of .34 standard deviations with drill and practice.

J. Kulik and his colleagues carried out three separate meta-analyses of findings on CBI. The first of these (J. Kulik, Kulik, & Cohen, 1980) examined applications of CBI in college classes. A total of 54 of the 59 studies located for this meta-analysis looked at achievement test results. Nearly two-thirds of these studies came from courses in mathematics, science, and engineering; many of the remaining studies came from psychology and the social sciences. The effect of CBI in a typical class was to raise student achievement by approximately .25 standard deviations, or from the 50th to the 60th percentile.

The second of the meta-analyses by Kulik and his colleagues covered 51 studies of CBI in grades 6 through 12 (J. Kulik, Bangert, & Williams, 1983). A total of 48 of the studies reported achievement test results. About half of these examined CBI effects on mathematics teaching, and about one-quarter examined CBI effects in other science areas. The studies covered a variety of uses of the computer: drill and practice, tutorials, management of instruction, simulation exercises, and practice in programming as a means of increasing cognitive skills. The average effect of CBI in the 48 studies was to raise achievement scores by .32 standard deviations, or from the 50th to the 63rd percentile.

The most recent of the meta-analyses by Kulik and his associates covered 29 comparative studies at the elementary school level (C. Kulik, Kulik, & Bangert-Downs, 1984). This meta-analysis showed clear positive effects of computer-based teaching, but the effects differed for off-line computer-managed instruction (CMI) and for interactive computer-assisted instruction (CAI). In 25 studies, CAI programs of drill and practice and tutorial instruction raised student achievement by 0.48 standard deviations, or from the 50th to the 68th percentile, or by ap-

proximately 5 months on a grade-equivalent scale. In four studies, CMI programs raised student achievement by only 0.07 standard deviations, or by only a trivial amount.

Achievement Effects and Study Features

Effects of computer-based teaching may be different at different instructional levels. Results from the area of mathematics teaching illustrate this point most clearly. Computer-based teaching appears to raise examination scores in mathematics by .40 standard deviations at the elementary level, by .30 standard deviations at the secondary level, and by only .10 standard deviations at the college level (J. Kulik, 1981). At the lower levels of instruction, learners appear to benefit more from the stimulation and guidance provided by a highly reactive teaching medium. It is not yet clear, however, that this relationship between CBI results and instructional level holds true in all content areas.

Short-term studies of CBI have sometimes reported stronger effects than have long-term studies. This may mean that the novelty of using a computer plays some role in its effects on students. If this is the case, the short-term studies give an exaggerated picture of the true effects of CBI. It is also possible to argue, however, that short-term studies are usually better controlled than are long-term studies. If this is true, the shorter studies may merit the more serious consideration. In either case, findings on the relationship between study duration and outcome are not strong and are not entirely consistent from meta-analysis to meta-analysis. The strongest support for a relationship between study length and size of effect comes from J. Kulik, Bangert, and Williams's (1983) meta-analysis of secondary school findings, and even in this study the difference in results from long- and short-term studies reached only borderline significance.

Meta-analysts have also reported other relationships between CBI results and study features, but these relationships are even less firmly established. Hartley (1978) found that CBI was relatively ineffective in the few studies where it was used as a complete replacement for conventional teaching. C. Kulik, Kulik, and Bangert-Downs (1983) found off-line computer-managed instruction to be far less effective than interactive computer-assisted instruction in elementary schools. J. Kulik, Bangert, and Williams's (1983) meta-analysis on secondary school applications of CBI found somewhat greater effectiveness in more recent implementations of CBI, reflecting, perhaps, an increase in the quality of CBI software in secondary schools in recent years. Other meta-analysts, however, have not found a time trend in study outcomes.

Other Effects

The positive effect that the computer has on students is not limited to the improvement of content learning. The computer also has positive effects in the attitudinal domain. J. Kulik, Bangert, and Williams (1983) found that students who learned with computer assistance developed far more favorable attitudes toward computers than did students who received all of their instruction by conventional means. Use of the computer in instruction may therefore help prepare students for the computer society in which they will live and work. With more than half of all workers projected to be using computers in their jobs by the end of this century, the effects of computer-based teaching on attitudes toward computers are of great potential importance.

J. Kulik, Bangert, and Williams (1983) also found that the computer has small but positive effects on secondary school students' attitudes toward school and toward the sub-

jects that they are learning with computer help. In 10 studies examining attitudes toward subject matter, for example, the average size of effect was .12 standard deviations; and in another 4 studies examining ratings of the quality of instruction, the average size effect was .19 standard deviations. Results from J. Kulik, Kulik, and Cohen's (1980) meta-analysis of college level studies were consistent with secondary level findings. The average effect of CBI at the college level was to improve attitudes toward instruction by .24 standard deviations and attitudes toward subject matter by .18 standard deviations.

Computer-based instruction also produced substantial savings in instructional time (J. Kulik, Bangert, & Williams, 1983; J. Kulik, Kulik, & Cohen, 1980). Several studies showed that students can learn more quickly with computer assistance than with conventional teaching methods. Although the claim of quicker learning has been made for programmed instruction also, findings for computer-based teaching are far more dramatic than are findings for programmed instruction. This time-saving effect of computer-based teaching is potentially as important as are its effects on student achievement.

FUTURE EVALUATIONS

Research studies have already documented the contributions that the computer is making to instruction. Computers have raised student achievement in numerous studies. They have given students a new appreciation for technology and have had positive effects on students' attitudes toward schools and teaching. Moreover, computers have helped teachers save instructional time.

The size of these contributions may at first glance seem small. The increases on examination scores, for example, have averaged less than one-half a standard deviation or less than 5 months on a grade-equivalent scale. But further reflection should reveal that increases of this magnitude are large enough to have major significance for education. Increases of even 1% in the effectiveness or efficiency of education can produce great benefits for society because of the vast size of the educational enterprise. The changes produced by computer-based teaching are far larger than this.

And yet there is no reason for researchers to be complacent and abandon the task of further evaluating computer-based teaching. The years ahead may turn out to be the most important ones ever in the development of computer-based teaching for the schools. They should also be important years in the evaluation of computer-based teaching. In the next few years, it may be possible to fill in the picture of effectiveness that has begun to emerge from evaluation studies.

The picture needs filling in, first of all, because computer hardware has been evolving rapidly. Evaluation studies have lagged far behind this development. Most evaluation studies have examined the effectiveness of programs written for mainframe computers and minicomputers. Terminals used in the studies were often primitive; learner time at the terminals was limited; computer response was sometimes slow, and "down time" was often high. The introduction of the microcomputer solves some of the problems that plagued early implementations of computer-based teaching, but it introduces complications of its own. Microcomputer-based systems have their own characteristics: their own software, their own management systems, and their own scale of operations. Teaching with microcomputers is worthy of study in its own right.

The pace of development of instructional software has also been increasing. The first instructional programs for computers did a limited number of tasks. They presented lessons, gave learners drill and practice on course materials, administered and scored tests, and managed instruction. These are basically tutorial functions, and they exploit only a small part of the computer's potential.

Recent applications have broadened teacher conceptions of the role that computers play in education (Taylor, 1980). In addition to serving a tutorial function, computers are now used by students as learning tools and even as "tutees." The computer is a tool for students when they use it as a calculator in mathematics and science assignments; as a map-maker in geography; as a facile, tireless performer in music; or as a text editor and copyist in English. The computer functions as a tutee when children "teach" it in a language that they understand. Few evaluation studies are available on these exciting new uses of the computer. More evaluation work is needed.

Evaluators also need to investigate a wider range of educational outcomes than they have in the past. They have repeatedly examined computer effects in such areas as pupil scores on final examinations, school attitudes, attitudes toward computers, and instructional efficiency. These are certainly important educational outcomes, but they are not the only instructional effects worth knowing about. In addition to scores on final examinations, teachers and educational planners need to know about long-range retention, effects on higher order skills, transfer of gains to other areas, and interpersonal outcomes of computer uses in the classroom. Only a few studies (e.g., Feldman & Sears, 1970; Ragosta, 1983) have examined such effects.

Finally, CBI evaluators must ultimately address the question, Why has the computer helped students to the extent it has? How does it influence student learning? Which features of the computer make it so effective? Is it the absolute consistency in the computer's response, or the computer's comparative impartiality? Does computer effectiveness stem from the novelty that the computer brings to instruction? Or is the immediacy of the computer's response the central thing? Are computer lessons equally effective when presented without electronic technology? How important is the social setting in which CBI is used? Process rather than outcome studies are needed to answer such questions, and process studies are needed in sufficient numbers for quantitative synthesis of results. It will take an enormous effort to produce the studies and to synthesize their findings, but judging by what has already been achieved, the effort may prove to be worthwhile.

SUMMARY

The effectiveness of technology in education has changed in the past, and it will undoubtedly change even more in the future. The "low" technologies of programmed and individualized instruction arrived with great fanfare in the 1950s and 1960s, promising to improve the process and products of education. But they did not make strong contributions to instructional effectiveness in their original forms. Programmed and individualized instruction raised student achievement by only small amounts (.10 standard deviations), did not have positive attitudinal effects on students, and did not produce dramatic effects on student learning time.

These "low" technologies had a strong influence on the development of computer-based teaching. Early tutorial programs incorporated features of Skinnerian programmed learning, and later programs incorporated the management systems developed for individualized instruction. Evaluation studies show that the high-technology offspring, however, have far exceeded their low-technology parents in instructional effectiveness. In a typical study, computer-based teaching raised student achievement by .40 standard deviations, dra-

matically affected the amount of time needed for teaching and learning, and significantly altered student attitudes toward computers.

Talented educators have already developed new applications for computers in education and new conceptions of the educational outcomes that computers effect. Educational evaluators are starting to test the value of these new conceptions in empirical studies. The years ahead therefore promise to be exciting ones that may answer major questions about the best ways to use computers in teaching.

REFERENCES

Alderman, D. L. (1978). *Evaluation of the TICCIT computer-assisted instructional system in the community college* (ETS PR 78–10). Princeton, NJ: Educational Testing Service.

Bangert, R. L., Kulik, J. A., & Kulik, C.-L. C. (1983). Individualized systems of instruction in secondary schools. *Review of Educational Research, 53,* 143–158.

Burns, P. K., & Bozeman, W. C. (1981). Computer-assisted instruction and mathematics achievement: Is there a relationship? *Educational Technology, 21,* 32–39.

Carnegie Commission on Higher Education. (1972). *The fourth revolution: Instructional technology in higher education.* New York: McGraw-Hill.

Carter, L. F. (1962). The challenge of automation in education. In J. E. Coulson (Ed.), *Programmed learning and computer-based instruction* (pp. 3–12). New York: John Wiley & Sons.

Chambers, J. A., & Sprecher, J. W. (1980). Computer-assisted instruction: Current trends and critical issues. *Communications of the ACM, 23,* 332–342.

Edwards, J., Norton, S., Taylor, S., Weiss, M., & Dusseldorp, R. (1975). How effective is

CAI? A review of the research. *Educational Leadership, 33,* 147–153.

Feldhusen, J., & Szabo, M. (1969). The advent of the educational heart transplant, computer-assisted instruction: A brief review of research. *Contemporary Education, 40,* 265–274.

Feldman, D. H., & Sears, P.S. (1970). Effects of computer-assisted instruction on children's behavior. *Educational Technology, 10,* 14.

Gage, N.L., & Berliner, D. C. (1979). *Educational psychology* (2nd ed.). Chicago: Rand McNally.

Glass, G. V. (1976). Primary, secondary, and meta-analysis of research. *Educational Researcher, 5,* 3–8.

Hartley, S. S. (1978). Meta-analysis of the effects of individually paced instruction in mathematics. *Dissertation Abstracts International 38*(7-A), 4003. (University Microfilms No. 77–29, 926)

Kulik, C.-L. C., Kulik, J., & Bangert-Downs, R. L. (1984, April). *Effects of computer-based education on elementary school pupils.* A symposium paper presented at the annual meeting of the American Educational Research Association, New Orleans.

Kulik, C.-L. C., Shwalb, B. J., & Kulik, J. A. (1982). Programmed instruction in secondary education: A meta-analysis of evaluation findings. *Journal of Educational Research, 75,* 133–138.

Kulik, J. A. (1981, April). *Integrating findings from different levels of instruction.* Paper presented at the annual meeting of the American Educational Research Association, Los Angeles. (ERIC Document Reproduction Service No. ED 208 040)

Kulik, J. A., Bangert, R. L., & Williams, G. W. (1983). Effects of computer-based teaching on secondary school students. *Journal of Educational Psychology, 75,* 19–26.

Kulik, J. A., Cohen, P. A., & Ebeling, B. J. (1980). Effectiveness of programmed instruction in higher education: A meta-analysis of findings. *Educational Evaluation and Policy Analysis, 2,* 51–64.

Kulik, J. A., Kulik, C.-L. C., & Cohen, P. A. (1980). Effectiveness of computer-based college teaching: A meta-analysis of findings. *Review of Educational Research, 50,* 525–544.

Miller, R. L. (1976). Individualized instruction in mathematics: A review of research. *The Mathematics Teacher, 69,* 345–351.

Murphy, R. T., & Appel, L. R. (1977). *Evaluation of the PLATO IV computer-based education system in the community colleges* (ETS PR 77–10). Princeton, NJ: Educational Testing Service.

Ragosta, M. (1983). Computer-assisted instruction and compensatory education: A longitudinal analysis. *Machine-Mediated Learning, 1,* 97–127.

Schoen, H. L. (1976). Self-paced instruction: How effective has it been in secondary and post-secondary schools. *The Mathematics Teacher, 69,* 352–357.

Schramm, W. (1964). *Four case studies of programmed instruction.* New York: Fund for the Advancement of Education.

Skinner, B. F. (1954). The science of learning and the art of teaching. *Harvard Educational Review, 24,* 86–97.

Taylor, R. P. (Ed.). (1980). *The computer in the school: Tutor, tool, tutee.* New York: Teachers College Press.

Vinsonhaler, J. F., & Bass, R. K. (1972). A summary of ten major studies on CAI drill and practice. *Educational Technology, 12,* 29–32.

CHAPTER 13

ARE COMPUTERS BAD FOR CHILDREN?

Seymour Papert
Laboratory for Computer Sciences
Massachusetts Institute for Technology
Cambridge, Massachusetts 02139

Articles critical of computers in education have recently begun to appear in the press. Suddenly, it seems that everyone now knows they are bad for children—or at least not very good.

In an article entitled "Computer Worship," in *Science 84*, Menosky (May 1984) attacked the idea that computer literacy will be increasingly important in the job market and, therefore, should be made available to all children through the educational system, predicting that computers will have no more than "some limited role in education" (p. 46). This article quoted Daniel McCraken (professor of computer science at the City College of New York and author of textbooks on computer languages) as saying, "I see computer literacy as the New Math of the 1980's" (p. 40). A grade school teacher/computer literacy instructor in Scarsdale, New York wondered why we should spend thousands of dollars "for an electronic workbook when a plain old $2.95 workbook with lots of drill-and-practice sheets will do just as well" (p. 45).

The entire summer 1984 issue of Columbia University's *Teachers College Record* was devoted to what they described as a "critical perspective" on the computer in education. Perhaps the mildest criticism here was that "Modern technology neither destroys nor transforms the traditional context of education; it simply augments" (Simpson, 1984, p. 629); and it concluded that "unless we spend the money on people, however, money spent on chips is money down the drain" (Simpson, 1984, p. 628). More severe was the warning that if Papert's educational philosophies are adopted, "we will be transformed into a culture of psychopaths" (Sardello, 1984, p. 631).

This chapter was completed with the editorial collaboration of Wynter Snow.

ANSWERING THE CRITICS

I want to discuss this criticism from two viewpoints. I shall argue that these critics are missing the whole point of how we can use computers in education. But first, I see this journalistic switch as a phenomenon that has little to do with education or children or computers. It has to do with the press: We are looking at the backlash side of an inevitable pendulum swing.

Journalistic Backlash

The need to attract the eyes of an audience is a crucial factor in the dynamics of media hype. Journalists first discovered that one of the most photogenic scenes of our age was a child in front of a computer screen. The light from the screen catches in the eyes and you get a really marvelous effect, a beautiful picture. It was published everywhere, always the same: bright-eyed, smiling children in front of a computer screen. And until recently, the story that went with it was euphoric. The computer was a panacea. It could do no wrong.

There came a point, however, when the public couldn't stand it anymore. The next thing that became newsworthy was that computers are bad. So the pendulum swung, and now the press could fill pages for another year or so with stories of how bad computers are.

It is ironic that the journalist who wrote "Computer Worship" described this pattern in that same summer issue of the *Teachers College Record*: "By the close of 1982, personal computers had been all the rage in the media, but the subject was getting stale. The educational uses of computers and the need for computer literacy quickly became the angle that generated at least another year's worth of additional news features" (Menosky, 1984, p. 617). His purpose was to condemn the media's earlier enthusiasm for computers as unwarranted and exaggerated, but the dynamics he cited are identical.

So I think the reasons why the press is now writing negatively about computers have very little to do with computers or education. But of course the journalists cannot admit this. They have to refer to seemingly scientific sources. Among these, the most frequently cited is by Pea and Kurland (1984), two researchers at the Bank Street College of Education. "In several studies comparing children who learned Logo with control groups who did not, researchers at Bank Street College's Center for Children and Technology have been surprised to find that, as Jan Hawkins put it, 'Logo promises more than it has delivered'" (Hassett, 1984, p. 26).

Missing the Point

What did Logo promise that it did not deliver? Pea and Kurland (1984) stated that they set out to research the "widespread belief . . . that through learning to program, children . . . will acquire powerfully general higher cognitive skills such as planning abilities [and] problem-solving heuristics" (p. 138). They found "expanded claims for the cognitive benefits of programming in a new generation of theoretical writings" (p. 142)— one of these being *Mindstorms*, in which they claimed that I argued that "cognitive benefits will emerge from taking 'powerful ideas' inherent in programming (such as recursion and variables) in 'mind-size bites' (e.g., procedures)" (p. 142). Pea and Kurland (1984) also stated that I have been "an outspoken advocate of the Piagetian account of knowledge acquisition through self-guided problem solving experiences, and [have] extensively influenced conceptions of learning programming, through 'a process that takes place without deliberate or organized teaching'" (p. 142).

The implication seemed to be that I believe children will learn Logo without being taught and will, at the same time, undergo something called "cognitive effects." But what did I really say?

The context of that last phrase is that my "model of successful learning is the way a child learns to talk, a process that takes place without deliberate and organized teaching" (Papert, 1980, p. 8). I did not and do not mean learning without teach*ers*. The baby doesn't learn to speak in isolation. Adults and other children interact with the baby all the time as teachers—but there is none of the paraphernalia of school, of the professional teacher systematically following an elaborate curriculum. No quizzes, no grades, no report cards or formal evaluations, yet everybody learns to speak.

Teachers of English might say that most speech isn't grammatical, but that's not the point. People learn something of immense complexity through a process that is radically different from what we see at school, sufficiently different to use names to distinguish between the two. I call this spontaneous process "Piagetian learning" and the other "instruction."

PIAGETIAN LEARNING VS. INSTRUCTION

Piaget informed us of what a magnificent and wonderful learner the child is. Each child reconstructs the knowledge of the culture in which that child lives—the mathematics and language, social structure, and so on. Piaget's image of the child is wonderful and inspiring, filled with an optimistic view that children can do anything. How disturbing then, to walk into a school and see how difficult it seems to be to teach the child such "basics" as the multiplication tables.

One of the most acute dilemmas posed by Piaget's work is: Why are some things learned so easily while other things are so difficult? Why is the child able to learn certain things—such as language—in this spontaneous, Piagetian way? Why does certain other knowledge seem to require instruction? What *is* the vital difference between Piagetian learning and instruction? This question is not carefully posed, if it's posed at all, in most educational research today. If I had to single out one theme of what I'm trying to do with education, I would pick that issue.

Once we adopt the goal of moving entire blocks of knowledge from the category of "needing instruction" into the far more effective, less expensive, and relatively painless one of "Piagetian learning," it leads to a complete shakeup in how we see education and the teacher's role. We stop seeing the teacher as someone who stands at the front of a room and hands out knowledge like so many sacks of potatoes. When we truly absorb the view that children are the architects and builders of their own knowledge, we see the problems of classrooms in an entirely different light.

Children may be the builders of their intellectual structures, but like other builders, they need materials. What are the bricks and stones, the little pieces that are put together into these edifices? I argued in *Mindstorms* that these raw materials are largely found in the culture. Knowledge and information are embedded in our language, in our biological reactions to the world, in the knowledge possessed by people in our environment. The pieces we use to build great structures are all around us.

Some areas of knowledge are supported by the rich presence of the needed materials in the surrounding culture. When that happens, the child builds easily and successfully, with minimal assistance. Certain other areas of knowledge (such as formal mathematics) do not seem to have readily available cultural materials, yet it is important for people growing up in our society to possess

some of these types of knowledge, so we invented school.

There is a second reason why mathematics—let's call the as-taught-in-school version "math"—why math is so hard to learn. Since the cultural building blocks are sparse, math usually becomes something imposed on children, so it acquires a bad name. Math becomes associated with all the anxiety and fears and dislikes and alienations that characterize mathophobia and aggravate the situation. Not only are the cultural materials not present, but toxins are added as well, poisons that prevent the instruction process from working even as well as it might.

This contrast—between the culturally based, Piagetian learning and the culturally alienated, school-based instruction—is the central challenge facing educators today. School is essentially limited in its ability to deal with these kinds of gaps in the cultural building blocks. You can reform the curriculum and invent better ways of teaching it, but as long as you're on the "instruction" side of this dichotomy, it's a makeshift operation.

Better practices in the classroom won't change the situation. These "difficult" pieces of knowledge will become readily learnable only if the culture changes, and that's a tall order. How can you change the culture? Quite obviously, you cannot. But you *can* become sensitive to the trends and forces that *are* changing the culture. Maybe you can also learn to guide those forces in fruitful directions. I see the computer as a potential means of transforming education from instruction into something closer to the Piagetian model.

GENERATING CULTURAL BUILDING BLOCKS WITH LOGO

The question of how to generate the cultural building blocks needed to learn mathematics in a Piagetian way was very much on my mind when I came to the Massachusetts Institute of Technology (M.I.T.) in the mid-1960s after spending 5 years with Piaget in Geneva. The personal computer was then just below the horizon as something that could enter into the culture and change the way people think, relate, and deal with different pieces of knowledge. So I began to see the computer as a new cultural element, a key to changing the culture. The origin of Logo was just this: What can we do with this computer culture? How can we intervene in it in a way that can influence social forces?

It was obvious that programming was going to develop tremendously. A lot of effort would be devoted to working out how to program computers, developing programming languages, and so on. It was very likely that people would start saying, "Well, maybe children should also learn to program." What might be missed, however, was the possibility that children and adults could program together, that programming could become a shared activity for people with different degrees of sophistication, knowledge, and development in the society.

Logo was specifically designed with this capability. It would have been much easier to make one language for children and another for adults, but our goal was to make the language meaningful for both children *and* adults, in fact for everybody at every age—although in different ways, of course. Such a language would have several results that *could* change the culture. The computer's owner and the child could genuinely share the enterprise of carrying out a programming project. The classroom teacher could genuinely share with the child the ability, the immersion, the sense of power, the sense of exploration, that programming a computer can bring (McCauley, 1983–84).

We expressed this concept in a slogan: that Logo has no threshold and no ceiling. Logo is often described as "a language for children," but this is misleading. Just as English has certain pieces that babies can easily grasp to start learning it, but has no cut-off between this and the language that philosophers, poets, and scientists use to express highly sophisticated ideas, Logo is continuous in this same sense. There's no baby language and then another, separate, grown-up language. There's continuity. No threshold—and no ceiling. Once inside, you can move progressively and continuously—perhaps through different levels of understanding and not without focused effort—into contact with deep and powerful concepts and ideas, ideas that in fact *feel* meaningful to the sophisticated mind.

The learning that takes place when this type of culture develops is radically different from what one experiences through instruction. My favorite example of this is one that I keep repeating. For a while, I felt apologetic about describing the same story over and over again. But by gradually distilling out a few paradigmatic situations, one proceeds in understanding the world. You can't expect to meet more than one or two a year, or to have a large supply of them, and this is one of my favorites.

The Lamplighter School Example

The first time I saw something develop that I would call a computer culture was in the Lamplighter School in Dallas. This site was written up only in a scattered way until recently, but there's now a beautiful description of it in sociologist Sherry Turkle's (1984) book, *The Second Self*, which describes people's involvement with computers. The chapter called "Child Programmers" recounts some work we did together on the growth of a computer culture.

This was a primary school—unusual in the United States—where the children ranged from 3½ or 4 years old through fourth grade, and there were about 300 children altogether. Fifty computers were brought into the school, which was a large enough ratio for certain cultural events to take place. In particular, the movement of children and computers got completely out of the teachers' control. The teachers could not watch everything that was happening—there was too much going on—but the children had ample opportunity to observe each other.

This school also had open architecture, a pod-like arrangement with an open area and four or five classrooms, so the younger children could see what the older children were doing, and there was a great deal of coming and going. The children could also come in at least an hour earlier or stay in the building afterward, and many did. If the computers had been boxed into the usual box classrooms—so that third grade students did third grade computer work in the privacy of the third grade classroom—or were kept in a computer lab to which students went for separate periods of 2 or 3 hours each week—under those conditions, the phenomena that I'm talking about couldn't have happened, or would have happened in a very different way.

A sense of appropriating the computer as "their thing" grew up among this community of children. This produced varieties of experts and different schools of thought about what to do with the computer and what was good style. For example, there was a hard-core scientist who thought a program should have something technical in it in order to be interesting: a new technique, a new command of the language, or a new way of getting something done. There were others who didn't think like that at all. They did want to master the technical aspect, but for them, the aesthetic of what was put up on the screen was more important. The computer was an instrument to create visual or sound effects—often considered to be extremely frivolous by the others. So there were many tensions and dilemmas within this computer culture. It was by no means monolithic or uniform.

When the computers were first brought into the school, the teachers met to decide

what each age level should learn, using their sense of what children at different ages could understand. When Logo is presented to children, it's always embedded in a microworld, usually Turtle Geometry. In this microworld, an object called a turtle draws lines on the screen when you give it Logo commands such as FORWARD 50 and RIGHT 90. This turtle microworld needs to be distinguished from Logo "proper"—the programming language used to manipulate the turtle—and from other microworlds as well. This school was using the first version of a slightly different microworld of dynamic turtles—called sprites—which could be made to move about freely on the screen.

In order to make this sprite move, you had to tell it both a speed and a direction, saying something like SETHEADING 270. The teachers reasoned, wrongly as it happens, that these dynamic sprites would be too "advanced" for the younger children because they didn't know about degrees, and numbers like 270 were pretty meaningless to them.

Now for me, saying we shouldn't talk to children about these numbers is like saying that babies can't talk, so we shouldn't talk to babies. That would be a good way to ensure that babies can't talk. In the case of language and what we know about acquiring it, we never doubt such a conclusion—but we have yet to think this way about mathematics.

So the teachers decided that the lower three classes would not get the dynamic, moving turtle because it was too rooted in directions and degrees and large numbers. They would get only the static turtle instead. This created a very unstable situation. The children in the lower grades began to work with what they were given, the static turtle that drew lines and geometric figures and drawings—which they enjoyed and learned a lot from—but they were seeing the older children doing other things. Soon, one of the second graders asked a fourth grader, "How do you do that?" And he kept asking until he understood enough to take back a little fragment of knowledge.

He didn't take back anything like a full understanding of what degrees are, or what 270 means. He took back a *little fragment*, a little bridge that he and his colleagues could work on. When I came in, he had 14 of his friends all working on what he described as "cracking the code." He had a way of thinking I had never seen or thought of. He said, "We've got the idea. Numbers are codes for directions. We haven't figured out the code, but we're working on it." A few months later, they had perfect control over all the directions, the entire 360 degrees through which the sprites could move.

Analysis in Terms of Cultural Learning

I'd like to contrast this kind of observation with the experiments typically done by educational psychologists and their colleagues, experiments that are supposedly "rigorous" and "scientific" merely because they use statistical analysis.

First of all, we didn't know in advance what this study might discover. It was serendipitous. But I think all learning and expansion of knowledge happens like that. Those children learned something about numbers and directions because they could pick out bits and pieces of Logo and experiment with them. And we learned something about how children can learn in a computer culture when those bits and pieces are embedded in a microworld.

Second, this happened at the social level, and it was made possible by social conditions that existed at that school. It could easily have been missed by the typical scheduling patterns of statistical samplings.

Third, it was fueled by some powerful feelings. Our more informal observations pick these up very easily, but statistical studies are narrowly and selectively focused, ignoring anything that isn't on their agenda of hypotheses.

When that boy told me they were cracking the code, there was a sense of subversion in his voice. He *knew* this was a taboo thing, and he *knew* that somebody had decided that this was stuff for older people. So the children were driven by the powerful desire to acquire what adults have—a force that gets nullified in this thing called school. In Piagetian, cultural learning, what you pick up, struggle with, and practice are those things that you see older people around you doing— whether it's dancing, singing, talking, mathematics, or working at the computer. You want to possess what you don't yet have *in the culture.*

These are important aspects of educational research, categories I would use to look at what effects computers have on children's learning. They contrast in almost every way with the research conducted in the Pea and Kurland Bank Street study.

PROGRAMMING AND PLANNING: ARE THEY AKIN?

Pea and Kurland (1984) stated quite explicitly that their purpose was to examine certain beliefs about "the" cognitive effects on children of learning programming, two beliefs in particular that "are polar opposites and neither is acceptable" (p. 138). Thus, we should recognize that from the start their bias was toward finding a "negative result."

Specifically, they decided that the obvious cognitive effect of learning to program computers should be an improvement in one's ability to plan. Why do they think that learning computer programming should increase one's ability to plan?

There is an explanation. In our culture, computer programs are seen as highly logical, analytic, structured plans. But in fact, I don't think many computer programmers think of them like that. And in practice, nothing could be further from the truth. This idea, that programming and planning are somehow akin, comes from the way in which computer programming has become an industry and production-line activity: The organization of the enterprise increasingly imposes systematic planning onto both programmers and programming. Karl Marx is far more relevant to explaining this phenomenon than is Jean Piaget. The idea is not about the cognitive structure of programming; it's about the way in which the programming industry is organized and the way in which the images of production have affected what we see as the official ideology of programming. Pea and Kurland are prisoners of a cultural process rooted in the material relations of production.

Planning as Personality

In any case, when we observe children, or when we observe adult programmers working in free environments, we see that planning is only one relatively minor aspect of programming. Far more fundamentally, planning is an expression of personality. Some people love to plan. They love the idea of working out in advance exactly what they want this thing to do, setting it up, designing it, and then making it do precisely that.

Other people absolutely hate planning. For them, it is anathema—as a way of programming or anything else. They want to jump in and make the computer do something. They'll do some little thing, a step in the direction they want to go, then look at what emerges and see how to make it do something more complicated. They want to elaborate on what they've created so far. The nicest description of this sort of thing that I know is Lévi-Strauss (1966) talking about the "bricolage" style of thinking of so-called primitive societies. That is, you don't work in a systematic way, applying general rules,

Instead, you draw on all your pockets of knowledge as you go along. With children we find both these types, the planners and the antiplanners.

Pea and Kurland, however, reflecting the social concept of programming, defined their test of programming's cognitive effect as whether or not it increases the children's planning ability. So they set up an experiment. None of the context is reported to us in their published papers; we are told nothing about the architecture or the interactions among the children or the adults. We are told only that these children have "had" 30 hours of Logo, whatever that means. Logo is the independent variable, and planning is the dependent variable, and you interpret the results as whether or not learning Logo has a cognitive effect.

Actually, it surprises me that Pea and Kurland didn't find a *negative correlation* with planning. That's probably because they didn't do the experiment very well. If we'd gone into that computer culture at Lamplighter School or some others where we've researched uses of the computer in more depth and detail, I think we'd find the children doing much *less* planning.

The reason for that is quite important. One of those toxins of school that I referred to earlier is the imposition of the planned, analytic mode of thinking on everybody, whether it fits their personality type or not. Our education systems then become highly biased toward the obsessive type of personality that likes the detail or the planning, and highly biased against people who, like myself, are more hysterical in personality type, more bricoleur, who prefer movement and change and like to make things happen.

One reason why school is experienced by bricoleur types as so constraining is that what happens to them is very similar to what happened to left-handed children when we forced them to write with their right hands: The consequences to them were disruptive and serious.

ENHANCING INDIVIDUAL STYLE IN THE LOGO ENVIRONMENT

My picture of what happens when children are allowed to explore Logo in their own style is that each child's individual style is strengthened. The planners are already fairly happy at school, in the math class anyway. They might be unhappy in the art class. But they're used to planning; they've done it all their lives. They plan in their Logo work too, but 40 or 60 hours of Logo in a study such as Pea and Kurland's can add little to their already extensive planning experience. It is the antiplanners who will show strong effects quickly. They are quite clearly unhappy in their traditional environments. One important reason is that they're being coerced into suppressing their nonplanning style of thinking and doing.

In a good Logo environment, one of the most exciting things that happens is that the antiplanners find themselves with support for their bricolage. In a sense, they get permission to express and be what they are. This complex technology, this very scientific and technical thing, can in fact be mastered in their style. So they feel liberated and allow their nonplanning style to blossom.

Something very similar shows up in the responses throughout the world to my book, *Mindstorms* (1980). Millions of people have felt a systematic put-down in the educational system, particularly in math class. Their natural way of thinking—with all its chaos and interaction and associations; its different, but equally valid, intuitions and thought—was dismissed as irrelevant and wrong. Then suddenly, somebody came along and said, "It's okay, go ahead and use your own style of thinking."

The same thing happens to children in a good Logo environment. I think the net effect of Logo is that the antiplanners, who are probably the majority, heave a sigh of relief and go to it in their natural way, with the overall amount of planning decreasing as well.

One can criticize the methodologies of experiments in many ways, but one that I would like to emphasize here is that the Pea and Kurland study mirrors a way of thinking about the computer as an agent—that it has an effect on the individual child. This is absolutely contrary to anything that is in the spirit of Piagetian learning, and it is contrary to our goals in designing Logo.

The computer cannot change education or affect children, any more than Logo can promise anything or deliver anything. Only *people* can do these things; or perhaps one might say only cultures can. Both computers and Logo can be used in many different ways, regardless of their capabilities and potentials. We can "curriculumize" Logo—chop it up into different "levels"—as many teachers have tried to do. Or we can use Logo as it was designed, as a way of creating new cultural building materials that make possible new forms of Piagetian learning. How each approach will work out remains to be seen. But what we know in advance is that the interesting question is *not* what happens when computers, with or without Logo, are injected into the school with neither curriculum *nor* culture.

REFERENCES

Hassett, J. (1984, September). Computers in the classroom. *Psychology Today*, 22–28.

Lévi-Strauss, C. (1966). *The savage mind.* Chicago: University of Chicago Press.

McCauley, J. (1983–84). Kepler. *The Computer Teacher, 11*(5), 15–22.

Menosky, J. A. (1984). Computer literacy and the press. *Teachers College Record, 85*, 615–621.

Menosky, J. A. (1984, May). Computer worship. *Science 84*, 40–46.

Papert, S. (1980). *Mindstorms: Children, computers and powerful ideas.* New York: Basic Books.

Pea, R. D., & Kurland, D. M. (1984). On the cognitive effects of learning computer programming. *New Ideas in Psychology, 2,* 137–168.

Sardello, R. J. (1984). The technological threat to education. *Teachers College Record, 85,* 631–639.

Simpson, B. (1984). Heading for the ha-ha. *Teachers College Record, 85,* 622–630.

Turkle, S. (1984). *The second self: Computers and the human spirit.* New York: Simon & Schuster.

CHAPTER 14

MICROCOMPUTERS AND YOUNG CHILDREN: A PUBLIC OR A PRIVATE AFFAIR?

Lois-ellin Datta
Institute for Program Evaluation
General Accounting Office
Washington, DC 20548

Four statements about public and private influences on microcomputers and young children seem justified. First, the relationship already is more a public affair than a private matter. Second, its conduct is inadequately examined with regard to expenditures and consequences. Third, the probable consequences, at least for the present generation, are of concern. Fourth, despite the new judicial and legislative terrain created by microcomputers and the uncertainties associated with this *terra parvo cognita*, some better policies may be available.

SOME DEFINITIONS

These assertions are discussed in the following sections. In this discussion, *microcomputers* refers to the microprocessor and its innards: the software through which it operates and the courseware through which it may instruct. It also means all attachments such as devices designed to serve as prostheses (e.g., voice synthesizers for talking books for the blind child) or to expand modalities of exploration (e.g., devices transforming body movements into sounds and colors (see Weir, 1981). It does *not* mean such commonly available learning technologies as television, which now is available in over 95% of all homes for children of all income levels.

Young children refers to children from 3 to 8 years of age. In most federal and state educational legislation, 3 years of age is the lower limit for authorized expenditures on or public responsibility for educational services. The commonly recognized transition from the preschool and early elementary school period to the upper elementary grades is 8 years of age. During this period, some form of education is generally accepted as a public affair. Below 3 years of age, there are few precedents for a public concern that is primarily educational in nature.

In this discussion, *a public affair* means some financial support or other enabling policy affecting who has access to what kind of microcomputer for what purposes. Thus, a corporate donation of microcomputers to elementary schools is a public affair if it is encouraged by tax write-offs as a public relations or advertising business expense, supported by public funds for cost-sharing, or stimulated by public officials who received salaries while they were obtaining donations of microcomputers from the private sector. When costs are borne by the public sector directly—through allocation of funds received—or indirectly—through forgiveness of costs that could be taxed—it is considered in part a public matter.

PUBLIC INFLUENCES ON MICROPROCESSORS AND YOUNG CHILDREN: ACCESS, UTILIZATION, QUALITY, AND CONTENT

There are many ways in which public policies can influence use of microcomputers by young children. These are illustrated in terms of influences on access, utilization, quality, and content.

Access

There are three major instruments of public policy with regard to access: the courts, indirect legislation, and direct legislation. (By *legislation* is meant decisions of elected bodies at federal and state levels and the regulations and operations developed by executive branches of government to carry out legislative intent.)

The Courts. For almost a generation, the courts have decided expansively in response to suits involving access to education. Examples include decisions affecting special programs for language minority children and for handicapped children. While this trend may have slowed or reversed somewhat, court-ordered changes arguably have had more far-reaching influences on access to education than have legislative or other actions. At present there are no court decisons directly influencing access to microcomputers by young children.

Indirect Public Support. Analysis of the federal and state tax system has shown that roughly $14 billion annually is involved, an amount almost as large as the approximately $15.8 billion annually of direct federal aid for postsecondary, secondary, and elementary education (Barro, 1983). Barro has argued that the cumulative effects of tax system supports for education are regressive. Less affluent taxpayers pay proportionally more and receive less than wealthier taxpayers, who have access to such devices as the deductability of state and local property and income taxes (the bulk of which are used for public education), exemptions for children over 21 who are students, and deductability for educational and business expenses that may involve microcomputers.

Table 14–1 illustrates some of these public influences on access. It is difficult to obtain detailed information on how much is involved in different types of deductions or how these tax deductible funds are spent. As an example, we do not know precisely how many individuals claim professional development deductions on their income tax (a gap now closed in the 1984 returns); how many of these claims involve purchase of microcomputers as part of these deductions; and how many of those claiming such deductions use the microcomputers in part for the education or recreation of children in the fam-

TABLE 14–1.
Examples of Public Influences on Microcomputers and Young Children: Access

- Allowing income tax deductions for computer camps as part of the child care deductions for working parents.

- Allowing income tax deductions for home computers that may be used part of the time for children's education where purchase and other costs are written off as business or professional expenses.

- Allowing depreciation of home computers as business or professional expenses including microcomputers used some of the time for children's education.

- Allowing charitable deductions for individuals or corporations donating new or used microcomputers to nonprofit organizations including public and private schools.

- Allowing tax-exempt foundations to donate new and used microcomputers to nonprofit organizations including public and private schools.

- Allowing public funds to pay salaries of public or private school officials while they are seeking donations of new or used microcomputers.

- Authorizing purchase of microcomputers from impact aid funds, educational block grant funds, and other legislation not specifically targeted on microcomputers.

- Authorizing distribution of educational funds in a manner conducive to purchasing more for some age or income groups than others.

- Authorizing distribution of funds in a manner that encourages purchase of equipment such as microcomputers versus other uses.

- Authorizing programs aimed directly at purchase of microcomputers in a manner that concentrates or disperses funds differentially by age or income group.

ily. We can speculate, however, that those likely to claim microcomputers as part of the equipment needed to earn income (e.g., in managing their financial affairs or as a specific aid in their professions) are likely to be wealthier, and that the cumulative effects of such tax deductions are to concentrate access to microprocessors in the home among the wealthier rather than the poorer families.

It is unclear whether lower costs or other forces eventually will narrow this gap. In the early 1950s, television sets were concentrated in wealthier homes and concern existed about inequitable educational results. As noted earlier, today virtually all homes have at least one television set. The television access gap now is in how many homes in different income brackets have two sets or more; how old the set is; and whether it is color with remote channel switches and videorecorder attachments. In the longer term, perhaps in 10 or 20 years, the prices of home microcomputers may drop to such low levels that almost every family will be able to acquire one, and they could be as ubiquitous as television sets.

Questions may still remain, however, about utilization: Extremely inexpensive pocket calculators are available, for example, but may not be as widely purchased or fully exploited as the learning devices they could be. One might expect that in the near future games played through television sets will be available widely but access at home to microcomputers with educational packages will continue to be concentrated among the wealthier and better educated, and that this will be encouraged by tax policies.

Direct Public Support. Federal legislation affecting access to microcomputers concentrates rather than disperses funds. Impact aid, for example, is concentrated in areas around military installations and with many civilian federal agencies. These, in turn, generally are upper or middle income areas rather than low income areas, due to hous-

ing patterns. Thus, Montgomery County, Maryland, a suburb of Washington, DC, with one of the nation's highest average incomes, enjoys a largesse of impact aid since many middle and upper echelon federal civilian employees reside there and there are many federal agencies located in the county.

Indirect Effects of Educational Legislation. The educational block grant program includes a distribution formula which requires that a proportional share of funds be allocated to private schools. The distribution formulae, combined with reductions in total funds, have the effect of providing small amounts of money to many individual schools. Compared to prior distribution of these funds, the block grants are a windfall for the relatively richer districts, relatively richer schools, and private schools. The small amounts available to individual schools and uncertainties about the stability of the program, in turn, have influenced decisions to purchase supplies and equipment where adequate monies are available for basic operating costs (as they tend to be for wealthier private schools) and to help pay for regular expenses in the hard-pressed public schools in low income areas. Thus, some educational legislation not aimed directly at microcomputers is having a major effect in rapidly expanding access to microcomputers, albeit more for children in private than in public schools, and more for schools in middle income and wealthier areas than for schools serving children from poorer families.

Access for Young Children. Legislation focuses on older-age children with one exception. The legislation administered by the Office of Special Education Programs enables the use of funds for children from 3 years of age through 21 years of age, and several sections of this legislation focus on young children. Through a variety of special programs, the Office has encouraged a strong emphasis on young children in the hope that early detection and remediation will reduce or prevent later learning disabilities. The Office has equally encouraged development and use of microcomputers and other learning technologies for young children. Support is available through development funds, research funds, demonstration funds, and service funds to provide access to these devices for young handicapped children of all income levels. Both policies and available funds are much greater with regard to microprocessor access for young children through Office of Special Education Programs-administered legislation than through other agencies in the federal government, and support is available widely, generously, and creatively. Since eligibility is determined by handicapping condition rather than family income or wealth, it should be noted this legislation also has the effect of dispersing microcomputer access across income levels. Nevertheless, it is not a counter-balance to other federal policies that cumulatively encourage greater access for children from better-off families.

Project Head Start and federal programs enabling day care support do not place priority on the purchase of microcomputers. At a meeting on microcomputers and young children, Head Start officials noted that while they were keenly aware of the potential of these devices, Head Start programs, which have not given teachers a raise in a decade and which, due to shifts in eligibility and funds available for food stamps and school lunch programs, are hard pressed to provide a nutritious breakfast or lunch to Head Start children, do not have the resources to buy microcomputers. Thus, nationally, Head Start is not providing direct support funds or seed money leadership through research, demonstration, or development programs with regard to increased access. There are no national efforts through day care programs or funds administered through the federal government to increase microcomputer access in day care centers.

With regard to programs administered through the Department of Education, most focus on elementary and secondary education. The discretionary fund awards aimed at expanding educational use of microcomputers have gone to projects at the upper elementary and older grades; schools using Chapter II and other funds also are concentrating their microcomputer purchases at these levels.

The third federal source of support for the purchase of microprocessors, the science education programs administered by the National Science Foundation, is aimed at secondary and postsecondary education.

To date, the private and foundation sectors have not emphasized early childhood education in their programs dealing with microcomputers and education. While individual businesses may be donating some microcomputers to day care centers and Head Start programs, the emphasis has been on upper elementary and secondary schools. Foundations supporting research and development on microcomputers and young children—for example, support for work at the Bank Street College of Education from the Xerox, Spencer, Sloan, Carnegie, and New York Times Company Foundations—aim more at quality improvements and inquiry into the teaching and learning process through microcomputers than at expanded access per se.

Utilization

Access to microcomputers is one element of policy. Utilization of microprocessors and the quality of the instructional materials and approaches have equally important consequences for children. In this discussion, "courseware" includes both materials, such as the Logo software, and approaches to use of the materials, such as free discovery, guided discovery, or direct instructional techniques.

Teacher comfort with and use of microcomputers has been regarded as the primary influence on whether and how children use microprocessors that nominally may be available at home or in school (Feurzeig, Horwitz, & Nickerson, 1981). Information is difficult to obtain on how many teachers take advantage of the educational and professional expense provisions in the income tax codes to purchase microcomputers and obtain training in how to use them. Many colleges and universities have departments of computer science, where demand greatly is outstripping the supply of instructors. Many other departments offer related courses that may attract teachers, and some offer courses in microprocessors and early childhood education, which are said to be major attractions for students. Colleges of teacher education also offer special summer programs. Both Stanford University and Harvard University, for example, are advertising summer institutes on microcomputers in education, promising to provide each participant with a variety of important microcomputer user skills, essential knowledge to become a microcomputer resource specialist, practical methods for integrating microcomputers into schools, and realistic strategies for coping with rapidly changing educational computing opportunities and needs.

In addition, many professional organizations concerned with education and young children offer workshops on microcomputers and include symposia and presentations in which experiences with and research on use of microcomputers in home and center settings are discussed. Head Start programs and many school systems support staff development through payment of tuition, fees, released time, and occasionally travel and per diem expenses. It probably is fair to say that most teachers, including early childhood educators, have within fairly easy geographic reach courses to teach them how to use microprocessors for themselves and for teaching young children. The courses are said to be well-attended, and workshops offering special training are sellouts.

There are, in addition, many newsletters dedicated to promoting microcomputer use for personal and instructional purposes (e.g., *Education Computer News*, 1984) and a plethora of books on microprocessors. Subscription to these journals and newsletters, like attendance at college and university courses on microcomputers and early childhood education, is similar in nature to other teacher education courses and journals that can be considered acceptable tax deductions.

While it is not clear that these materials will meet the needs of all educators of young children—from those who are computer terrific to those who are terminal cases—it is clear that there are many offerings and that many are taking advantage of them. What is more uncertain is who is paying and with what distributional effects with regard to utilization. We do not know how many educators of young children are paying all or part of their own training expenses, how many use tax deductions to obtain some public support, how many are receiving training through the schools or day care centers with which they work, and whether the combination of new teachers who grew up computer friendly and those eager to catch up with the new technology are adequate for encouraging effective utilization.

Again, speculatively, teachers in schools rich in access to microcomputers are more likely than teachers in schools with meager access to microcomputers to seek and receive training in their use. If this is so, utilization, like access, may be more concentrated in middle income and wealthier schools. It also seems plausible that parents able to purchase microcomputers for business or personal use at home are better prepared to help their children use the microprocessors than are parents whose at-home access may depend on library or school loans of the equipment.

Public Expenditures on Teacher Training

Teacher inservice training traditionally has received considerable resources, but the jury is still out on how much teacher inservice is being supported through traditional sources that have been block granted, and of this, how much is aimed at funding microcomputer training.

The Office of Special Education Programs continues to have authorized and appropriated funds for teacher training, including funds aimed at young children's development through use of learning technologies.

National Science Foundation science education funds include substantial set-asides for teacher preservice and inservice training, including helping teachers better use microcomputers in the classroom. These programs are targeted, however, at upper elementary grades and beyond.

The Head Start program and day care programs have no initiatives in this area. Skill in using microcomputers for child development is not part of the Child Development Associates certification requirements.

The U. S. Department of Education, through the Secretary's discretionary funds and the National Institute of Education, does have an initiative in the learning, teaching, and computer area. The program includes support for demonstrations showing exemplary use of microcomputers in classrooms with teacher training components and research on what teachers need to know to use microcomputers effectively. These efforts are directed, however, at upper elementary and secondary levels. None emphasizes young children and their teachers. This also was true of earlier demonstrations supported jointly by the National Science Foundation and the National Institute of Education. These awards brought classroom teachers and computer experts together to show how effective computer approaches could be developed by classroom teachers. The projects spanned upper elementary through postsecondary years, in the mathematics/science areas only. However, the Institute now is supporting a research center on computers whose work may include some studies of young children and their use of

learning technologies as well as studies of their parents and teachers.

Teacher preparation for new emphases (educating handicapped children, bilingual education, and now microcomputers in the classroom) has been seen as a public responsibility. Current policies continue to support this with regard to teacher preparation for using microcomputers in the classroom, but training for the early childhood educator seems to be absent, low, or modest, rather than of central priority in national initiatives.

Quality

Public policies have varied considerably with regard to quality, which involves adequate attention to developing, testing and publicizing instructional materials and methods. At one time, public funds supported numerous curriculum development programs through conceptualization, development, testing, revision, and field-testing stages. In some instances, support extended through dissemination and marketing (for example, the direct and indirect support for the development of "Sesame Street," and, with less universally acclaimed results, curricula such as *Man: A Course of Study*). Prior to 1980, the National Institute of Education, the Libraries and Learning Technologies Program of the Education Department, and the National Science Foundation supported courseware development for computers. Efforts in the microcomputer area were halted in 1981 (for example, the joint National Science Foundation/National Institute of Education program). The reasons were philosophical: belief that curriculum development was a matter for the private sector and that federal support was an inappropriate intrusion into the state and local process of determining instructional priorities, approaches, and content. For a variety of reasons, this posture is no longer so rigid, and some funds for courseware development are available in some areas. As will be noted later, however, federal support of curriculum development is a policy of no-man's-land.

The extent to which the many points of influence on utilization and quality of microcomputers illustrated in Tables 14–2 and 14–3 actually are exercised is difficult to estimate. As many others have noted, the condition of information on the condition of education is more tantalizing than satisfying. Fairly extensive public support through tax deductions and direct and indirect legislation is probable. Public encouragement, through requirements for computer science training for high school graduation and, in some states, for teacher certification, is another influence with probably extensive consequences. Availability of courses in and research on microcomputers and early childhood education is growing rapidly, but inservice training for parents and caregivers as well as teachers of young children has low priority for national resources and attention. What there is, is a grass roots, individual, and locally encouraged effort.

Influence on Content

Table 14–4 illustrates some points of influence on the content of microcomputer materials through public funds and encouragement. Encouragement through courseware development has focused on mathematics and science. As noted in studies reported in this book and elsewhere, some exciting work is under way on using microcomputers to help children learn to read and compose, for second language acquisition, and for general cognitive development.

A related content emphasis is computer literacy. As noted earlier, many states now have required computer science units for high school graduation. Such a requirement was recommended by the National Commission on Excellence in Education, and it appears on the College Entrance Examination Board guidelines on skills required for succeeding in college work. Some colleges are wiring dormitories for individual student microcomputers; some are purchasing mi-

TABLE 14–2.
Examples of Public Influences on Microcomputers and Young Children: Utilization

- Allowing income tax deductions for teachers who are obtaining training in computer programming and microcomputer use as legitimate business and professional expenses.

- Allowing income tax deductions for teacher purchase of supplies and other equipment (e.g., books and instruction manuals) related to microprocessors.

- Allowing charitable deductions for individuals or corporations running training programs for teachers.

- Allowing tax-exempt foundations and funds to pay the costs of teacher inservice training, of developing materials for installation and inservice training, and the salaries of trainers promoting use of microcomputers for education in public or private schools.

- Allowing public funds to be used to pay salaries of public or private school officials while they seek donations of training services and materials for teachers.

- Allowing businesses selling microcomputers to deduct, as a business expense, costs of training programs offered as part of the sales package.

- Authorizing public funds to be used for teacher training and teacher training materials from impact aid, block grants, and other legislation not specially aimed at microcomputer utilization.

- Authorizing programs aimed directly at training teachers to use microcomputers for instruction, such as summer workshops, forgivable teacher loans, and inservice training.

TABLE 14-3.
Examples of Public Influences on Microcomputers and Young Children: Quality

- Court decisions affecting ownership and copyrights of software and courseware produced by for-profit organizations.
- Allowing tax-exempt foundations and funds to support development and testing of microcomputer software and courseware.
- Allowing public funds to be used for the development and testing of software and courseware in legislation not specifically targeted at learning technologies.
- Authorizing programs for development and testing of courseware and software; authorizing dissemination of information about these products; authorizing distribution of products developed through public funds at below market prices via subsidies for thin market distribution.

- Allowing or authorizing programs aimed at defining standards of quality, reviewing educational microcomputer materials in terms of standards of quality, or—through quasi-independent bodies—establishing standards of quality.
- Allowing payment of salaries and other expenses of public officials to meet with industry representatives to encourage or promote standards of quality.
- Support of television and radio programs on Public Broadcasting Service channels aimed at children, parents, or teachers that emphasize computers and how to use them.

crocomputers for all students and faculty; others have regarded student ownership of a microcomputer and skill in using it as a prerequisite in some majors.

What is meant by *computer literacy* can vary from a smattering of terms to considerable command of one or more languages and the ability to design computer programs. How this latter skill is acquired may

be most important for early childhood policy. Learning quickly and effectively to operate a device such as a word processor probably is well within the capacity of many who do not receive training until after high school. What seems more problematic is how extremely high levels of fluency in computer design, operations, and utilization develop. Early access may be one element, although

TABLE 14-4.
Examples of Public Influence on Microcomputers and Young Children: Content

- Targeting categorical funds on certain areas, such as mathematics and science, for equipment purchase, courseware development, and teacher training.
- Requiring minimum hours of training in computer science for high school graduation or teacher certification.
- Allowing staff whose salaries and expenses are paid through public funds to participate in courseware development.

- Entering into agreements with courseware developers to purchase a minimum number of units of a specific course, if the producer agrees to develop these.
- Establishing public bodies reviewing and deciding on courseware purchases for public educational systems.
- Court decisions affecting instructional content, such as instruction in creationism.

as other chapters in this book indicate, there are more questions than answers about cognitive effects of different instructional opportunities provided through microcomputers. Some schools have a high enough concentration of students fluent in computer languages to form clubs. Most participants are young men, and most schools having such clubs are in the affluent neighborhoods. The comic strip "Bloom County" includes a pre-adolescent computer whiz from an apparently well-to-do black family, a child with his own microcomputer and seemingly unlimited telephone access—a pointed contrast to the more typical spread in opportunity to become fluent at early ages in microcomputer use.

A PUBLIC AND A PRIVATE AFFAIR

It has been argued that the issue of microcomputers and young children already is a public affair, one that favors middle income and wealthier children and one that emphasizes elementary and secondary education over earlier ages. It also is, as Table 14–5 illustrates, a private affair.

While information again is scarce, the cumulative influences of the private sector appear to be congruent with those in the public sector. The two reinforce rather than counter-balance each other with regard to access, utilization, quality, and content.

As examples:

- With some notable exceptions, private sector donations seem to focus on elementary and secondary schools rather than preschools.
- Through home purchases, more middle and upper income children are likely to have access to microcomputers at home than do low income children.
- Some private sector groups concerned with curriculum development have ar-

gued particularly strongly against use of microcomputers in the preschool and early grades, blocking proposed federal assistance that might have reached some low income children.

- Parental and community groups have been particularly successful in providing microcomputer laboratories and microcomputers for classroom use to children in middle and upper income neighborhood schools.
- Middle and upper income parents have been primary supporters of the burgeoning computer summer camps and after-school computer clubs and training programs. One computer day camp ("TIC," 1984), which has had a waiting list for all sessions, serves children 7 to 16 years of age. The camp offers programming at beginning, intermediate, and advanced levels in Logo, BASIC, Pascal, and machine assembly languages, applied to typing and word processing, data management, music generation, graphics, and animation, voice synthesis, and electronic hardware projects. The fee is $300 for a two-week session, with five sessions available during the full summer for a total cost of $1200. The brochure comments,

> We believe that the kind of intense interaction that occurs between kids and computers have positive benefits: it can improve math and reasoning skills, reading ability and attitudes toward learning . . . guided exploration on a computer can hone intellectual skills, teach problem solving and improve the ability to communicate. . . . ("TIC," 1984).

Another camp offers a minimum of 3 hours of computer instruction a day in programming robotics and artificial intelligence ("Kids to Compute," 1984).

TABLE 14–5.
Some Examples of Private Influences on Microcomputers and Young Children

Access

- Decisions by privately owned corporations to target hardware, software, or courseware development on home or school markets.
- Decisions of privately owned corporations to target training opportunities to different sectors of potential markets (e.g., teacher training seminars, computer camps).
- Decisions of individuals to purchase equipment for private use including buying microprocessors for their children, rather than other equally expensive materials.
- Decisions by various organizations to emphasize access to microcomputers for educational purposes.
- Decisions by various organizations to block use of public funds to provide access to microcomputers for educational purposes.

Utilization and Quality

- Decisions by privately owned corporations to donate training to private or public school teachers in microprocessor use.
- Decisions by individuals to donate time and skills for teacher training or instructional program development.
- Decisions by various organizations to place high priority on encouraging utilization in schools.
- Decisions by individuals on what microcomputer and what materials to purchase for their children's use.
- Decisions by individuals on how much of their own time or how much family emphasis will be given to use of microprocessors and learning computer languages.
- Decisions by individuals on how much of their own time will be spent on developing courseware for educational use by their children.

Content

- Decisions by privately owned corporations to invest in developing materials for one content area or type of use rather than another (e.g., recreational versus educational use, aggressive action versus cooperative modes).
- Decisions by organizations to encourage one content area (e.g., science and mathematics) over another in purchasing materials for private or public schools.
- Decisions by individuals in purchasing, developing, or borrowing courseware in one content area or of one program type rather than another.
- Cumulative influences of reports and articles leading to decisions such as those above (e.g., effects of a widely read magazine article emphasizing the cognitive benefits of a certain language or program).
- Cumulative effects of broader trends with more private than public components (e.g., beliefs about the importance of different styles of microcomputer usage or content for boys in contrast to girls).

- The ways in which computers are used in middle and upper income schools differs from the ways in which children attending schools in lower income neighborhoods use them: for exploration, discovery, problem solving, and programming in the former but for rote drill and practice in the latter.

Despite the efforts of many school leaders to attract equivalent resources and foster equivalent use, some of which have led to establishment of computer-oriented magnet schools and expanded access for lower income children, the concern arises that in the near future computers could contribute to educational resegregation with regard to income.

There certainly is no national or state policy with such an intention. Rather, emerging trends seem associated with some long-standing cultural patterns (e.g., gender differences), the cumulative influences of public decisions (such as the distributional formulae for Chapter II of the Elementary and Secondary Education Act) intended to increase local flexibility and greater equality in federal support, and of private decisions (such as the decision to give a child an inexpensive home computer versus an equivalently priced electronic game). And in this sense, these cumulative influences also could contribute to the maintenance of past patterns of distinctions made along lines of race, gender, and ethnicity.

It might seem a fairly easy matter to decide otherwise. There are, however, difficulties that make shifts in policy somewhat more problematic. Some of these are considered next.

Importance of Courseware Relative to Hardware

Access to microcomputers seems a first priority, yet many argue that without first-rate courseware, the microcomputer is no better or worse than any other teaching device. It is far from cheap and easy to create first-rate instructional materials for microcomputers. Most classroom teachers do not have the time and resources, let alone the mix of programming, instructional, and graphic skills to do the job. Writing the materials now is a cottage industry. The cost would be particularly high if most materials were tested for educational effectiveness, which they now are not. The market for school system purchases is thin and uncertain at present.

Copyright laws are at present almost equally uncertain, which increases the risk of aiming for the home market. The computer industry is beginning to crack down on illegal copying of courseware and software. Some firms, for example, are using difficult-to-copy, lock-type disks, risking the higher price these create in competition for the school market. Some firms are making very strong, public protests to schools and school districts caught in extensive copying, risking good will. However, the cost to the computer industry of detection and prosecution of copyright violators could be exorbitant. The incentives may be greater for flooding the market with courseware produced at the lowest possible cost rather than investing in the expensive production costs of developing, testing, and revising. New projects reviewing courseware quality may contribute to creating a floor to an acceptable quality in materials, but if past is prologue, market forces alone in this area may be insufficient to go beyond a floor quality that is low to the ground indeed.

If the microcomputer is to be more than another doll corner, someone has to pay to create good materials. If the public pays, there are legitimate fears about inappropriate government control of content. What might start out as an introduction to mathematics, for example, might begin with the equivalent of a minute's prayer. Good, from some perspectives; not so good from others if paid for from public funds. The Corporation for Public Broadcasting has developed procedures to assure appropriate influences on public television program content and to keep the government at arm's length (or more). The agency paying for development of a program has no say in what goes over the air, except in the most general terms. The problems and costs of adequate representation of various segments of the community, however, are substantial. When public funds pay for curriculum, fears of inappropriate control increase, time and costs soar, and, because of relative investments, the eventual results may be constrictive to producers. If there were a large government award to produce early childhood courseware, the winner could dominate the industry since competitors would not have such a subsidy for development of their materials. Again, from some perspectives, this is not desirable.

Importance of Utilization over Courseware

The best curricula rarely are self-instructional. The same seems true of computer learning. The differences in actual use of classroom microprocessors among teachers who were computer fluent and those who were not (reported by Sheingold, Kane, and Endreweit, 1983) suggest the influence of teacher attitudes and training. Many teachers seem highly motivated to learn how to use microcomputers in the classroom and could be expected to take advantage of training opportunities.

Noting that haphazard computer purchases involving machine-specific, inadequate software lead to expensive hardware sitting idle, several federal legislators have introduced bills to help schools become more sophisticated purchasers; presumably, those in the purchasing departments would be as interested as teachers in taking advantage of guidance on how to invest computer purchase funds more wisely in order to improve utilization.

Effective investment to increase home utilization and support is a more uncertain business. The prevalence of children of scientists among outstanding young scientists illustrates the influence of home values and opportunities on scientific interests and development. Making microcomputers available through library or school loans, with coordinated programs for parents, might help equalize utilization. Since such opportunities would be voluntary, this might exacerbate resegregational effects, however; volunteers for such training usually are parents already highly motivated to cover every bet for their children.

With regard to teacher training, it is unclear how rapidly the next generation of early childhood educators will become computer fluent and fill positions in the field. By the time an adequate national program to bring most early childhood educators up to speed in microcomputers can be installed, the problem already may have been solved. To neglect current teachers may create a lost generation of teachers and children; on the other hand, inservice training may not be the best answer.

Importance of Early Versus Later or Continued Access

As of this writing, there is nationally less than one microcomputer per public school. The microcomputers that are in schools are not necessarily used for instructional purposes. Most elementary and secondary school children have fewer than 10 minutes per week of individual access to a microcomputer, at least through the public school system. If a national objective were that every child from kindergarten through 12th grade should have 1 hour of access to a microcomputer weekly, we would be years distant from this somewhat modest objective.

Microcomputers and programs seem to be changing rapidly. For example, a major new language, ADA, is being adopted by the Department of Defense. The language is based on the same LISP logic embodied in a language, Logo, that is used often for young children's manipulation of microprocessors. It is not unlikely that to acquire and maintain competence in computer languages requires considerable, extended, and up-to-date access (Char, 1983). This argues for early and extended access to microprocessors. But ways to provide such access are not easy. Were the devices to be made available through preschools and schools, this might be seen as improper enticement away from the home and family that could be unacceptable to many people. To bring the devices into the homes or to make them available through libraries might benefit most those parents and families who are already computer-aware. To provide free microcomputers to individual families could risk low utilization for a high expenditure.

While these issues do not exhaust the policy dilemmas, they may illustrate some of the reasons why apparently simple policy changes (a microcomputer in every Head Start classroom, for example) may be neither wise nor simple to implement.

SOME POLICY POSSIBILITIES

It does not seem likely that the near future holds a major shift in the trends resulting from public and private influences on microcomputers and young children. It seems desirable, however, to consider how to (1) provide more direct examination of the consequences of cumulative policies and (2) improve access, utilization, and quality of microcomputer opportunities and materials for young children, particularly those from low income families. The possibilities suggested here may be useful, should better information and improvement of access, utili-

zation, and quality be accepted as policy objectives.

Examination

As a minimum, we need better information about microcomputers and young children. Much of the discussion to this point has been speculative, based on information that sometimes has been solidly researched and analyzed, but too frequently for policy purposes is anecdotal or of uncertain completeness and quality. The first set of options, then, deals with examining the condition of education with regard to young children and microcomputers.

- Support, through agencies such as the National Center on Educational Statistics, regular surveys of access, utilization, and quality of microcomputer use and materials in public and private schools.
- Obtain, through the regular Census Bureau household surveys, national information on access, utilization, and quality of microcomputer use in homes.
- Analyze, through long-term awards to groups skilled in policy analysis, changes in patterns of access, utilization, and quality by age group, family income, ethnicity, and gender.
- Review, through long-term awards to groups skilled in policy analysis, court decisions, and direct and indirect legislative influences on how much money is available to whom for access, utilization, and quality improvement in educational use of microcomputers and associated courseware.
- Discuss, through regular sessions in organizations concerned with the education of young children, what is happening in access, utilization, and quality of materials.

Improvement

As a minimum, some relatively low cost approaches to improving access, utilization, and quality that already are being tried with some apparent success could be more widely disseminated. Utilization and quality are concerns affecting all young children: Within resources already being allocated to microcomputers and young children, more could be done to obtain greater benefits. The second set of options focuses on improvements.

- Encourage donation of older microcomputers to early childhood programs.
- Establish microcomputer lending libraries at a variety of community institutions (for example, at churches as well as libraries) for home use.
- Develop user-friendly materials for home use by parents who are themselves computer inexperienced.
- Involve youth and older children who are computer fluent in working with young children and their teachers on microprocessors in schools.
- Use a wide variety of opportunities to increase even short-term access to microprocessors for families and young children (e.g., microcomputer "corners" in shopping malls and grocery stores, mobile computer-equipped vans).
- Expand information exchanges on teacher- or parent-developed courseware or other instructional materials through groups such as ERIC/Early Childhood Education.
- Expand Public Broadcasting Service programming aimed at parents and teachers, including support for follow-up dissemination of training tapes derived from these programs.

Particularly for Low Income Children and Families

At a minimum, the risks of educational resegregation demand attention to access, utilization, and quality for low income children. Extrapolating from the experience with low income children and television, cheap hardware in itself will not be sufficient to bridge a potential gap in sophisticated understanding and use of microcomputers. Children who have grown up playing Space Invaders may not be able to catch up later with children who have grown up writing programs to create new games. The third set of options focuses on low income children.

- Provide summer computer day camp opportunities for low income children.
- Encourage expanded day and weekend use of already available school microcomputer facilities through staffing by volunteer organizations.
- Inform the teachers of low income children (as well as other teachers) of the tax write-offs that may be available to them for purchase of and training in microcomputer use.*
- Support group purchase prices for microcomputers through teacher organizations, particularly chapters serving low income children.
- Emphasize recruiting big sisters and brothers, foster grandparents and similar volunteers who have microcomputers and are willing to teach the children and their teachers how to use them.

---

*Changing tax laws with regard to home use of microprocessors may affect the conditions under which all or part of the costs are deductible. Readers would need to consult their tax advisors for individual use of information in this chapter.

- Consider developing a special Head Start initiative aimed at expanding access and utilization through donations and volunteer efforts in all Head Start centers.
- Consider special recognition of training for and skills in using microcomputers for early childhood instruction in the Child Development Associate program.
- Explore ways in which microcomputer programs and approaches developed initially for handicapped children through Office of Special Education projects could be made available to local programs for low income young children.

The approaches sketched here are illustrative. Some would require additional funds (for example, summer computer day camps for low income children). Some would encourage wider use of existing tax deductions and thus incur public costs (for example, increasing teacher awareness of tax write-offs). Most involve leadership and a focusing of energy on microprocessors for educational purposes (for example, better use of materials, equipment, and skills developed through programs for handicapped young children for Head Start and similar programs).

CONCLUSIONS

Some conclusions are implicit in proposing that these approaches be considered, in addition to other proposals under consideration in some states and some federal legislation that are even more far-reaching. There is, as other chapters in this book indicate, much that is inconsistent in current findings, much that is disputed, and much that

needs to be studied (see Char, 1983). These information and values gaps may argue against further efforts to promote access to microcomputers by young children. In addition, as prices drop, any current concerns for levels and distribution of access to microcomputers may be self-correcting problems within a generation. Both points of view would imply making haste slowly.

On the other hand, the nation has struggled so hard to reduce the correlations among gender, race, income, educational opportunity, and subsequent economic opportunity that to permit the gap to spread yet again, if we can avoid this, may exact a higher social price than the costs of trying to close it, with regard to microcomputer access, utilization, and quality. It also should be noted that other nations are considerably bolder (Nicholson, 1983). "Improvement" is a limp, vague policy, compared to more ambitious goals such as achieving computer literacy for new generations of children. Great Britain, for example, has subsidized development of extremely low cost microcomputers, software, and courseware. One in every five homes, and all classrooms in all schools, now are said to have a microcomputer, including classes serving young children.

So assertive a policy results from a very high priority being placed on microcomputers as learning devices. The United States may not have reached this conclusion. At the least, however, we can conclude that the by-products of policies intended to achieve other purposes are too little attention to microprocessors and young children in terms of access, utilization, and quality, particularly for children of the poorest families. Because of (a) the long-term consequences of resegregational effects of differential computer skills and (b) uncertainties about how far and how fast children who try to catch up in high school and beyond can go, greater attention is needed to what is happening with microcomputers and young children.

REFERENCES

Barro, S. (1983, October). *Federal tax expenditures for education: Concepts, measures, and policy implications.* Washington, DC: Decision Resources.

Char, C. A. (1983). *Research and design issues concerning development of educational software for children* (Technical Report No. 14). New York: Bank Street College of Education, Center for Children and Technology.

Education Computer News. (1984). Arlington, VA: Capitol Publications.

Feurzeig, W., Horwitz, P., & Nickerson, R. (1981, October). *Microcomputers in education* (Report No. 4798). Prepared for Department of Health, Education and Welfare, National Institute of Education; and Ministry for the Development of Human Intelligence, Republic of Venezuela. Cambridge, MA: Bolt, Beranek and Newman. (ERIC Document Reproduction Service No. ED 208 901)

Kids to compute at summer camp. (1984, April 20). *Education Daily,* p. 2.

Nicholson, R. B. (1983, December). Using computers, TV and other innovative ideas. *New Report: National Academy of Sciences, 33*(10), 20–24.

Sheingold, K., Kane, J. H., & Endreweit, M. (1983). Microcomputer use in schools: Developing a research agenda. *Harvard Educational Review, 53,* 412–432.

TIC Computer Camp [Brochure] (1984). Arlington, VA: Technology Instruction Corporation.

Weir, S. (1981). *Logo as an information prosthetic for the handicapped* (Working Paper No. 9). Cambridge, MA: Massachusetts Institute of Technology, Division for Studies and Research in Education.

AUTHOR INDEX

SUBJECT INDEX

Access, 182, 185
ADA language, 193–194
Adaptive Firmware Card, 153–154
Advanced Instant Logo, 141
Affective potential, 84–85
Aggression
  and generalized arousal, 64
  object, 66
  video games tests, 66–67
Algorithms, importance, 91, 99–100
Anderton, Nancy, 95
Arcade games, 50, 62, 92–93
  See also Video games
Arousal
  cooperative and competitive tests, 67–68
  emotional, 62–63
  generalized, *See* Generalized arousal
  theory, 62–63
Artificial Intelligence Laboratory, 104
Associative fluency, 79
Associative play, 51

Bank Street studies, 8, 173
BANK STREET WRITER program, 139–140
Bitzer, Donald, 162
Block grant program, 184
Body syntonicity, 106, 119–121
Box-score reviews, 163–164
Bricoleur thinking types, 178–179
Bunderson, Victor, 162

CAI, *See* Computer-assisted instruction
Calculators, 20, 137
Carnegie Commission on Higher Education, 160
Caterpillar program, 133
Catharsis, 63, 69
CBI, *See* Computer-based instruction
Center for Young Children (CYC), 74, 132
Challenge, 15–16
CMI, *See* Computer-managed instruction
Cognitive development, 29–30
Cognitive maps, 90
Cognitive objective, 142
Cognitive potential, 84–85
Cohen, Bert, 105
Collaboration, 30, 51
Collective symbolism, 79–80
Color, with Logo, 108–109
Communication
  by computer algorithm, 100
  for handicapped children, 149
Computer camps, 183, 190
Computer Discovery Project, 132
Computer literacy, 137–138, 188–190
Computer-assisted instruction (CAI), 9, 13, 165
Computer-based instruction (CBI), 162
  quantitative syntheses, 164–166
  review articles, 163–164
Computer-managed instruction (CMI), 165

The Computing Teacher, 149
Concept learning, 104, 105
Connections, between media, 30–31
Conrad, John, 94
Consonants and vowels, 96
Constructive play, 51, 75
Control
  as computer attraction, 77–78
  environmental, for handicapped children, 150
  personal, 16
  and self-esteem, 107
  of software, 5, 88, 91, 92–93
  through play, 81
Cooperation, 46
Cooperative play, 51
Cornell, Jean, 127
Corporation for Public Broadcasting, 192–193
Counting Bee, 40
Courseware, *See* Software
Court decisions, 182–183
Creative Crayon program, 48, 75–77, 134
Creative thinking, 135
Creative writing, 139–140
Curiosity, 16
Curriculum
  development, federal support, 187–188
  for handicapped children, 147
  individualized, 43–44
  in preschool, computer use, 46–47
  for young children, 132
CYC, *See* Center for Young Children

Debugging, 118–119
Defense, U. S. Department of, 194
Delta Drawing program, 141–142
Dexterity, 39, 132
Digest of Software Reviews, 149
Discovery learning, 6, 18, 74, 123, 147
Distances, estimating, 112–113
Divergent thinking, 79, 82, 83, 135
Dolch spelling program, 97–98
Dramatic play, 51, 75, 80
Duckworth, Eleanor, 142

Edison, Thomas Alva, quote from, 21–22
Education, 149
Education Computer News, 186
Education, National Institute of, 187
Education, U. S. Department of, 185, 187
Educational Testing Service (ETS), 162
Ego syntonicity, 119–121
Electronic Easel program, 136
Electronic Learning, 149
Emotional arousal, 62–63
Environmental control, 150
Environmental experience, 92
ETS, *See* Educational Testing Service
Evolution, theories of, 100
Experiential learning, 121, 132